ETHIOPIA

Yves-Marie Stranger was born in Exeter, Devon, and grew up shepherding goats on the family farm in the French Pyrenees. After leading horse treks in the Showan highlands, Yves-Marie now works as a translator and editor in French, English and Amharic, and divides his time between Ethiopia and France. He is the author of *Ces pas qui trop vite s'effacent* and *Le Syllabaire Abyssin*, and runs the publishing house Uthiopia – Utopia in Ethiopia.

You can contact Yves-Marie via YvesMarieStranger.com or Uthiopia.com

ETHIOPIA

Through Writers' Eyes

Edited by
YVES-MARIE STRANGER

ELAND

First published in 2016 by Eland Publishing Ltd,
61 Exmouth Market, London ECIR 4QL
with the support of the French embassy in Ethiopia

Editorial Content © Yves-Marie Stranger

All extracts © of the authors,
as attributed in the text and acknowledgements.

ISBN   978 1 78060 077 2

Cover image:
*Priest walking the rock edge path to Mariam Korkor Church,
Tigray, Ethiopia* © Cultura RM Exclusive/Philip Lee Harvey

Text set in Great Britain by Antony Gray
Printed in Spain by GraphyCems, Navarra

In Memoriam

Jean-Michel Cornu de Lenclos

Saigon, Vietnam 1956,
Phnom Pen, Cambodia, 2014

'Like all those possessing a library, Aurelian was aware that
he was guilty of not knowing his in its entirety.'

The Theologians, JORGE LUIS BORGES

'Believe nothing that is written in books, until you
observe them and find them to be true.'

Hatata, ZARA YACOB

'They're using pancakes as spoons!'
'Ooo, let's see what else they do wrong.'

The Simpsons visit Little Ethiopia

Disclaimer

I thank early readers for their advice and discerning criticism – but claim as my own any Abyssinian idiosyncrasies in the choices retained here. Spellings, however idiosyncratic, have been kept, for the larger part, as in their original renderings, save when they would have presented the reader with unnecessary difficulties. The word *Ethiopian* will be used throughout this book, where contemporary usage would often divide the people into their smallest common denominators. There is nothing wrong *per se* in this essentialism – 'Unity in Diversity' is after all one of the Federal Republic's mottoes. But if Ethiopia has indeed long been famous for its multiplicity, this reductive view seems to hark back to the Italian invaders' catalogue-like definition for the country: 'Ethiopia: the Museum of Peoples'. While there is indeed beauty in diversity, the ties that bind are stronger than the dividing chasms that rend the Ethiopian high plateau. The texts anthologised here are of their time and may use vocabulary, or express ideas, in a way that is considered derogatory today. Terms such as 'Fuzzy-Wuzzy' (for Beni Amer), 'Galla' (for Oromo), 'Falasha' (for Beta Israel), or 'Moor' (for Arabs and Muslims), are to be read as historical. Any lack of correction of these terms should in no way be understood as an endorsement of their contemporary usage by the editor or the publishers.

Y-M S

Acknowledgements

Many thanks to Eloi Ficquet, Solomon Demeke, Lydia Stranger, Abebe Zegeye, Deborah Ghirmai and Fabio Ferraresi for reading first drafts, and to Jean-Michel le Dain (and the French Embassy in Ethiopia) for their willingness to support the translation of a number of texts which were only available to this day in French. The task of sourcing rare travel accounts would have been near impossible without the friendly help of the staff of the libraries of the French Centre for Ethiopian Studies in Kebena, and of the Library of Ethiopian Studies itself, in the melancholic palace that became Addis Ababa University's first abode. A number of authors have kindly given their permission for extracts from their books to feature here: Sébastien de Courtois, Hugues Fontaine, Philip Marsden, Dervla Murphy, Kevin Rushby, Ian Campbell, Jacques Mercier, Aberra Jembere's son Nurlin Aberra (and Shama Books), Charlie Walker, Aida Edemariam and Sammy Asfaw. Warm thanks to all of them. Eloi Ficquet also kindly allowed me to use an extract from the *Chronicle of the Imans of Wollo* that he was yet to publish. We also acknowledge permission to reprint other copyright material as follows: Penguin Books Ltd for permission for the extract from *Remote People* by Evelyn Waugh (© Evelyn Waugh 1932), Curtis Brown Group Ltd, London on behalf of Thomas Packenham for permission to quote from *The Mountains of Rasselas* (© Thomas Packenham, 1959), Curtis Brown Group Ltd, London on behalf of the Beneficiary of the Estate of Wilfred Thesiger for permission to use an extract from *The Life of My Choice* (© Wilfred Thesiger, 1980) and the *Guardian* for permission to use the article by Aida Edemariam from 1 September 2007.

Remerciements aussi à Joseph Stranger for tracking down books; to Rose Baring and Andrew R. Knight for their *Gypaetus barbatus*-eyed editing, as well as to Yoadan Girma for her impeccable translating and secretarial skills. Special thanks to Richard and Rita Pankhurst, who not only allowed me to quote from Richard's book (*Travellers in Ethiopia*), but also to republish here his informative article on 'Caves Around Addis Ababa' from the *Ethiopian Observer*. Et un grand merci à Mark Ellingham, from Sort of Books – without whom the library of Mount Abora would have continued to lack an indispensable, if necessarily summary, appendix.

Y-M S

Contents

3 ERA OF THE PRINCES (1700–1855)

4 EUCALYPTOPOLIS (1855–1974)

5 GOODBYE ABYSSINIA, HELLO ETHIOPIA (1930–2015)

6 UTHIOPIA

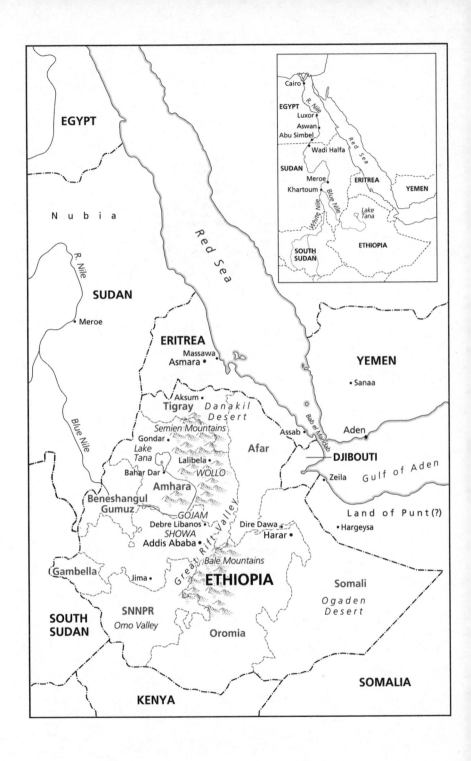

GENESIS

Introduction

Can the Ethiopian change his skin –
can the leopard change its spots?

JEREMIAH 13:23

Jorge Luis Borges – who once wrote a fable called *The Immortal* that began and circuitously ended inside the margins of Ethiopia – set forth that 'all good authors create their precursors'. In turn, following in his footsteps, one could venture to say that all countries worth their salt create their own geography – from myths, old maps and wishful thinking.

Today, we may be sure Ethiopia is a country in north-east Africa, but the country's borders have not always been so well defined. Depending on the whims and knowledge of writers and geographers, Ethiopia was at times made up of all of sub-Saharan Africa – with a coastline that wandered from the Red Sea to the Atlantic Ocean – or was solely the area circumscribed between the northern reach of Egypt's desert, the confluence of the Blue and White Niles and the Atbara river. In a later incarnation, the country became a saintly empire administered by an anointed priest-king, known as Prester John: an empire so munificent and kaleidoscopic that it was found in the Congo, in Mongolia, in Syria and, finally, in the Christian kingdom of the hinterlands of the Red Sea. The Greek Bible had the spawn of Shem, Kush and Ham go and multiply in Egypt and Aethiopia – a tale later reprised in a legend that has Axum's first

capital founded by none other than Ityopis, son of Kush. Later the
Ethiopian Queen Kandace's eunuch is converted by the Apostle Philip
on the road to Damascus – and returns to convert queen and kingdom
to Christianity. Research has revealed that biblical transcribers and
interpreters had rendered Kandace from the Meroitic for *Queen* or
Queen Mother. This title, in various guises and local languages, was
used until the twentieth century to denote the Ethiopian queen.

It is this intertexual play carried out on a mind's eye map, which is
so fascinating to the amateur Ethiopianist, and to the visitor to
Ethiopia. No country can be better grasped from the depths of an
armchair, and a library is as good a place as any to make out the ancient
contours of the land of Prester John, Mandeville and Rasselas, as well
as the new outlines of a country that today is attempting with great
vigour to shake off the modern myth it was saddled with – of Korem
and the 1970s famine, of the Derg's Red Terror, and of poverty and
refugee camps. The BBC's John Buerk and Jonathan Dimbleby's
pronouncements on Ethiopia have had as much, if not more,
resonance in the modern era as all of the Classical and Enlightenment
authors put together. And yet – when John Buerk began his famous
intervention at dawn in Korem, he too harked back to the text and the
myth, when he intoned on camera those now famous words: 'Dawn,
and as the sun breaks through the piercing chill of night on the plain
outside Korem, it lights up a biblical famine, now, in the twentieth
century.'

One could be forgiven for thinking that these references are so
many worn-out palimpsests now lying unused by the young, and
certainly never used by Ethiopians themselves. But one would be
wrong. For however bland and annoying those references to biblical
imagery may seem to be the epithet 'biblical' is etched on the land
itself. For a country that has so many illiterates, the Ethiopians' own
knowledge of historical works, myths, and books referencing their
country is quite astounding. As is their respect for the word, for
rhetoric and their love of poetry. Since time immemorial, 'magic
scrolls', consisting in wide-eyed angel sketches and verses from the
Psalms of David, have been worn tightly rolled up in cartouches
around necks to ward off the evil eye. And it is said that Emperor Zera

Yacob (1399–1468) – himself a scholar who penned various religious treatises – so much believed in the power of the word that he promulgated that all his subjects should have 'I renounce Satan' tattooed on their wrists.

Ethiopia likes to call itself a country of the Book and – from rustic magic scrolls to the carefully wrought *Liber Axumae* horse-skin vellum – the word is often seen as panacea as well as origin. Witness the practice of granting children names to tease out self-fulfilling prophecy: *Kassahun* (Be-My-Compensation); *Afewerk* (Mouth-of-Gold); *Assefa* (Expand-the-Borders). But, if a naturalistic novel such as *Love unto the Grave*, by the author and politician Addis Alemayehu (I-Saw-a-New-World, as his name can be rendered into English), is much loved, it is not so much because it has been read, but because it has been broadcast over the radio countless times since it was written after World War II.

Today, Ethiopia would like to shed some of its biblical imagery, at least when it comes to that stock phrase 'a biblical famine'. A quick glance round a bookshop will reveal that most Amharic-language bestsellers today stray far from biblical exegesis: cheap translations of . . . Agatha Christie and Danielle Steel, although you can also find a book such as *Anna Karenina*. The themes and language of nineteenth-century Russia translate surprisingly well both into Amharic and into Ethiopian reality. And *Anna Karenina* has also been broadcast over the radio to great acclaim. But if Ethiopia is overwhelmingly religious and devout – and not just Christian, as the country has one of the oldest Muslim cultures in the world – Ethiopia, always a land of paradox, is a religious country that has been led by lay regimes for more than forty years, first by the avowedly atheistic regime of the military Derg junta, and today by the secular government of the Federal Democratic Republic of Ethiopia. Although Ethiopia likes to portray itself as monotheistic and monolithic – both to itself and to the outside world – the reality is much more complex. Beliefs in spirits, good and bad, and possession cults are widespread throughout the country. Seers and oracles are consulted by Muslim and Christian alike (they often pay their respects in the same shrines), and *adbars* (trees that harbour spirits) are covered in clarified butter near to Addis Ababa to this day. There is also a special class of lay clergy in the Orthodox Church, the *debtara* (loosely translated as deacon), which specialises in writing out charms, and calculating people's futures with numerology, often based on the Psalms of David. But an outsider would never know this: little is written on the subject, less is spoken. Jacques Mercier's *Asres* (anthologised here), an intimate portrait of a seer, charlatan and wise men, is as good a portrait as you will find of this invisible but all-pervasive spiritual world.

All happy countries resemble each other, while all unhappy countries are unhappy in their own special way – Ethiopia, always idiosyncratic in its economic malpractices and a byword for famine, has now been at peace for over twenty years and has become a stabilising influence in East Africa. The building blocks for the country's long-term stability and growth are rapidly being set up. The economy is booming, roads are being built, and the bulging population, now said to be around one hundred million, is vastly made up of youth hungry for change. Hydroelectric dams bisect all of the country's great rivers, and the biggest dam of them all, the Renaissance Dam, is being laid across that river famous since antiquity, the Nile. This last dam is seen as a threat by Egyptians – a colonial-era, British-brokered treaty grants them close to 90 per cent of the river's water – and as a cure to all their woes by Ethiopians, who feel aggrieved by such a markedly unjust treaty, and feel, rightly or wrongly, that if they harness their country's water resources, prosperity and riches will come at last to their homeland, nay, will restore their country to its position of eminence among the world's nations:

> O Nile, you are the majestic blood line of my African glory
> That shower my blessings upon the starved of the world
> You are the eloquence that rings the Ethiopian bell
> > across the deaf world.

TSEGAYE GEBRE-MEDHIN* ('NILE')

---

* Tsegaye Gebre-Medhin (1936–2006), Ethiopian poet, dramatist and writer. Also well known for his translations into Amharic of Shakespeare and Molière.

Fast-growing populations can be a bonanza, or a time bomb, so it is too early today to say if this new vision of a prosperous, water-powered Ethiopia will become a reality. But as the word renaissance implies, for there to be a rebirth, there must have been a first par-turition, and modern Ethiopian youth, with their Facebook pages and love of mobile phones, still hark back to a perceived manifest destiny for Ethiopia first cast by Greek writers looking up the Nile and along the shores of the Red Sea to a remote other – the 'most distant men' as Homer called them.

Contemporary young Ethiopians often wear t-shirts featuring the Emperor Theodore to mark their support for their national heritage. Theodore is the wild, unhinged figure of Ethiopian unity from the mid-nineteenth century. He would have industrialised his country by the force of his will, but ended up taking his own life on his mountain redoubt of Magdala rather than surrender to Robert Napier (later 1st Baron Napier of *Magdala*) and the British expeditionary force sent from India to bring him to reason.

The emperor is an obvious romantic icon. And his beautiful and delicate face, with its typical Ethiopian braids, is a common sight on t-shirts and bar murals in Addis Ababa. Theodore has the advantage of being shrouded in the mists of time, in a country that is diverse religiously and ethnically. His massacres and divisions have long been forgotten (Theodore had a particular inclination for throwing trussed-up prisoners off cliffs). Moreover, the noble hero featured on t-shirts lived in a time when photography had barely made its appearance on the scene, and had certainly not reached his mountain-top fortress. The quasi-official portrait that today's Ethiopian youth like so much is in fact a line drawing made by an English newspaper artist whose editor needed illustrations for the increasingly popular articles on the Napier expedition. The artist's remit was 'to draw a noble Ethiopian emperor'. And this he did, with great success.

A similar artistic licence is the recent vogue for the name *Rasselas* – you can meet young people in Addis Ababa and Little Ethiopia in Washington DC proudly bearing the name – which although familiar to Western readers of Doctor Johnson's *The History of Rasselas, Prince of Abissinia*, should not really be a name in Ethiopia at all. Johnson invented the portmanteau moniker by combining the title *Ras*, an equivalent to Duke, and the name Selas, that he had encountered in his first literary endeavour: a translation (from the French) of Jeronimo Lobos's Ethiopian *Itinerário*, in which Ras Selas features prominently as the brother of the Ethiopian emperor and a staunch supporter of Catholicism. It seems that this trope of substituting titles for names – calling the *Hendeke* Kandace, the *queen* Queen – is an Ethiopian speciality. Witness the name (and title) Ras Tafari, or *Duke Who-is-Fearsome*, Haile Selassie's pre-coronation name, which gave the *Ras* moniker Rastafarians themselves often claim as mantle – an exodus to a promised land in which all men will be, if not kings, at least dukes . . .

But no matter – in today's Ethiopia (a Greek word), you can meet young men called Rasselas (an English novelist's invention by way of a translation of a book by a Portuguese Jesuit), proudly displaying t-shirts featuring a British newspaper artist's vision of what an Ethiopian emperor should look like. Ethiopia continues to create its precursors with great energy. *Vive la renaissance!*

YVES-MARIE STRANGER

FROM *Le Syllabaire Abyssin*, 2016

Lucy in the Sky with Diamonds

Lucy already had a burnt face back then, spindly legs, and arms that hung down by her thighs as she shuffled along the river. She sought out frogs, nesting birds and fawns hidden among the bushes. She did not know the age she had reached, Lucy, although she was of age to give birth – her first blood had been received with coming of age rites in which she was isolated on a distant hill. Her ilk had covered her whole body in cataplasms of clay, mingled with green and red leaves and purple berries.

Lucy wallows in the peat bogs along the river, having spent the morning foraging, from dawn to high noon. It smells good on the river bank, and the cavity in which Lucy curls up cools her extremities and trunk. Midges cannot alight on her splattered skin nor can mosquitoes pierce the muddy crust. Lucy loses her odour; there is only her breath, which is slight, to betray her to big cats, apes and to those of her ilk. She sinks into the bog, disgruntled warthogs thrashing about before taking flight. Lucy reposes, at ease, wrapped up in her second skin of moist earths. Lucy has a dream, always the same. She dreams of a vast cavern, of obscure shadows, with a roof of twinkling stars. Lucy lies on her back in her dream, and in front of her face are invisible walls. She can touch them, look at them, but cannot go through them. On the other side of these walls, pale spectres press themselves. They examine her, weighing and measuring her up with their gaze. These spectral apparitions seem themselves to be holding their breath – as if they did not wish for Lucy to detect their presence.

Lucy wakes up, in fits and starts. She remembers headlong races in the savannah. She recalls the sound and odour of dry grasses crackling

as they are consumed during the dry season fires. She remembers wild
escapes from the fire itself, as her ilk ran in the company of antelopes,
dikdik, sabre-toothed tigers and caves hyenas. The dikdik were no
more afraid of Lucy and hers, than the latter hesitated to brush
up against hyena during the time of the fire. It is the truce of the
savannah. Flee as fast as possible, as far as your legs will carry you. The
fire running out – no more vegetation to consume, a liquid barrier: all
then slink away. Dikdik make for boulders, hers coming together in a
glade. Who is missing? Who stumbled? Who is now lying, their hot
body still smoking in the pretty savannah? One of her ilk picks up a
smoking ember and places it down in the middle of the glade. That
evening, the predatory shadows come up against a new invisible wall
and the sleep of all is untroubled.

Lucy also remembers helter-skelter races through the trees with
her play companions – they swing from branch to branch, squabbling
with monkeys over ripe fruit and dove nests lined with fat chicks. They
tear out the fluff from their chests before biting into them like warm
figs. The great apes are hairier, stronger; they swing better, they climb
quicker. But it is them, Lucy and her ilk, who push them back into the
forests, along the river, when they find an antelope, a smoking zebra
on the plain, brought down and scorched by the fire. They tear off
shreds of skin and flesh, eating these soft meats as much with their
fingers as with their teeth. They gnaw bones, break them with rocks
and suck on the marrow. Lucy looks up. She looks towards the heights
of the mountains to the west, a barrier like a great green and white
wall, a mottled mix of cliffs, boulders and forest. This is the end of the
low plains full of silt-laden rivers, and of countless herds of beasts, in
which her ilk range, from rains to dry season, between too abundant
waters and green grasses, and the droughts and their storms of fire.

When the dry season of the year of her blood came, a bad wind
began to blow, such as the fire breathes itself, a hot tongue which
precedes the lick of the flame and harries you on as surely as the arm
projects the hand in front of itself. This wind blew even before the
fire, drying out the plain and making the grasses as brittle and
transparent as dragonfly wings. When the sky's fire came down – the
black clouds that tore themselves up on the western wall had been

massing for several days already – the savannah erupted in a sea
of flames in such a manner as Lucy could not remember, and the
escape of her ilk and of all that had leg and wing was desperate. A
cavalcade of dust, smoke and flame full of the acrid smell of the fire
itself and of a thousand beasts pressed against one another in the
heart of the raging storm: the jackal against the hyrax, the mottled
cheetah beside the maroon antelope – the leopard leaping on together
with the scampering baboon.

The river bank was as she remembered it, and the marshy bog
alone seemed still in the midst of the fury of the universe, as Lucy slid
her body into the mire. Only the tingling of smoke in her nose, the
glowing embers rising to the skies, and the iridescent purple and
yellow reflections beyond the trees of the river bank, to remind her of
the raging fire. Lucy never knew the exact moment in which the
smoke stopped prickling her nose, as she never knew if she was
awaking from, rather than entering, a long dream, in which diamonds
studded the roof of her cavern for eternity.

Le Syllabaire Abyssin recounts the lives of 33 Ethiopian figures
(corresponding to the 33 main symbols of the Ethiopian syllabary),
and echoes Marcel Schwob's *Imaginary Lives*. This is the life of Lucy
(*Australopithecus Afarensis*), one of our oldest ancestors, who lived
around 3.4 million years ago and whose skeleton was found in 1974
in the Afar Depression. The Beatles song 'Lucy in the Sky with
Diamonds' was playing that day on the dig – and the name stuck.

HERODOTUS

FROM *The Histories*, 440 BC

The Most Remote of Men

I went as far as Elephantine to see what I could with my own eyes, but for the country still further south I had to be content with what I was told in answer to my questions. South of Elephantine the country is inhabited by Ethiopians [. . .] Beyond the island is a great lake, and round its shores live nomadic tribes of Ethiopians. After crossing the lake one comes again to the stream of the Nile, which flows into it [. . .] After forty days' journey on land along the river, one takes another boat and in twelve days reaches a big city named Meroë, said to be the capital city of the Ethiopians. The inhabitants worship Zeus and Dionysus alone of the Gods, holding them in great honour. There is an oracle of Zeus there, and they make war according to its pro-nouncements, taking it from both the occasion and the object of their various expeditions [. . .] After this Cambyses [the King of Persia] took counsel with himself, and planned three expeditions. One was against the Carthaginians, another against the Ammonians, and a third against the long-lived Ethiopians, who dwelt in that part of Libya which borders upon the southern sea [. . .] while his spies went into Ethiopia, under the pretence of carrying presents to the king, but in reality to take note of all they saw, and especially to observe whether there was really what is called 'the table of the Sun' in Ethiopia. Now the table of the Sun according to the accounts given of it may be thus described: it is a meadow in the skirts of their city full of the boiled flesh of all manner of beasts, which the magistrates are careful to store with meat every night, and where whoever likes may come and eat during the day. The people of the land say that the earth itself brings forth the food. Such is the description which is given of this table.

The Ethiopians to whom this embassy was sent are said to be the tallest and handsomest men in the whole world. In their customs they differ greatly from the rest of mankind, and particularly in the way they choose their kings; for they find out the man who is the tallest of all the citizens, and of strength equal to his height, and appoint him to rule over them [. . .] The spies were told that most of them lived to be a hundred and twenty years old, while some even went beyond that age – they ate boiled flesh, and had for their drink nothing but milk. Among these Ethiopians copper is of all metals the most scarce and valuable. Also, last of all, they were allowed to behold the coffins of the Ethiopians, which are made – according to report – of crystal, after the following fashion: when the dead body has been dried, either in the Egyptian, or in some other manner, they cover the whole with gypsum, and adorn it with painting until it is as like the living man as possible. Then they place the body in a crystal pillar which has been hollowed out to receive it, crystal being dug up in great abundance in their country, and of a kind very easy to work. You may see the corpse through the pillar within which it lies; and it neither gives out any unpleasant odour, nor is it in any respect unseemly; yet there is no part that is not as plainly visible as if the body were bare. The next of kin keep the crystal pillar in their houses for a full year from the time of the death, and give it the first fruits continually, and honour it with sacrifice. After the year is out they bear the pillar forth, and set it up near the town [. . .]

Where the south declines towards the setting sun lies the country called Ethiopia, the last inhabited land in that direction. There gold is obtained in great plenty, huge elephants abound, with wild trees of all sorts, and ebony; and the men are taller, handsomer, and longer lived than anywhere else. The Ethiopians were clothed in the skins of leopards and lions, and had long bows made of the stem of the palm-leaf, not less than four cubits in length. On these they laid short arrows made of reed, and armed at the tip, not with iron, but with a piece of stone, sharpened to a point, of the kind used in engraving seals. They carried likewise spears, the head of which was the sharpened horn of an antelope; and in addition they had knotted clubs. When they went into battle they painted their bodies, half with chalk, and half with vermilion.

*

Herodotus (*c.*484–425 BC), 'The Father of History', referenced
Ethiopia and Ethiopians widely in his *Histories* – the question being
what exactly he was referring to. The word Ethiopia is itself a Greek
invention for anyone with 'a burnt face', and Aethiopia shorthand for
the foreigner, the other, the barbarian from countries far away (that is
to say beyond Egypt and Libya) – indeed Herodotus, like Homer,
calls the Ethiopians 'the most distant of men', and he and other Greek
writers imagine their gods playing and resting in this most exotic of
locales – and we all know that when it comes to sending the gods off
somewhere, it is better to choose a place so distant as to both make a
good story, and so that you don't need to worry too much about the
details.

Of the details of Herodotus' own life, George Rawlinson said that
'The data are so few – they rest upon such late and slight authority;
they are so improbable or so contradictory, that to compile them into
a biography is like building a house of cards, which the first breath of
criticism will blow to the ground.' It has often been said that he never
travelled from Greece – let alone made it to Egypt, and that most of
his writings on such distant people as the Ethiopians are nothing but
invention, story and myth – and indeed Herodotus since his own
times has also been known as 'The Father of Lies'. But despite this, he
remains the main source for many antique references and, if the
flooding of the Nile is not due to snow melt inside the continent, it
remains that as many elements as have been found to be fabricated
have been corroborated by modern historiography. And Ethiopia
today does indeed exist, if only because Herodotus put pen to paper
and made the name part of the known world.

STRABO

FROM *Geographica*, *c.*7 BC, first 'modern' edition 1469

The Foodies' Guide to the Horn of Africa

In the intervening space, a branch of the river Astaboras discharges itself. It has its source in a lake, and empties part of its waters into the bay, but the larger portion it contributes to the Nile. Then follow six islands, called Latomiae, after these the Sabaïtic mouth, as it is called, and in the inland parts a fortress built by Suchus. Then a lake called Elaea, and the island of Strato; next Saba, a port, and a hunting-ground for elephants of the same name. The country deep in the interior is called Tenessis [this could roughly correspond to modern Eritrea]. It is occupied by those Egyptians who took refuge from the government of Psamtik III. They are surnamed Sembritae , as being strangers. They are governed by a queen, to whom also Meroë, an island in the Nile near these places, is subject. Above this, at no great distance, is another island in the river, a settlement occupied by the same fugitives. From Meroë to this sea is a journey of fifteen days for an active person. Near Meroë is the confluence of the Astaboras, the Astapus, and of the Astasobas [the White and Blue Niles].

On the banks of these rivers live the Rhizophagi [root-eaters] and Heleii [marsh-men]. They have their name from digging roots in the adjacent marsh, bruising them with stones, and forming them into cakes, which they dry in the sun for food. These countries are the haunts of lions. The wild beasts are driven out of these places, at the time of the rising of the dog-star, by large gnats. Near these people live the Spermophagi [seed-eaters], who, when seeds of plants fail, subsist upon seeds of trees, which they prepare in the same manner as the Rhizophagi prepare their roots. Next to Elaea are the watch-towers of Demetrius, and the altars of Conan. In the interior Indian

reeds grow in abundance. The country there is called the country of
Coracius [modern-day Eritrea].

Far in the interior was a place called Endera [modern Tigray, in
Ethiopia] inhabited by a naked tribe who use bows and reed arrows,
the points of which are hardened in the fire. They generally shoot the
animals from trees, sometimes from the ground. They have numerous
herds of wild cattle among them, on the flesh of which they subsist,
and on that of other wild animals. When they have taken nothing in
the chase, they dress dried skins upon hot coals, and are satisfied with
food of this kind. It is their custom to propose trials of skill in archery
for those who have not attained manhood. Next to the altars of Conan
is the port of Melinus, and above it is a fortress called that of Coraus
and the chase of Coraus, also another fortress and more hunting-
grounds. Then follows the harbour of Antiphilus, and above this a
tribe, the Creophagi , whose men are circumcised and whose women
are excised after the Jewish custom.

Further still towards the south are the Cynamolgi, called by the
natives Agrii, with long hair and long beards, who keep a breed of very
large dogs for hunting the Indian cattle which come into their country
from the neighbouring district, driven there either by wild beasts or
by scarcity of pasturage. The time of their incursion is from the
summer solstice to the middle of winter. Next to the harbour of
Antiphilus is a port called the Grove of the Colobi [the Mutilated],
the city Berenice of the Sabae, and Sabae, a considerable city; then the
grove of Eumenes.

Above is the city Darada, and a hunting-ground for elephants,
called 'At the Well'. The district is inhabited by the Elephantophagi
[Elephant-eaters], who are occupied in hunting them. When they
descry from the trees a herd of elephants directing their course
through the forest, they do not then attack, but they approach by
stealth and hamstring the hindmost stragglers from the herd. Some
kill them with bows and arrows, the latter being dipped in the gall of
serpents. The shooting with the bow is performed by three men, two,
advancing in front, hold the bow, and one draws the string. Others
remark the trees against which the elephant is accustomed to rest,
and, approaching on the opposite side, cut the trunk of the tree low

down. When the animal comes and leans against it, the tree and the elephant fall down together. The elephant is unable to rise, because its legs are formed of one piece of bone which is inflexible; the hunters leap down from the trees, kill it, and cut it in pieces. The nomads call the hunters Acatharti, or impure.

Above this nation is situated a small tribe, the Struthophagi [Bird-eaters], in whose country are birds of the size of deer, which are unable to fly, but run with the swiftness of the ostrich. Some hunt them with bows and arrows, others covered with the skins of birds. They hide the right hand in the neck of the skin, and move it as the birds move their necks. With the left hand they scatter grain from a bag suspended to the side; they thus entice the birds, until they drive them into pits, where the hunters despatch them with cudgels. The skins are used both as clothes and as coverings for beds. The Ethiopians called Simi are at war with these people, and use as weapons the horns of antelopes.

Bordering on this people is a nation blacker in complexion than the others, shorter in stature, and very short-lived. They rarely live beyond forty years; for the flesh of their bodies is eaten up with worms. Their food consists of locusts, which the south-west and west winds, when they blow violently in the spring-time, drive in bodies into the country. The inhabitants catch them by throwing into the ravines materials which cause a great deal of smoke, and light them gently. The locusts, as they fly across the smoke, are blinded and fall down. They are pounded with salt, made into cakes, and eaten as food. Above these people is situated a desert tract with extensive pastures. It was abandoned in consequence of the multitudes of scorpions and tarantulas, called tetragnathi [four-jawed], which formerly abounded to so great a degree as to occasion a complete desertion of the place long since by its inhabitants.

Next to the harbour of Eumenes, as far as Deire and the straits opposite the six islands, live the Ichthyophagi, Creophagi, and Colobi, who extend into the interior. Many hunting-grounds for elephants, and obscure cities and islands, lie in front of the coast. The greater part are nomads; husbandmen are few in number. In the country occupied by some of these nations styrax grows in large quantity. The

Icthyophagi, on the ebbing of the tide, collect fish, which they cast upon the rocks and dry in the sun. When they have well-broiled them, the bones are piled in heaps, and the flesh trodden with the feet is made into cakes, which are again exposed to the sun and used as food. In bad weather, when fish cannot be procured, the bones of which they have made heaps are pounded, made into cakes and eaten, but they suck the fresh bones. Some also live upon shellfish, when they are fattened, which is done by throwing them into holes and standing pools of the sea, where they are supplied with small fish, and used as food when other fish are scarce. They have various kinds of places for preserving and feeding fish, from whence they derive their supply.

Some of the inhabitants of that part of the coast which is without water go inland every five days, accompanied by all their families, with songs and rejoicings, to the watering places, where, throwing themselves on their faces, they drink as beasts until their stomachs are distended like a drum. They then return again to the sea-coast. They dwell in caves or cabins, with roofs consisting of beams and rafters made of the bones and spines of whales, and covered with branches of the olive tree. The Chelonophagi [Turtle-eaters] live under the cover of shells (of turtles), which are large enough to be used as boats. Some make of the sea-weed, which is thrown up in large quantities, lofty and hill-like heaps, which are hollowed out, and underneath which they live. They cast out the dead, which are carried away by the tide, as food for fish.

Strabo (64 BC – AD 24) was a Greek geographer, philosopher and historian, born in modern-day Amsya, Turkey, just 75 kilometres from the Black Sea. Unlike Herodotus, who compiled fragments from earlier writers and was said to have not even travelled out of Greece, Strabo travelled far and wide, and the observations in his *Geographica* are often based on first-hand experience, or on first-hand accounts he collected himself. Strabo began travelling as a student, first moving to Nysa (Sultanhisar, Turkey) where he studied rhetoric and grammar and developed a lifelong love for Homer, before continuing to Rome where he studied philosophy with Xenarchus and, importantly,

geography under Tyrannion of Amisus. He completed his education
with Athenodorus Cananites, a well-connected philosopher who gave
him insights into stoicism. Strabo is most famous for his *Geographica*,
which seeks to be descriptive and utilitarian in its perspective – of
practical use for travellers, generals and traders – and as such was
widely circulated and used after his death. He is said to have visited
'Ethiopia', but it is unsure what is meant by this term, which probably
refers here to Nubia.

ACTS OF THE APOSTLES

FROM New Testament, fifth book, c. AD 80–90

A Eunuch's Endowment

Then the angel of the Lord spoke to Philip, 'Get up and head south on the road that goes down from Jerusalem to Gaza, the desert route.' So he got up and set out. Now there was an Ethiopian eunuch, a court official of the Candace, that is, the Queen of the Ethiopians, in charge of her entire treasury, who had come to Jerusalem to worship, and was returning home. Seated in his chariot, he was reading the prophet Isaiah. The Spirit said to Philip, 'Go and join up with that chariot.' Philip ran up and heard him reading Isaiah the prophet and said, 'Do you understand what you are reading?' He replied, 'How can I, unless someone instructs me?' So he invited Philip to get in and sit with him. This was the scripture passage he was reading: Like a sheep he was led to the slaughter, and as a lamb before its shearer is silent, so he opened not his mouth. In his humiliation justice was denied him. Who will tell of his posterity? For his life is taken from the earth. Then the eunuch said to Philip in reply, 'I beg you, about whom is the prophet saying this? About himself, or about someone else?' Then Philip opened his mouth and, beginning with this scripture passage, he proclaimed Jesus to him. As they travelled along the road they came to some water, and the eunuch said, 'Look, there is water. What is to prevent my being baptised?' Then he ordered the chariot to stop, and Philip and the eunuch both went down into the water, and he baptised him. When they came out of the water, the Spirit of the Lord snatched Philip away, and the eunuch saw him no more, but continued on his way rejoicing.

The anonymous writers of *The Acts of the Apostles* are recounting an early version of the conversion of 'Ethiopia' – how Queen Kandace became a Christian after her own eunuch's conversion. As we have seen in the Introduction, Kandace means 'Ruling Queen', and we do not know for sure which queen's conversion is being alluded to in this story. What we do know is that Kandace was a queen of Meroe – a kingdom often given the name Ethiopia but in fact in modern-day Sudan. Ethiopia itself, with Axum as its capital, would only truly be proselytised from the fourth century onwards, and retains Christianity at its core to this day. The various Nubian and Sudanese Christian kingdoms, no doubt first converted by Egyptian Coptic missionaries, toppled one after another to Islam, with the last shrivelled-up Christian pocket falling at the beginning of the sixteenth century.

LUCIUS CASSIUS DIO

FROM *Roman History*, AD 180–235

What did the Romans ever do for Ethiopia?

About this same time the Ethiopians, who dwell beyond Egypt, advanced as far as the city called Elephantine [modern-day Aswan in Egypt], with the Candace as their leader, ravaging everything they encountered. At Elephantine, however, learning that Gaius Petronius, the governor of Egypt, was already moving, they hastily retreated before he arrived, hoping to make good their escape. But being overtaken on the road, they were defeated and thus drew him after them into their own country. There, too, he fought successfully with them, and took Napata, their capital, among other cities. This place was razed to the ground, and a garrison left at another point; for Petronius, finding himself unable either to advance farther, on account of the sand and the heat, or advantageously to remain where he was with his entire army, withdrew, taking the greater part of it with him. Thereupon the Ethiopians attacked the garrisons, but he again proceeded against them, rescued his own men, and compelled the Candace to make terms with him.

Dio Cassius's (*c.* AD 155–235) history of Rome in eighty volumes was written in Greek over several decades and has survived into the modern era in many fragmentary texts, which give us insights both into actual happenings and into mythical stories and events in Roman history. Besides Rome, Italy and its empire, in which Dio served as a senator, a governor and even as a proconsul in Africa, his history gives early glimpses of 'far away' lands, such as Ethiopia – and even Britain, where Dio is one of only three authors to recount the revolt of the Celts under Boudica.

EZANA

FROM Rock Inscription, *c.* AD 350

Ezana was Here

Through the might of the Lord of All I took the field against the
Nubians when the people of Noba revolted, when they boasted and
said 'He will not cross over the Takkaze,' said the Nubians, when
they did violence to the peoples Mangurto and Hasa and Barya, and
the Black Nubians waged war on the Red Nubians and a second and
a third time broke their oath and without consideration slew their
neighbours and plundered our envoys and messengers whom I had
sent to interrogate them, robbing them of their possessions and
seizing their lances. When I sent again and they did not hear me, and
reviled me, and made off, I took the field against them. And I armed
myself with the power of the Lord of the Land and fought on the
Takkaze at the ford of Kemalke. And thereupon they fled and stood
not still, and I pursued the fugitives twenty-three days slaying them
and capturing others and taking plunder from them, where I came;
while prisoners and plunder were brought back by my own people
who marched out; while I burnt their towns, those of masonry and
those of straw, and seized their corn and their bronze and the dried
meat and the images in their temples and destroyed the stocks of
corn and cotton; and the enemy plunged into the river Seda, and
many perished in the water, the number I know not, and as their
vessels foundered a multitude of people, men and women were
drowned [. . .]

And I arrived at Kush, slaying them and taking others prisoner at
the junction of the rivers Seda and Takkaze. And on the day after my
arrival I dispatched into the field the troop of Mahaza and the
Damawa and Falha and Sera up the Seda against the towns of masonry
and of straw; their towns of masonry are called Alwa, Daro. And they

slew and took prisoners and threw them into the water and they returned safe and sound, after they had terrified their enemies and had conquered through the power of the Lord of the Land. And I sent the troop Halen and the troop Laken and the troop Sabarat and Falha and Sera down the Seda against the towns of straw of the Nubians and Negues; the towns of masonry of the Kasu which the Nubians had taken were Tabito, Fertoti; and they arrived at the territory of the Red Nubians, and my people returned safe and sound after they had taken prisoners and slain others and had seized their plunder through the power of the Lord of Heaven. And I erected a throne at the junction of the rivers Seda and Takkaze, opposite the town of masonry which is on this peninsula.

Ezana (*c.*325–*c.*370), the first King of Axum to convert to Christianity, is attested by many sources – epigraphic, literary and numismatic. He is referred to in various documents from the Mediterranean Greek/Roman world as having accepted Christianity and having the bishop Frumentius by his side. There are various stellae and victory slabs written in Greek, Sabean and Geez that attest not only to Ezana's subjugation of various foes but also – in the later victory inscription to commemorate the expedition against the Nobatae of Nubia – of the king's own subjugation to a new monotheistic creed: Christianity. Coinage also attests to the kingdom's adoption of a new official religion with the symbol of the cross making its appearance later in the king's rule.

TYRANNIUS RUFINUS

FROM *The Church History of Rufinus*, c. AD 403

From the Monk's Mouth

One Metrodorus, a philosopher, is said to have penetrated to further India [i.e. Ethiopia] in order to view places and see the world. Inspired by his example, one Meropius, a philosopher of Tyre, wished to visit India [probably Ethiopia] with a similar object, taking with him two small boys who were related to him and whom he was educating in the humanities. The younger of them was called Aedesius, the other Frumentius. When, having seen and taken note of what his soul fed upon, the philosopher had begun to return, the ship on which he travelled put in for water or some other necessary at a certain port. It is the custom of the barbarians of these parts that, if ever the neighbouring tribes report that their treaty with the Romans is broken, all Romans found among them should be massacred. The philosopher's ship was boarded; all with himself were put to the sword.

The boys were found studying under a tree and preparing their lessons, and, preserved by the mercy of the barbarians, were taken to the king [this would probably be King Ella Amida]. He made one of them, Aedesius, his cupbearer. Frumentius, whom he had perceived to be sagacious and prudent, he made his treasurer and secretary. Thereafter, they were held in great honour and affection by the king. The king died, leaving his wife with an infant son [Ezana] as heir to the bereaved kingdom. He gave the young men liberty to do what they pleased but the queen besought them with tears, since she had no more faithful subjects in the whole kingdom, to share with her the cares of governing the kingdom until her son should grow up, especially Frumentius, whose ability was equal to guiding the kingdom – for the other, though loyal and honest of heart, was simple.

While they lived there and Frumentius held the reins of government in his hands, God stirred up his heart and he began to search
out with care those of the Roman merchants who were Christians
and to give them great influence and to urge them to establish in
various places religious buildings to which they might resort for
prayer in the Roman manner. He himself, moreover, did the same
and so encouraged the others, attracting them with his favour and his
benefits, providing them with whatever was needed, supplying sites
for buildings and other necessaries, and in every way promoting the
growth of the seed of Christianity in the country. When the prince
for whom they exercised the regency had grown up, they completed
and faithfully delivered over their trust, and, though the queen and
her son sought greatly to detain them and begged them to remain,
they returned to the Roman Empire.

Aedesius hastened to Tyre to revisit his parents and relatives.
Frumentius went to Alexandria, saying that it was not right to hide
the work of God. He laid the whole affair before the bishop and
urged him to look for some worthy man to send as bishop over the
many Christians already congregated and the churches built on
barbarian soil. Then Athanasius – for he had recently assumed the
episcopate – having carefully weighed and considered Frumentius'
words and deeds, declared in a council of the priests: 'What other
man shall we find in whom the Spirit of God is as in you, who can
accomplish these things?' And he consecrated him and bade him
return in the grace of God whence he had come. And when he had
arrived in India [Ethiopia] as bishop, such grace is said to have been
given to him by God that apostolic miracles were wrought by him
and a countless number of barbarians were converted by him to the
faith. From which time Christian peoples and churches have been
created in the parts of India [Ethiopia] and the priesthood has begun.
These facts I know not from common report but from the mouth of
Aedesius himself, who had been Frumentius' companion and was
later made a priest in Tyre.

*

Tyrannius Rufinus or Rufinus of Aquileia (344–410) was a monk,
historian and theologian. Born in Italy to Christian parents, after a

meeting with Jerome in the monastic community where he lived, Rufinus travelled to Alexandria where he studied under Didymus the Blind. During his time in Egypt, Rufinus cultivated relationships with the Desert Ascetics and when he later left to live in Jerusalem, he set up a monastery on the Mount of Olives, which combined elements of the ascetic life with a life of learning and theology. He renewed his friendship with Jerome before the two became embroiled in a series of published theological controversies. In later years Rufinus went back to Italy.

PROCOPIUS OF CAESAREA

FROM *The Wars of Justinian*, AD 551

War by Proxy in the Red Sea

At that time the idea occurred to the Emperor Justinian to ally himself
with the Ethiopians and the Omeritae, in order to injure the Persians
[. . .] About opposite the Omeritae on the opposite mainland dwell
the Ethiopians who are called Auxumitae, because their king resides
in the city of Auxomis. And the expanse of sea which lies between
is crossed in a voyage of five days and nights, when a moderately
favouring wind blows [. . .]

From the city of Auxomis to the Egyptian boundaries of the
Roman domain, where the city called Elephantine is situated, is a
journey of thirty days for an unencumbered traveller. Within that
space many nations are settled, and among them the Blemmyae and
the Nobatae, who are very large nations. But the Blemmyae dwell in
the central portion of the country, while the Nobatae possess the
territory about the River Nile. Formerly this was not the limit of the
Roman Empire, but it lay beyond there as far as one would advance
in a seven days' journey; but the Roman Emperor Diocletian came
there, and observed that the tribute from these places was of the
smallest possible account, since the land is at that point extremely
narrow – for rocks rise to an exceedingly great height at no great
distance from the Nile and spread over the rest of the country –
while a very large body of soldiers had been stationed there from of
old, the maintenance of which was an excessive burden upon the
public; and at the same time the Nobatae who formerly dwelt about
the city of Premnis used to plunder the whole region; so he persuaded these barbarians to move from their own habitations, and to
settle along the River Nile, promising to bestow upon them great
cities and land both extensive and incomparably better than that

which they had previously occupied. For in this way he thought
that they would no longer harass the country about Pselchis at least,
and that they would possess themselves of the land given them, as
being their own, and would probably beat off the Blemmyae and the
other barbarians.

And since this pleased the Nobatae, they made the migration
immediately, just as Diocletian directed them, and took possession of
all the Roman cities and the land on both sides of the River beyond
the city of Elephantine. Then it was that this emperor decreed that to
them and to the Blemmyae a fixed sum of gold should be given every
year with the stipulation that they should no longer plunder the land
of the Romans. And they receive this gold even up to my time, but
none the less they overrun the country there. Thus, it seems that with
all barbarians there is no means of compelling them to keep faith with
the Romans except through the fear of soldiers to hold them in check.
And yet this emperor went so far as to select a certain island in the
River Nile close to the city of Elephantine and there constructed a
very strong fortress in which he established certain temples and altars
for the Romans and these barbarians in common, and he settled
priests of both nations in this fortress, thinking that the friendship
between them would be secure by reason of their sharing the things
sacred to them. And for this reason he named the place Philae. Now,
both these nations, the Blemmyae and the Nobatae, believe in all the
gods in which the Greeks believe, and they also reverence Isis and
Osiris, and not least of all Priapus. But the Blemmyae are accustomed
also to sacrifice human beings to the Sun. These sanctuaries in Philae
were kept by these barbarians even up to my time, but the Emperor
Justinian decided to tear them down [. . .]

At about the time of this war Ellestheaeus, the king of the
Ethiopians, who was a Christian and a most devoted adherent of this
faith, discovered that a number of the Omeritae on the opposite
mainland [southern Arabia] were oppressing the Christians there
outrageously; many of these rascals were Jews, and many of them held
in reverence the old faith which men of the present day call Hellenic.
He therefore collected a fleet of ships and an army and came against
them, and he conquered them in battle and slew both the king and

many of the Omeritae. He then set up in his stead a Christian king, an Omeritae by birth, by name Esimiphaeus, and, after ordaining that he should pay a tribute to the Ethiopians every year, he returned to his home. In this Ethiopian army many slaves and all who were readily disposed to crime were quite unwilling to follow the king back, but were left behind and remained there because of their desire for the land of the Omeritae; for it is an extremely goodly land.

These fellows at a time not long after this, in company with certain others, rose against the king Esimiphaeus and put him in confinement in one of the fortresses there, and established another king over the Omeritae, Abramus by name. Now this Abramus was a Christian, but a slave of a Roman citizen who was engaged in the business of shipping in the city of Adulis in Ethiopia. When Ellestheaeus learned this, he was eager to punish Abramus together with those who had revolted with him for their injustice to Esimiphaeus, and he sent against them an army of three thousand men with one of his relatives as commander. This army, once there, was no longer willing to return home, but they wished to remain where they were in a goodly land, and so without the knowledge of their commander they opened negotiations with Abramus; then when they came to an engagement with their opponents, just as the fighting began, they killed their commander and joined the ranks of the enemy, and so remained there. But Ellestheaeus was greatly moved with anger and sent still another army against them; this force engaged with Abramus and his men, and, after suffering a severe defeat in the battle, straightway returned home. Thereafter the king of the Ethiopians became afraid, and sent no further expeditions against Abramus. After the death of Ellestheaeus, Abramus agreed to pay tribute to the king of the Ethiopians who succeeded him, and in this way he strengthened his rule. But this happened at a later time.

At that time, when Ellestheaeus was reigning over the Ethiopians, and Esimiphaeus over the Omeritae, the Emperor Justinian sent an ambassador, Julianus, demanding that both nations on account of their community of religion should make common cause with the Romans in the war against the Persians; for he purposed that the Ethiopians, by purchasing silk from India and selling it among the Romans, might themselves gain much money, while causing the Romans to profit in only one way, namely, that they be no longer compelled to pay over their money to their enemy. (This is the silk of which they are accustomed to make the garments which of old the Greeks called 'Medic', but which at the present time they name 'Seric'.) As for the Omeritae, it was desired that they should establish Caïsus, the fugitive, as captain over the Maddeni, and with a great army of their own people and of the Maddene Saracens make an invasion into the land of the Persians. This Caïsus was by birth of the captain's rank and an exceptionally able warrior, but he had killed one of the relatives of Esimiphaeus and was a fugitive in a land which is utterly destitute of human habitation.

So each king, promising to put this demand into effect, dismissed the ambassador, but neither one of them did the things agreed upon by them. For it was impossible for the Ethiopians to buy silk from the Indians, for the Persian merchants always locate themselves at the very harbours where the Indian ships first put in (since they inhabit the adjoining country), and are accustomed to buy the whole cargoes; and it seemed to the Omeritae a difficult thing to cross a country which was a desert and which extended so far that a long time was required for the journey across it, and then to go against such a people much more warlike than themselves. Later on Abramus too, when at length he had established his power most securely, promised the Emperor Justinian many times to invade the land of Persia, but only once began the journey and then straightway turned back. Such then were the relations which the Romans had with the Ethiopians and the Omeritae.

Procopius of Caesarea (500–560) figures as the last prominent historian of the ancient world, and was the main historian of the sixth century, writing such works as *The Wars of Justinian*, *The Buildings of Justinian* and his prominent work *Secret History*. Although he positioned himself as a historian in the mould of Herodotus or Thucydides, Procopius was both a much more engaged writer – accompanying General Belasarius to vanquish the Vandals in North

Africa and writing extensively about it – and a much more 'modern'
one – in the modern sense of modern – when he wrote in a titillating
manner about all sorts of scandalous goings on – real or imagined –
at the Byzantine court of Justinian ('The Emperor suddenly rose
from his throne and walked about, and indeed he was never wont to
remain sitting for long, and immediately Justinian's head vanished,
while the rest of his body seemed to ebb and flow; whereat
the beholder stood aghast and fearful, wondering if his eyes were
deceiving him' or, 'And Theodora often, even in the theatre, in the
sight of all the people, she removed her costume and stood nude in
their midst, except for a girdle about the groin: not that she was
abashed at revealing that, too, to the audience, but because there was
a law against appearing altogether naked on the stage, without
at least this much of a fig-leaf'). Almost nothing is known about
Procopius' early life – apart from what he tells us in his own writings –
save that he was born in Caesarea in Palaestina Prima and became a
barrister, before becoming Belisarius' legal adviser.

THEOPHANES THE CONFESSOR

FROM *Chronicles of Theophanes*, AD 810–815

The Ambassador Julian Visits Emperor Kaleb

In the same year, the Romans and Persians broke their peace. The Persian war was renewed because of the embassy of the Homeritan Indians [the Himyarite Arabs] to the Romans. The Romans sent the Magistrianos Julian from Alexandria down the Nile River and through the Indian Ocean [the Red Sea] with sacral letters to Arethas [King Kaleb], the king of the Ethiopians. King Arethas [Kaleb] received him with great joy, since Arethas longed after the Roman Emperor's friendship.

On his return, this same Julian reported that King Arethas was naked when he received him but had round his kidneys a loincloth of linen and gold thread. On his belly he wore linen with precious pearls; his bracelets had five spikes, and he wore gold armlets by his hands. He had a linen and gold cloth turban round his head, with four cords hanging down from both its straps.

He stood on a carriage drawn by four standing elephants which had a yoke and four wheels. Like any stately carriage, it was ornamented with golden petals, just as are the carriages of provincial governors. While he stood upon it, he held in his hands a small gilded shield and two gold javelins. His counsellors were all armed, and sang musical tunes.

When the Roman ambassador was brought in and had performed the prostration, he was ordered to rise by the king and was led before him. Arethas accepted the Emperor's sacral letters and tenderly kissed the seal which had the Emperor's image. He also accepted Julian's gifts and greatly rejoiced.

When he read the letter, he found that it was urgent for him to arm himself against the Persian king, devastate Persian territory near him, and in the future no longer make covenants with the Persian. Rather, the letter arranged that the land of the Homeritai would conduct its business with Egyptian Alexandria by way of the Nile River.

In the sight of the envoy, King Arethas immediately began to campaign: he set war in motion against the Persians and sent out his Saracens. He himself also went off against Persian territory and pillaged all of it in that area. After conquering, King Arethas gave Julian a kiss of peace on the head and sent him off with a large retinue and many gifts.

Theophanes the Confessor (*c.*760–*c.*818), Byzantine aristocrat, monk and chronicler, a saint to both the Orthodox and Catholic Churches. Theophanes continued the chronicle of his friend Syncellus at the latter's request and his *Chronicles* is a precious compilation of dates, events and earlier writings since lost. Theophanes, an orphan at an early age, was married at twelve but convinced his wife to take a vow of celibacy. He founded monasteries and became a well-known and robust protector of the use of icons, a position for which he would later be persecuted and sent into exile in Samothrace, where he quickly died.

COSMAS INDICOPLEUSTES

FROM *The Christian Topography*, AD 550

The Gold Trade in Ethiopia

That country known as that of Sasu is itself near the Ocean, just as the Ocean is near the frankincense country, in which there are many gold mines. The King of the Axumites accordingly, every other year, through the governor of Agew sends thither special agents to bargain for the gold, and these are accompanied by many other traders – upwards, say, of five hundred – bound on the same errand as themselves. They take along with them to the mining district oxen, lumps of salt, and iron, and when they reach its neighbourhood they make a halt at a certain spot and form an encampment, which they fence round with a great hedge of thorns. Within this they live, and having slaughtered the oxen, cut them in pieces, and lay the pieces on the top of thorns, along with the lumps of salt and the iron. Then come the natives bringing gold in nuggets like peas, called *tancharas*, and lay one or two or more of these upon what pleases them – the pieces of flesh or the salt or the iron, and then they retire to some distance off. Then the owner of the meat approaches, and if he is satisfied he takes the gold away, and upon seeing this its owner comes and takes the flesh or the salt or the iron. If, however, he is not satisfied, he leaves the gold, when the native seeing that he has not taken it, comes and either puts down more gold, or takes up what he had laid down, and goes away. Such is the mode in which business is transacted with the people of that country, because their language is different and interpreters are hardly to be found.

The time they stay in that country is five days more or less, according as the natives more or less readily coming forward buy up all their wares. On the journey homeward they all agree to travel well-armed, since some of the tribes through whose country they must pass might threaten to attack them from a desire to rob them of their gold. The space of six months is taken up with this trading expedition, including both the going and the returning. In going they march very slowly, chiefly because of the cattle, but in returning they quicken their pace lest on the way, they should be overtaken by winter and its rains. For the sources of the River Nile lie somewhere in these parts, and in winter, on account of the heavy rains, the numerous rivers which they generate obstruct the path of the traveller. The people there have their winter at the time we have our summer. It begins in the month Epiphi of the Egyptians and continues till Thoth – that is to say June through August – and during the three months the rain falls in torrents, and makes a multitude of rivers all of which flow into the Nile [. . .]

Cosmas Indicopleustes – 'Cosmas who sailed to India' – did just that several times in the sixth century, during the reign of Emperor Justinian. He was a Greek trader from Alexandria and an Eastern Christian; he was therefore interested in maps, cartography and geography from a simply utilitarian motive but, as well, from a theological point of view, and his work, the *Christian Topography*, is interesting both for its wonderful mapping and for the theological geography that Cosmas sees, or superposes, on to the worlds he explored. Cosmas' first-hand accounts – if that is truly what they are – of India, Sri Lanka, of the Indian Ocean and Red Sea trade routes, and of the Axum Empire, are precious testimonials. His accounts of Ethiopia in particular are an extremely rare window on to the land and customs of Axum – a country that, due to the rise of Islam in the Red Sea, soon turned inward and stopped its trading and cultural exchanges with both the Mediterranean and the Indian subcontinent. Cosmas, after much seafaring, finished life as a hermit.

ANONYMOUS

FROM *The Periplus of the Red Sea, c.* AD 100

A Rough Guide to Ethiopia

Of the designated ports on the Erythraean Sea, and the market-towns around it, the first is the Egyptian port of Mussel Harbour. To those sailing down from that place, on the right hand, after eighteen hundred stadia, there is Berenice. The harbours of both are at the boundary of Egypt, and are bays opening from the Erythraean Sea.

On the right-hand coast next below Berenice is the country of the Berbers. Along the shore are the Fish-Eaters, living in scattered caves in the narrow valleys. Further inland are the Berbers, and beyond them the Wild-flesh-Eaters and Calf-Eaters, each tribe governed by its chief; and behind them, further inland, in the country towards the west, there lies a city called Meroe.

Below the Calf-Eaters there is a little market-town on the shore after sailing about four thousand stadia from Berenice, called Ptolemais of the Hunts, from which the hunters started for the interior under the dynasty of the Ptolemies. This market-town has the true land-tortoise in small quantity; it is white and smaller in the shells. And here also is found a little ivory like that of Adulis. But the place has no harbour and is reached only by small boats.

Below Ptolemais of the Hunts, at a distance of about three thousand stadia, there is Adulis, a port established by law, lying at the inner end of a bay that runs in toward the south. Before the harbour lies the so-called Mountain Island, about two hundred stadia seaward from the very head of the bay, with the shores of the mainland close to it on both sides. Ships bound for this port now anchor here because of attacks from the land. They used formerly to anchor at the very head of the bay, by an island called Diodorus, close to the shore, which could be reached on foot from the land; by which means the barbarous natives attacked the island. Opposite Mountain Island, on the mainland twenty stadia from shore, lies Adulis, a fair-sized village, from which there is a three days' journey to Coloe, an inland town and the first market for ivory. From that place to the city of the people called Axumites there is a five days' journey more; to that place all the ivory is brought from the country beyond the Nile through the district called Cyeneum, and thence to Adulis. Practically the whole number of elephants and rhinoceros that are killed live in the places inland, although at rare intervals they are hunted on the seacoast even near Adulis. Before the harbour of that market-town, out at sea on the right hand, there lie a great many little sandy islands called Alalaei, yielding tortoise-shell, which is brought to market there by the Fish-Eaters.

And about eight hundred stadia beyond there is another very deep bay, with a great mound of sand piled up at the right of the entrance; at the bottom of which the opsian stone is found, and this is the only place where it is produced. These places, from the Calf-Eaters to the other Berber country, are governed by Zoscales; who is miserly in his ways and always striving for more, but otherwise upright, and acquainted with Greek literature.

There are imported into these places, undressed cloth made in Egypt for the Berbers; robes from Arsinoe; cloaks of poor quality dyed in colours; double-fringed linen mantles; many articles of flint glass, and others of murrhine, made in Diospolis; and brass, which is used for ornament and in cut pieces instead of coin; sheets of soft copper, used for cooking-utensils and cut up for bracelets and anklets for the women; iron, which is made into spears used against the elephants and other wild beasts, and in their wars. Besides these, small axes are imported, and adzes and swords; copper drinking-cups, round and large; a little coin for those coming to the market; wine of Laodicea and Italy, not much; olive oil, not much; for the king, gold and silver plate made after the fashion of the country, and for clothing, military cloaks, and thin coats of skin, of no great value. Likewise from the district of Ariaca across this sea, there are imported Indian iron, and steel, and Indian cotton cloth; the broad cloth called monache and that called sagmatogene, and girdles, and coats of skin and mallow-coloured cloth, and a few muslins, and coloured lac.

There are exported from these places ivory, and tortoise-shell and rhinoceros-horn. The most from Egypt is brought to this market from the month of January to September, that is, from Tybi to Thoth; but seasonably they put to sea about the month of September.

From this place the Arabian Gulf trends toward the east and becomes narrowest just before the Gulf of Avalites. After about four thousand stadia, for those sailing eastward along the same coast, there are other Berber market-towns, known as the 'far-side' ports; lying at intervals one after the other, without harbours but having roadsteads where ships can anchor and lie in good weather. The first is called Avalites; to this place the voyage from Arabia to the far-side coast is the shortest. Here there is a small market-town called Avalites, which must be reached by boats and rafts. There are imported into this place, flint glass, assorted; juice of sour grapes from Diospolis; dressed cloth, assorted, made for the Berbers; wheat, wine, and a little tin. There are exported from the same place, and sometimes by the Berbers themselves crossing on rafts to Ocelis and Muza on the opposite shore, spices, a little ivory, tortoise-shell, and a very little myrrh, but better than the rest. And the Berbers who live in the place are very unruly.

After Avalites there is another market-town, better than this, called Malao, distant a sail of about eight hundred stadia. The anchorage is an open roadstead, sheltered by a spit running out from the east. Here the natives are more peaceable. There are imported into this place the things already mentioned, and many tunics, cloaks from Arsinoe, dressed and dyed; drinking-cups, sheets of soft copper in small quantity, iron, and gold and silver coin, not much. There are exported from these places myrrh, a little frankincense, the harder cinnamon, duaca, Indian copal and macir, which are imported into Arabia; and slaves, but rarely.

Two days' sail, or three, beyond Malao is the market-town of Mundus, where the ships lie at anchor more safely behind a projecting island close to the shore. There are imported into this place the things previously set forth, and from it likewise are exported the merchandise already stated, and the incense called mocrotu. And the traders living here are more quarrelsome.

Beyond Mundus, sailing toward the east, after another two days' sail, or three, you reach Mosyllum, on a beach, with a bad anchorage. There are imported here the same things already mentioned, also silver plate, a very little iron, and glass. There are shipped from the place a great quantity of cinnamon (so that this market-town requires ships of larger size), and fragrant gums, spices, a little tortoise-shell, and mocrotu (poorer than that of Mundus), frankincense, ivory and myrrh in small quantities.

Sailing along the coast beyond Mosyllum, after a two days' course you come to the so-called Little Nile River, and a fine spring, and a small laurel-grove, and Cape Elephant. Then the shore recedes into a bay, and has a river, called Elephant, and a large laurel-grove called Acannae; where alone is produced the far-side frankincense, in great quantity and of the best grade.

Beyond this place, the coast trending toward the south, there is the Market and Cape of Spices, an abrupt promontory, at the very end of the Berber coast toward the east. The anchorage is dangerous at times from the groundswell, because the place is exposed to the north. A sign of an approaching storm which is peculiar to the place, is that the deep water becomes more turbid and changes its colour. When this happens they all run to a large promontory called Tabae, which offers safe shelter. There are imported into this market-town the things already mentioned; and there are produced in it cinnamon (and its different varieties, gizir, asypha, areho, iriagia, and moto) and frankincense.

Beyond Tabae, after four hundred stadia, there is the village of Pano. And then, after sailing four hundred stadia along a promontory, toward which place the current also draws you, there is another market-town called Opone, into which the same things are imported as those already mentioned, and in it the greatest quantity of cinnamon is produced (the arebo and moto), and slaves of the better sort, which are brought to Egypt in increasing numbers; and a great quantity of tortoise-shell, better than that found elsewhere.

The voyage to all these far-side market-towns is made from Egypt about the month of July, that is Epiphi. And ships are also customarily fitted out from the places across this sea, from Ariaca and Barygaza, bringing to these far-side market-towns the products of their own places; wheat, rice, clarified butter, sesame oil, cotton cloth, and girdles, and honey from the reed called sacchari. Some make the voyage especially to these market-towns, and others exchange their cargoes while sailing along the coast. This country is not subject to a King, but each market-town is ruled by its separate chief.

Beyond Opone, the shore trending more toward the south, first there are the small and great bluffs of Azania; this coast is destitute of harbours, but there are places where ships can lie at anchor, the shore being abrupt; and this course is of six days, the direction being south-west. Then come the small and great beach for another six days' course and after that in order, the Courses of Azania, the first being called Sarapion and the next Nicon; and after that several rivers and other anchorages, one after the other, separately a rest and a run for each day, seven in all, until the Pyralax islands and what is called the channel; beyond which, a little to the south of south-west, after two courses of a day and night along the Ausanitic coast, is the island Menuthias, about three hundred stadia from the mainland, low and wooded, in which there are rivers and many kinds of birds and the mountain-tortoise. There are no wild beasts except the crocodiles; but there they do not attack men. In this place there are sewed boats, and canoes hollowed from single logs, which they use for fishing and catching tortoise. In this island they also catch them in a peculiar way, in wicker baskets, which they fasten across the channel-opening between the breakers.

Two days' sail beyond, there lies the very last market-town of the continent of Azania, which is called Rhapta; which has its name from the sewed boats [rhapton ploiarion] already mentioned; in which there is ivory in great quantity, and tortoise-shell. Along this coast live men of piratical habits, very great in stature, and under separate chiefs for each place. The Mapharitic chief governs it under some ancient right that subjects it to the sovereignty of the state that is become first in Arabia. And the people of Muza now hold it under his authority, and send thither many large ships; using Arab captains and agents, who are familiar with the natives and intermarry with them, and who know the whole coast and understand the language.

There are imported into these markets the lances made at Muza especially for this trade, and hatchets and daggers and awls, and various kinds of glass; and at some places a little wine, and wheat, not for trade, but to serve for getting the good-will of the savages. There are exported from these places a great quantity of ivory, but inferior to that of Adulis, and rhinoceros-horn and tortoise-shell (which is in best demand after that from India), and a little palm-oil.

And these markets of Azania are the very last of the continent that stretches down on the right hand from Berenice; for beyond these places the unexplored ocean curves around toward the west, and running along by the regions to the south of Aethiopia and Libya and Africa, it mingles with the western sea.

The anonymous author of the *Periplus* has good first-hand knowledge of the ports and seas between Egypt and India – to the Romans, this whole area was the 'Red Sea'. And from Berenice Troglodytica to Bucephalus Alexandria by way of Eudaemon Arabia, the account would remain unsurpassed in its wealth of accurate detail for centuries to come.

EDWARD GIBBON

FROM *History of the Decline and Fall of the Roman Empire*,
1776–1788

The Decline and Fall of Ethiopia in Arabia

Justinian had been reproached for his alliance with the Aethiopians, as
if he had attempted to introduce a people of savage negroes into the
system of civilised society. But the friends of the Roman empire,
the Axumites, or Abyssinians, may be always distinguished from the
original natives of Africa. The hand of nature has flattened the noses
of the Negroes, covered their heads with shaggy wool, and tinged
their skin with inherent and indelible blackness. But the olive complexion of the Abyssinians, their hair, shape, and features, distinctly
mark them as a colony of Arabs; and this descent is confirmed by
the resemblance of language and manners, the report of an ancient
emigration, and the narrow interval between the shores of the Red
Sea. Christianity had raised that nation above the level of African
barbarism: their intercourse with Egypt, and the successors of
Constantine, had communicated the rudiments of the arts and
sciences; their vessels traded to the Isle of Ceylon, and seven
kingdoms obeyed the Negus or supreme prince of Abyssinia. The
independence of the Homerites, who reigned in the rich and happy
Arabia, was first violated by an Aethiopian conqueror: he drew his
hereditary claim from the Queen of Sheba, and his ambition was
sanctified by religious zeal. The Jews, powerful and active in exile, had
seduced the mind of Dunaan, prince of the Homerites. They urged
him to retaliate the persecution inflicted by the Imperial laws on
their unfortunate brethren: some Roman merchants were injuriously
treated; and several Christians of Negra were honoured with the crown
of martyrdom. The churches of Arabia implored the protection of the
Abyssinian monarch. The Negus passed the Red Sea with a fleet and

army, deprived the Jewish proselyte of his kingdom and life, and extinguished a race of princes, who had ruled above two thousand years the sequestered region of myrrh and frankincense. The conqueror immediately announced the victory of the gospel, requested an orthodox patriarch, and so warmly professed his friendship to the Roman empire, that Justinian was flattered by the hope of diverting the silk trade through the channel of Abyssinia, and of exciting the forces of Arabia against the Persian king. Nonnosus, descended from a family of ambassadors, was named by the emperor to execute this important commission. He wisely declined the shorter, but more dangerous, road, through the sandy deserts of Nubia; ascended the Nile, embarked on the Red Sea, and safely landed at the African port of Adulis. From Adulis to the royal city of Axum is no more than fifty leagues, in a direct line; but the winding passes of the mountains detained the ambassador fifteen days; and as he traversed the forests, he saw, and vaguely computed, about five thousand wild elephants. The capital, according to his report, was large and populous; and the village of Axum is still conspicuous by the regal coronations, by the ruins of a Christian temple, and by sixteen or seventeen obelisks inscribed with Grecian characters. But the Negus gave audience in the open field, seated on a lofty chariot, which was drawn by four elephants, superbly caparisoned, and surrounded by his nobles and musicians. He was clad in a linen garment and cap, holding in his hand two javelins and a light shield; and, although his nakedness was imperfectly covered, he displayed the Barbaric pomp of gold chains, collars, and bracelets, richly adorned with pearls and precious stones. The ambassador of Justinian knelt; the Negus raised him from the ground, embraced Nonnosus, kissed the seal, perused the letter, accepted the Roman alliance, and, brandishing his weapons, denounced implacable war against the worshippers of fire. But the proposal of the silk trade was eluded; and notwithstanding the assurances, and perhaps the wishes, of the Abyssinians, these hostile menaces evaporated without effect. The Homerites were unwilling to abandon their aromatic groves, to explore a sandy desert, and to encounter, after all their fatigues, a formidable nation from whom they had never received any personal injuries. Instead of enlarging his conquests, the king of Aethiopia was incapable of defending his possessions. Abrahah, the slave of a Roman merchant of Adulis, assumed the sceptre of the Homerites; the troops of Africa were seduced by the luxury of the climate; and Justinian solicited the friendship of the usurper, who honoured with a slight tribute the supremacy of his prince. After a long series of prosperity, the power of Abrahah was overthrown before the gates of Mecca; and his children were despoiled by the Persian conqueror; and the Aethiopians were finally expelled from the continent of Asia. This narrative of obscure and remote events is not foreign to the decline and fall of the Roman Empire. If a Christian power had been maintained in Arabia, Mahomet must have been crushed in his cradle, and Abyssinia would have prevented a revolution which has changed the civil and religious state of the world.

Edward Gibbon's (1737–1794) *Decline and Fall* and his subsequent literary fame came after earlier lesser auspicious works, such as the *History of Switzerland* (unpublished during his lifetime) and *Mémoires Littéraires de la Grande-Bretagne* (a flop). While Herodotus is considered the Father of History, the founding of modern history is often ascribed to Gibbon himself. The latter, if given to witty and ironic descriptions which have not been to everyone's taste – as well as charges against religion – does at least rely heavily on primary sources, and eschews the hitherto common practice of simply compiling events already compiled by others. It is interesting here to hear the prejudices of the modern European mind in comparison to the descriptions given by classical writers. Gibbon lived comfortably off the proceeds of the estate left to him by his father, and was able to dedicate his life to his literary endeavours.

SURAT 105 AL-FIL (THE ELEPHANT)

FROM The Koran

Have you not heard how your Lord treated the companions
of the elephant?
Did He not upset their plans and thwart them?
And He sent against them flocks of birds,
Casting upon them pebbles of hardened clay,
Making them like chewed up straw.

The Koran. The mention of Ethiopians in the Surat Al-Fil denotes
the importance of Abyssinia in the Red Sea both in terms of regional
geopolitics and of ideology and cultural influence. Al-Fil tells the
story of how Abraha (the Abyssinian viceroy sent to invade Yemen
on the bidding of Byzantium), tried to attack Mecca, apparently
unsuccessfully, with the help of war elephants in AD 570. This was
the same year that the Prophet Mohammed was born, and the 'Year
of the Elephant' is to this day a commonly accepted manner of
designating that auspicious year. During the first Hegira, some of
Mohammed's followers found refuge at the court of the Abyssinian
king – the just Nejashi of Muslim lore. This event was commemorated
by the Prophet himself in his hadith 'Do not wage war on the
Abyssinians' – with the caveat 'if they don't attack you first . . . ' A
darker counterpart is to be found in the warning about a 'bandy-
legged Ethiopian' (another hadith), whose apparition is said to
announce the beginning of the end of times. However the importance
of Ethiopians in early Islam is underlined by the fact that the religion's
first muezzin, Bilal, who called the faithful to prayer, was one.

BYRON KHUN DE PROROCK

FROM *Dead Men Do Tell Tales*, 1942

Massua first came into prominence 3000 years ago in the time of the Queen of Sheba. Nearby are the ruins of Adulis. Once this city stood on the shores of the Red Sea, at the mouth of the River Saba. Then the river carried a great amount of silt. Before the Saba dried and stopped flowing, it had formed a long delta which left Adulis 7 miles from the sea.

Using this harbour, the Queen of Sheba opened up trade with Arabia and even Asia. Like Hannibal, she crossed the mountains of Ethiopia between Axum and Adulis with elephants, bringing with her vast numbers of slaves, soldiers, and nobles. With a fabulous treasure of gold and precious stones, she probably embarked from this port to make her conquest of Solomon's imagination and heart.

This Queen combined the fascination of Cleopatra with the commercial instincts of a modern business tycoon. Ethiopians have never been good traders; and for centuries they have left commerce to Greeks and Phoenicians. There is one theory that the Queen was of Phoenician and Semitic blood; in any event she conversed fluently and got on well with Solomon. The emperor, Haile Selassie, a direct descendant of that Queen, has great powers of fascination.

Adulis and the caravan trail that led from there to 'The Mountains of the Moon' where the legendary gold mines were located seems not to have appeared in history again until the days of two other African Queens, Candace and Berenice. One seduced the General of the Roman Army and persuaded him not to invade her country; the other was sufficiently wealthy to buy off the Persians. And each of these incidents saved Ethiopia from being conquered.

Ethiopia is next heard about through the activities of another strange woman, Judith, who was a very astute Jewess. Oddly, she possessed an enormous harem comprised of many nationalities – a harem full of men. Next came the semi-legendary empire in Ethiopia of Prester John. He ruled in the Middle Ages, and even sent a delegation to the Vatican in Rome, but, without ever promising allegiance and obedience to the Pope.

From Massua the yacht had gone to Assab, 'The Forbidden'. This is a place few people have ever heard of; it is the ancient Assoba and I believe it may be some day an important centre for petroleum. Once it was an important port of embarkation for slaves going to Persia and Arabia. Caravan trails many centuries old lead from the cluster of white, Arab houses and tin-roofed Italian military barracks. One goes to the rich Aussa Sultanate, and the other crosses the Danakil desert and goes on to the highlands of African Thibet. There were found those mysterious Hebrew tablets which may someday substantiate the legend of the Jewish Falasha people – the Lost Tribe of Israel.

Almost two million people of Hebrew descent live isolated in the Ethiopian mountains of Southern Godjam. Noses, skulls, customs, and traditions are typically Jewish, and the people follow the old Mosaic Law to the letter. Their Rabbis dress, and carry out the sacred rites of the calendar, just as they did in the days of Moses and Solomon. They have had no slightest contact with the outside world for centuries. They are the only manufacturing people in Ethiopia. Though their methods are primitive, they make fine jewellery, pottery, and cloth. Coming among them is like going back, magically, 3000 years into that time in the history of Palestine when Solomon reigned.

The Falasha Jews are said to be very wealthy, but their riches are never apparent; when a stranger appears, everything of value, indicative of their accumulated wealth, is concealed. Persecuted through the ages, they have learnt that displaying their riches is the surest way to attract invaders. The Ethiopians look down on these people, and the Falasha Jews in turn consider the Ethiopians as far inferior to themselves. My own belief, and it is borne out by many Ethiopian legends, is that they are descendants of a lost tribe of Israel.

*

Count Byron Khun de Prorock – born Francis Byron Kuhn –
(1896–1954) is the original Indiana Jones from the 1920s and 1930s.
He was acclaimed by the public for his articles, documentary films
and books and loathed in equal measure by 'true' archaeologists who
– quite rightly it seems – saw little more in him than a sensationalist
and media-hungry tomb-raider. After working on the excavations of
Carthage (and very seriously so: he was the holder of the Norton
Lectureship in 1922–23), Prorock organised a series of daring
expeditions that became more and more fantastical as he acquired
fame: he claimed to have found Atlantis in North Africa, then the
biblical land of Ophir, before stumbling upon the very temple where
Alexander the Great became a god . . . In his books, with names such
as *Digging for Lost African Gods, In Quest of Lost Worlds* and the
Ethiopian-based *Dead Men Do Tell Tales*, it is difficult to make out
what is truth and what confabulation. In *Dead Men*, Prorock ('Not a
count and certainly no archaeologist' as a colleague happily summed
him up) finds Ophir between Ethiopia and Sudan, and searches for
King Solomon's mines (which were, it appears, a top priority during
the Italian invasion of Ethiopia).

2

ABYSSINIANS AND ORANGES (1500–1700)

Introduction

> From the Ethiop's land a messenger
> This moment has reached us, news of grave import
> Brings he – be pleased to hear him!
>
> VERDI, Aida, ACT I, SCENE I

The relationship between the Portuguese and the Ethiopians between the fifteenth and seventeenth centuries was one of uneasy co-operation, turning to conflict. In the beginning the Portuguese, like the knights of yore, rode from the Red Sea shore into the misty hinterland of Ethiopia to save a Christian monarch, Prester John, from the Moor – or so the chivalric romance of the Portuguese in Ethiopia reads. In it, Prester John stands for King Arthur, Dom Christóvão da Gama is a Lancelot without reproach and Pero Paez a wise but conflicted sage who has the ear of kings – but whose fanatical successors undermine his painstakingly wrought foundations of mutual respect and understanding in a few decades. The romance ends in wild acts of cruelty and hanged priests; with exiled patriarchs in Goa calling for troops to put the Ethiopian king through his paces and convert his Coptic Christian people to Catholicism by force; and Ethiopia closing its borders to foreigners, with special orders to behead any Jesuit attempting to enter the kingdom.

In the second half of the fifteenth century, the kingdom of Portugal surged on to the great seas, their enemy the Turk, their goal India and its spices. Henry the Navigator set up his famous school for mariners and sent out envoys. Their mission was to find a route to India that avoided the dominions of the Turks, and to make contact with a mysterious king known as The Prester John of the Indies. This Prester John had been lurking in the margins of the story books, a shady figure woven from early references to a Presbyter in Syria; Nestorian accounts of a good Christian king in Asia, located by some in Xanadu, by others among the Jacobites of southern India; and a trickle of information from Jerusalem on a just and mighty king living somewhere to the south. A ninth-century Jewish traveller, El Dani (from the lost tribe of Dan), told of Jewish kingdoms on the banks of Ghion, and despite the paucity of the information given on Africa itself, El Dani's tale was welcomed by some as true while others saw him as just another windbag, a teller of tall tales.

The Prester's famous twelfth-century letter to the Pope sought to set the record straight: far from being Jewish, the kingdom was ruled by a just and mighty Christian king, who lived in a palace of lapis lazuli with moats of molten gold. The letter is certainly a fake, but the message was received, amplified and seized upon by adventurers, politicians and prelates. This Prester John was a Christian king willing to forge an alliance with western Christendom. The Portuguese envoys making their way down the coast of West Africa asked at each mooring if the land of the Prester was still far, and were often told that yes, just such a king does exist, but a little farther inland, a little further down the coast . . .

After several unsuccessful attempts, it fell to Pero da Covilha in 1495 to reach this Prester John, who at the time of his visit was Eskender, the young Emperor of Ethiopia, whose title is *Negusa Nagast*, King of Kings. Da Covilha travelled disguised as a merchant from Morocco (he spoke good Arabic), and, before even setting foot on the African coast, he had been the first Christian to reach Mecca, had made his way to India, and sent back instructions to Portugal on how best to sail to India by way of the Cape of Good Hope. But, after these voyages, and despite his instrumental role in initiating the age of great discoveries, Pero da Covilha disappeared into the interior of the continent and was not heard of again – until a Portuguese embassy visited Ethiopia in 1521 led by Rodrigo da Lima. The expedition's chaplain, Francisco Alvarez, recounted in his *True Description of a Voyage to the Prester John of the Indies*, how the embassy discovered an ageing da Covilha at the Ethiopian king's court. Plied with land grants and goods, he had all he could want for but had never been allowed to leave. The embassy spent seven years in the kingdom, and Alvarez' testimony is precious, as it is the first truthful account of the lands, the peoples and their customs. Of Lalibela he wrote famously: 'As to these marvels in Lalibela, I tire of describing them more as I am sure of not being believed.' Relations with the Prester – who was vaguely interested in the tall tales about himself, but not that much – were cordial enough, but again, not much more. The embassy was allowed to leave.

Shortly after their departure, events in Ethiopia took a dramatic turn. The Muslim populations of the east, until then nominally vassals of the Ethiopian kings, rose up and laid waste most of the kingdom in a series of daring campaigns led by Imam Ahmad ibn Ibrahim al-Ghazi – nicknamed *Gragn*, the left-handed one, in popular, Christian–Ethiopian culture. An envoy was sent hurriedly to Lisbon, but took seven years to get there, at the end of which Christóvão da Gama, with four hundred soldiers, was sent to save Ethiopia from Imam Ahmad. Christóvão rode up into the highlands and was himself beheaded, before the Portuguese and Abyssinian troops rallied, killed Imam Ahmad and put paid to the Muslim threat more or less for good.

Most of the Portuguese soldiers remained in the country, and this was the opening of a little-known chapter in the history of the Horn of Africa. For the next one hundred and fifty years, the descendants of those soldiers, the *Burtukan* (or Oranges as they became known – it is thought that the Portuguese first brought the fruit to Ethiopia, and it was given their name, with a B since the P of *Portugan* was difficult to pronounce), and Jesuit priests – often Portuguese it is true, but also Spanish, Indian, Catalan, Genovese – vied for the fortunes and the faith of Ethiopia. Missionaries, along with stonemasons and musical instruments were dispatched to the mountain kingdom to influence and hopefully convert the population. The Jesuits were ultimately expelled in 1632, and the last remaining priests were hounded and hanged; a large community of Catholics subsisted until the 1660s, when they are told to renounce their faith or go into exile, which many do, to Sennar in Sudan, where perhaps they thought they could put their war skills to good use as mercenaries. The descendants of the Portuguese soldiers became a sort of Praetorian Guard for Ethiopian Emperors, as well as the chief builders of bridges and castles. Oral traditions tell of a dispute in which Emperor Fasilides incurred the wrath of his priests by having two Portuguese sisters in his harem at the same time – a harem was just fine, but sisters was pushing the boundaries of orthodoxy.

Today, it is still common for Ethiopians, especially from Gondar and Zegue, to claim Portuguese blood. But if a smattering of Portuguese limestone buildings can still be found throughout Gojjam and the Lake Tana basin, and although a surprising number of islanders on Lake Tana have green eyes, the main legacy of the Portuguese lies in the books they penned. Starting with Francisco Alvarez, and continuing with Pero Paez, Jeronimo Lobo, Manoel de Almeida, and without forgetting all the correspondence that is kept in the archives of the Vatican, the Jesuits left a monument in writing that is invaluable, and, unlike previous accounts, is often to the point and informative.

Francisco Alvarez' book in particular is not only well informed, but also precious for its depiction of the country on the eve of the jihad led from Harar by Imam Ahmad, and before what is now known as the Oromo migrations, a momentous population movement which saw many of what had been the old heartlands of Abyssinia shift to different tongues and different cultures. The *Futuh Al-Habasha* (*The Conquest of Abyssinia*), a chronicle written by one of Ahmad's followers, is another invaluable book of these times: recounting the plundering of many churches and monasteries and thus revealing how prosperous the country was, giving a voice to the invaders and shedding light on the other side of the story. For these Muslim warriors saw themselves, of course, as just as chivalrous as the Portuguese and Christian kings they battled against. Recent historiography seems to have taken to calling these struggles 'an Ethiopian civil war'. Perhaps this is just plain silly, but it seeks to address a legitimate grievance in Ethiopia about historical writing which sees anything other than the Christian

Abyssinians as foreign and alien. That said, all of the authors here write with the opinions and prejudices of their time and are best read together, as a sort of historical thesis and antithesis.

These writings initiated what is known today as Ethiopian Studies, by way of the collaboration between Gregorius, an Ethiopian Catholic monk, and Job Ludolf, a German orientalist. And although the country did go into a form of lockdown for a while, this was squarely aimed at Catholic zealots. Armenian, Arab and French travellers continued to make their way to the court in Gondar, and trade in slaves and ivory was as brisk and profitable as ever. The Portuguese writings became the measure for all subsequent travellers, who read them and sometimes denigrated them while still constantly referencing them. Even Samuel Johnson's *Rasselas* is, in a manner, a spin-off from his translation of Jeronimo Lobo's *Travels in Ethiopia*. Lobo was quite trustworthy – he accurately described the source of the Blue Nile – but he was also an authority on the unicorn, which he described as living in great numbers in a region not far from that very source. Thus, the Portuguese era is a chapter on the threshold of science, with accurate descriptions of watercourses and languages, but with a unicorn or two thrown in for good measure, lest we forget Prester John of the Indies!

ANONYMOUS

FROM *The Life of the Holy Lalibela*, thirteenth century

And now listen, dear friends, you who are seeking the benedictions of the grace of the righteous and who are burning with love for Lalibela, so that you will make your delights from the account of his good fight, which percolates as water into the entrails, as marrow into the bone. For it is a shower of praises not even absorbed by the high heat of summer. So open wide the ears of your hearts. I begin, as much as the imperfections of my tongue and the shortcomings of my knowledge allow me, to speak of some of his numerous prodigies. I cannot enumerate one by one the accomplishments of this blessed one, but only a small number amongst them, so that your hearts will rejoice in learning of them, for the sight of the righteous rejoices much more than a well laid table can satiate, than thirst is quenched by wine and mead; she possesses more smoothness than oil and fat, as the prophet says: His words are softer than butter. As to you, it is good that you should wear his faith as you would clothes, that you fold yourself in it as you would in a veil, and that you honour this man as you honour the angels, the prophets, the apostles, the righteous, martyrs, virgins and monks, for he is of one piece with them. May his prayer and his intercession, his succour and the hope of his benediction remain with the servant of God, our Queen, Walatta Iyasus, with Walatta Hiruta Selase, with all you here who are present, and who have come from far and wide to seek shelter in the shade of his wings; may he not leave your side till the end of centuries. Amen.

Birth of Lalibela

There was in Ethiopia a city named Roha, the hometown of the blessed Lalibela, and in this city lived a man belonging to one of the greatest noblest and richest families in gold, in silver, in vestments, in precious cloth, in menservants and maidservants. This man was named Jan Seyum; he married and begat a son, who became this illustrious saint, mysteriously called Lalibela. I shall now explain the significance of this name and why it was given him.

When his mother brought him into the world, there came a great swarm of bees which stuck to him as they do with honey, and his mother saw these bees swarming around her child, like the army around the king. In that time the spirit of prophecy came down upon her and she said: 'The bees know that this child is great.' That is why she gave him the name of Lalibela, which means: 'The bees have recognised his grace.'

(. . .)

Description of the ten monolithic churches in the sky

Having said these words, God showed him the great houses made of a single stone. The number of these churches is ten and each one is of a particular construction, colour, and aspect. Some have narrow entrances and vast chambers, while others whose entrance is large are narrow inside. Their walls are very long and very high and amongst these churches, there are those which are higher than others and which have a particular colour. Some are reddish, others of the colour of the baltet stone, others of the colour of the zagas, others of the colour of the dust of kebo; there are those which possess great dimensions; others are larger than the others by the measure of . . .

Translated by YVES-MARIE STRANGER

Gebre Mesqel Lalibela (early thirteenth century), is more often styled Lalibela, which is thought to mean 'the bees have anointed his sovereignty' in Agaw. Lalibela was a monarch from the Zagwe dynasty, later overthrown by the 'rightful' descendants of Saba and Solomon. Nevertheless, the king's recognised role in building the rock-hewn churches of Roha (now known as Lalibela), have secured Lalibela an important place in Ethiopian history. He remains an important saint in the orthodox calendar to this day and this anonymous account of his life (or *gedl* in Amharic) is an important document of those times.

ALESSANDRO ZORZI

FROM *The Itinerario of Alessandro Zorzi,*
collected 1519–24 in Venice

Mapping the Journey

Brother Thomas of the Order of St Dominic, who came from Rome and is a native of the city of Barara, where are the Patriarch and Presta Davit (notwithstanding that the said Presta is still in the city of Zorgi), being of that country and almost from the middle of the kingdom of the said Presta, wherefore it seemed to me reasonable that he should know almost all the kingdoms, provinces, cities, mountains and rivers about it in the east, west, south and north, and the other places. I therefore took him to our house, and showing him the drawing I had made from the notes written above, I questioned him as well as I could seeing the little Latin that he had, about which he replied, first:

That in the province of Amarra, in the mountains, rises a branch of the Nile; and so likewise in the mountains of Cafat in the province of Gogiam rises the other branch that joins it going north; and in the province of Nubi it joins another main branch of the Nile coming from the west and enclosing the island of Meroe, coming from the springs of Nias, i.e. Black. He says that all (branches) united fall over the cataract and flow through Egypt, passing Cairo and going by its delta in several branches into the Mediterranean Sea beside Alexandria.

Item, he also gave me to understand that on the east and south side of the mountains of Cafat rises another river called Auas, which was little less than the Nile, diving in the province of Orab; and one branch passing by the side of the city of Barara, going southwards to the city of Us or Vis; the other branch going farther southwards by the province of Mogar (and then) eastwards by the province of Satai; both branches uniting in the province of Fesegar, and going northwards by the province of Doaro, and then by Bali and entering the province of Giamora, and on into the province of Adel, went into the Red Sea, where is the commercial city of [Zelo] or Barbara, with a good harbour, south of the Adem, which is the emporium of India and the gateway for all the spice and cloth and other things that come by land to Barara.

Item, another great river not less than the Nile which is called Ubi, which has its source in the south towards the Cape of Good Hope in the Southern Ocean, where sail the Portuguese also, where are great mountains on latitude 24 south towards the Antarctic Pole, where it is very cold and snows when the sun is in Cancer; and so rising on longitude 50 in the great province of Adia, and running northwards through the provinces of Teso and Voge and through Gorage, and so between the province of Damot and Naria through the province of Conce, it reaches the province of Gange and enters the Ocean on the east by several mouths at the city of Quiloa, captured by the Portuguese. The said river Ubi [it is understood, and the said river] receives on both right and left banks many other rivers and torrents so as to make it a great river. And from this place on the ships of Combaia, that reach the said ports, and also on those of the Portuguese, much merchandise goes by land to Barara, which is a shorter way than that from Gelo emporium and Barara. But that from Gelo is the chief because it is opposite Adem and Arabia Felix and Persia and India. Note that the other Brother Thomas of the Order of St Francis told me that (the) queen (of) Ganger made war on the Presta and since has made peace and pays him tribute, and that the people would not have a king but a queen; and Ganger is bounded on the south by the Ocean.

Item, the said Brother Thomas says that: From Barara going west-wards to the province of Mogar is 240 miles – from Mogar to the province of Cafat, 150 miles – from Cafat to Debian province through which passes the Nile, 800 miles – from Debain to Quara, 120 miles – from Quara one goes towards Tunici

Item, from Barara to Bosge south-westwards over the plain, 180 miles – from Bosge to Damot province over the plain (Christians), 180 miles from Damot to Naria province (Christians), 240 miles from Naria to Sicondi province (. . . Christians), 240 miles from Sicondi to Ulamo province, idolaters, 300 miles, and hot because it is under

Capricorn, and fugitive scorched Ethiopians with curly hair, idolaters, bestial, with ugly faces.

Which province of Ulamo is very great and goes (he says) to the sea, but he knows not its size; and there are great mountains and great heat, but that from Barara to Sicondi one goes over a plain and some hills, where go those who would go to the Lake of Sacala, and to avoid the great mountains that are on the way from Barara to Sacala they make their way from there to the province of Sicondi, because from the said province of Sicondi they go between the south and south-east to the province of Gamo, which is 440 miles; and from Gamo province to Sacala lake is 180 miles.

Sacala is a very great lake of sweet water that is 600 or 700 miles round, with estates and castles inhabited by Christians that have arrived recently with ('per') a captain of the Presta who, having transgressed, in order to escape with his life, fled hither from Barara from Presta John; and reaching this lake with his people he built a great church of St George in the midst of an island that is in the middle of the lake and is as big as Corfu; and here he captured a great city. And also round the lake are great mountains, and valleys great and small, where run streams, torrents and rivers and rivulets into the said lake, and (there is) a great valley that goes to the province of Gamo on the way to Secondi, as I said above; but the great mountains are on the east side of the lake, and these continue southward; and it is the same towards Barara in the middle of the journey; and then it is flat or merely hilly as far as the Auas river, and then flat to Barara; and on latitude 22 south, there is the great province of Adia, where rises a very great river called Ubi, that runs through several provinces and goes into the Indian Sea at the city and island of Quiloa in the east, and so it flows with various rivers and streamlets from right and left.

From Adia the said river Ubi goes to Teso – from Teso it goes to Gorage – from Gorage it goes to Conce province – from Conce it goes to the port of Gange (where they go once a year for the fair) to the Indian Sea where is Quiloa.

By another way go the merchants from Barara to the Red Sea, where is Barbara and the mouth of the river Auas; and some say that mouth is at Zelo port and City. And the said Brother Thomas says the mouth is at Barbara whence comes various merchandise to Barara from Adem and Persia Combaia and India.

And the Portuguese follow another route; they go by the Red Sea to Messoa port, at which they have made a strong castle to prevent spices from going by the Arabian Sea to Algidem; and so too the said Portuguese carry spices to the province of the Presta, and chiefly to Axon, which is said to be one of the greatest cities in those provinces, and another and greater Rome for grandeur and splendid buildings, ancient and wondrous; and that there are there columns as great as the campanile of San Marco in Venice, with great arches also and worked stones with great Chaldaean letters that few can read. Which city Ptolemy mentions in his Geography, putting it on latitude 10 and calling it Auxuma.

And the said Brother Thomas says that it is very hot there, beyond all comparison hotter than in Barara, although it is about on the equator; and that there it is cool and temperate, and that the said Portuguese carry (goods) by land from the said port of Mesoa to Axon and other provinces of the Presta as far as Barara; which trade-route is the finest and best by reason of the many cities to the right and the left until one comes to Barara and Vis, which is a warehouse and country of storehouses, as is mercantile Venice; and there at present is Andrea Corsali, a Florentine who is going to print Chaldaean books in the said country. And he has a great warehouse both there and in Barara; through that country passes the river Auas, so that the said way is thronged with merchandise and people that go unceasingly from place to place, full of cities, castles, villages, rivers, plains, hills, as here is the road to Rome.

And that coming from Messoa to Barara on the right hand as far as the branch of the Nile (the country) is occupied by cities and castles and estates, and beyond the Nile are provinces of Presta Davit. Starting from Axon westwards beyond the Nile is the province of Zagade, which on the north is bounded by the province of Nubi, where are infidels and bad men; and in the said province of Zagade the said Presta has cities and castles and estates and monasteries and hermitages. And the province of Zagade is bounded on the south by the great province of Agau and Dembrian along the Nile, on both sides of which are woods with churches and many hermits. And south of the province of Dembrian on the said branch of the Nile is the province of Basender, and then the great province of Gogian, where in the mountains of Caffat rises the said branch of the Nile; in all those provinces beyond the Nile in the west the inhabitants are under the said Presta.

On the left hand departing eastwards [sic] from the said port of Mesoa are more provinces (as I have noted) as far as the other trade-route that comes from Barbara, sea-port, and from Gelo, going to Barara; but the said way is more mountainous, sandy and wild, though there are some cities and castles and estates, where goes (?) also the river Auas. But beyond the said way towards the east are wild places full of scrub, woods, sand, and towards the sea mountains and various animals and bestial herdsmen; yet once a year at the fairs they pass through the city of the said Presta, (coming) from the Ocean from Melinde, city and port, from India, and from Chiloa, city and port, where goes river Ubi that comes from the north towards the Cape of Good Hope. And so too they come from the other mountains of Adia and from the province of Teso, that goes towards Mocembeque and Zefala, where at Cefala is the mouth of a great river, and where is the mine of gold which is not so good as that which comes from the mountains of Caffat.

Alessandro Zorzi (*c.*1470–1538). A cartographer from Venice, Zorzi is the author of a number of manuscripts conserved in the Biblioteca Nazionale in Florence known as the Codice Alberico. The Venetian doge Foscarini relates that Zorzi travelled 'for about 20 years, visiting Cyprus (twice), Alexandria, England, Spain and Flanders' and that he 'made notes about customs and antiquities and made drawings of the more interesting ones'. His *Itinerario* is a fragmentary collection of detailed voyages told to him in person in Venice by Ethiopian and foreign travellers. It is a kind of Rough Guide to the routes leading to 'Prester John', and provides precious testimony on the state of Abyssinia before the upheavals of the sixteenth century.

FRANCISCO ALVAREZ

FROM *A True Relation of the Lands of Prester John*, 1540

Has Anybody Seen the Road to Prester John?

On Monday, the 17th of October, we set out, thinking that we should this day reach the court and camp, because we had gone to halt at a league from it. Then it seemed to us that they intended to take us there next day very early. While we were in this hope, there came to us a great lord, who is called by title Adugraz, which means chief major domo, he said that he was come to protect us and give us what we had need of. This gentleman told us to mount at once and come with him. We got ready, as it appeared that he was going to take us to the court: he took a turn backwards, not by the road we had come by, but he turned with us round some hills and we returned back more than a league, he telling us not to be in any ill humour, as the Prester was coming in that direction where we were going, and indeed six or seven horsemen were going in front of us on very good horses, skirmishing and amusing themselves, and a great many mules. They conducted us behind some hills, and the gentleman lodged himself in his tent, and ordered us to be lodged near him in our poor tent, such as we had brought for the journey, and ordered us to be provided with all that was necessary, and we were much put out of the way; and the Prester was coming to halt near where we were. On Wednesday in the morning they brought us a large round tent saying that the Prester John sent us that tent and that nobody had a tent such as that except him, and the churches, and that his tent belonged to him when he was on a journey. So we remained till Friday without knowing what we were to do. The captain who guarded us and the friar warned us to look well after our goods, as there were many thieves in the country, and the Franks who were in the country also

told us so: they further told us that there were agents and captains of
thieves, and that they paid dues of what they stole.

On Friday, the 20th of October, at the hour of tierce, the friar came
to us in great haste, for the Prester John had sent to call us, and that
we should bring what we had brought for him, and also all our
baggage, as he wished to see it. The ambassador ordered all that to be
loaded which the captain-major had sent for him, and no more. We
dressed ourselves and arranged ourselves very well, God be praised;
and many people came to accompany us. So we went in order from
the place we started from as far as a great entrance, where we saw the
tents pitched in a great plain, that is, certain white tents, and, in front
of the white ones, one very large red tent pitched, which they say is set
up for great feasts or receptions. In front of these pitched tents were
set up two rows of arches covered with white and red cotton cloths,
that is, an arch covered with red and the next with white: not covered
but rolled round the arch, like a stole on the pole of a cross, and so
these arches were continued to the end; there may have been quite
twenty arches in each row, and in width and height they were like the
small arches of a cloister. One row may have been apart from the
other about the distance of a game of quoits. There were many people
collected together; so many that they would exceed twenty thousand
persons. All these people were in a semi-circle, and removed a good
way off on each side; the smartest people were standing much nearer
to the arches. Among these smarter people were many canons and
church people with caps like mitres, but with points upwards of
coloured silk stuffs, and some of them of scarlet cloth: and there were
other people very well dressed. In front of these well-dressed people
were four horses, that is, two on one side and two on the other,
saddled and caparisoned with rich brocade covering; what armour-
plating or arms were underneath I do not know. These horses had
diadems high above their ears, they came down to the bits of the
bridle, with large plumes on them. Below these were many other
good horses saddled but not arrayed like these four, and all the heads
of all of them were on a level, making a line like the people. Then, in
a line behind these horses (because the crowd was much and thick),

there were honourable men, who were not clothed except from the waist downwards, with many thin white cotton cloths, and crowded, standing one before the other. It is the custom, before the King and before the great lords who rule, to have men who carry whips of a short stick and a long thong, and when they strike in the air they make a great noise, and make the people stand off. Of these a hundred walked before us, and with their noise a man could not be heard. The people riding horses and mules, who came with us, dismounted a long way off, and we still rode on a good distance, and then dismounted at about a crossbow-shot from the tent, or the distance of a game of mancai. Those who conducted us did us a courtesy and we to them, for we had been already taught and this courtesy is to lower the right hand to the ground. In this space of a crossbow shot there came to us fully sixty men like courtiers or macebearers and they came half-running, because they are accustomed so to run with all the messages of the Prester. These came dressed in shirts and good silk cloths, and over their shoulders or shoulder, and below, they were covered with grey skins with much hair on them; it was said they were lion skins. These men wore above the skins collars of gold badly wrought, and other jewels and false stones, and rich pieces round their necks. They also wore girdles of silk coloured ribands, in width and weaving like horse girths, except that they were long and had long fringes reaching to the ground. These men came as many on one side as on the other, and accompanied us as far as the first row of arches, for we did not pass these. Before we arrived at these arches, there were four captive lions where we had to pass, and in fact passed. These lions were bound with great chains. In the middle of the field, in the shade of these first arches, stood four honourable men, among whom was one of the two greatest lords that are in the court of the Prester, and who is called by title Betudete. Of these there are two, one serves on the right hand, the other on the left hand. They said that he of the right hand was at war with the Moors, and he of the left hand was this one here. The other three who stood here were great men. Before these four we did as did those who conducted us. On reaching them we remained a good while without speaking to them, nor they to us. On this there came an old priest, who they say is a relation and the confessor of the Prester, with a cloak of white Indian cloth of the fashion of a burnoose, and a cap like those of the others who stood apart. The title of this man is Cabeata, and he is the second person in these kingdoms. This priest came out of the said tent which would yet be two casts of quoits from the arches. Of the four men who were with us at the arches, three went half way to receive him, and the Betudete, who was the greatest lord of them, remained with us; and when the others came up he also advanced three or four steps, and so all five came to us. On reaching him, the Cabeata asked the ambassador what he wanted and where he came from. The ambassador answered that he came from India, and was bringing an embassy to the Prester John, from the captain-major and governor of the Indies for the King of Portugal. With this he returned to the Prester, and with these questions, and ceremonious courtesies, he came three times. Twice the ambassador answered him in the same manner, and the third time he said, I do not know what to say of it. The Cabeata said: Say what you want and I will tell it to the King. The ambassador replied that he would not give his embassage except to his Highness, and that he would not send to say anything except that he and his company sent to kiss his hands, and that they gave great thanks to God for having fulfilled their desires and having brought Christians together with Christians, and for their being the first. With this answer the Cabeata returned and came back directly with another message, when the above-mentioned persons went to receive him as before: and on reaching us he said that Prester John sent to say that we should deliver to him what the great captain had sent him. Then the ambassador asked us what he ought to do, and that each of us should say whatever he thought of it. We all said that we thought that he should give him what was sent. Then the ambassador delivered it to him piece by piece, and, besides, four bales of pepper which were for our own expenses. When it was received it was all carried to the tents, and all afterwards brought back to the arches where we were. And they came and stretched the tent cloths which we had given on the arches, and so with the other stuffs. Having set everything in sight of the people, they caused silence to be made, and the chief justice of the court made a speech in a very loud voice, declaiming, piece by piece, all the things

which the captain-major had sent to the Prester John, and that all were
to give thanks to the Lord because Christians had come together with
Christians, and that if there were here any whom it grieved, that they
might weep, and any that rejoiced at it, that they might sing. And the
great crowd of people who were near by gave a great shout as in praise
of God, and it lasted a good while; and with that they dismissed us. We
went to lodge at the distance of a long gunshot from the tents of the
Prester, where they had already pitched the tent which they had sent
us, and there we remained and also the goods which remained to us.

When our baggage came and was brought we began to see by
experience the warning which was given us of thieves, because on
the road they had taken by force from a servant who attended us,
four tinned copper vessels, and other four of porcelain, and also
other small kitchen articles, and because the servant had attempted
to defend himself they had given him a great wound in one leg. The
ambassador ordered him to be taken care of (of these pieces none
appeared again). As soon as we were lodged the Prester John sent us
three great white loaves, and many jars of mead and a cow. The
messengers who brought this said that Prester John sent it, and that
they would give us immediately fifty cows and as many jars of wine.
The following Saturday, the 21st day, he sent us an infinite quantity
of bread and wine, and many dainties of meat of various kinds, and
very well arranged: and the same happened on Sunday, when, among
many other dainties, he sent us a calf whole in bread, that is to say in
a pie, so well dressed that we could not get tired of it. On Monday the
friar came to us to say that if the ambassador would give all the pepper
to the Prester John, that he would order food to be given to him and
to his company, as far as Masua. And they ceased giving us food,
neither did the fifty cows nor the jars of wine come. In the meantime
they prohibited all the Franks who were in this country from speaking
to any of us: and also they told us not to go out of our tent, that such
was the custom of all those who come to this court, until they had had
speech with the king not to go forth from their tents. We well knew
later that such was their custom, and on account of this prohibition
they kept prisoner a Portuguese, nicknamed the Sheep, who came to

speak to us on the road, and one of the Franks, saying, that they came
to tell us the things of the court. This Sheep ran away one night with
his chains from the custody of a eunuch who guarded him, and came
to our tent. Next morning they came to fetch him, but the ambassador
would not give him up, but sent the factor and the interpreter to go
and ask the Betudete from him, why he ordered Portuguese to be put
in irons, and had them so ill-treated by slave eunuchs. The Betudete
answered, saying: who had bid us come here, that Matheus had not
been to Portugal by order of the Prester John, nor of Queen Helena;
and that if the slave had cast irons on the Portuguese, that the
Portuguese should in turn cast them on the slave, and that this was
the justice of the country.

[. . .]

Because many times I mention Franks, I wish to say that when Lopo
Soarez, captain-major and governor, went from India and came to
Jiddah with a large fleet, in which I also was, there were in the said
place of Jiddah sixty Christian men captives of the Turks. These
Christians were of many nations. These who are at the court say that
they were all waiting for the favour of God and the entry of the
Portuguese into Jiddah to join with them; and, because the fleet of
Lopo Soarez did not make the land, they remained there. A few days
after that, sixteen of these white men, with as many other Abyssinians
of this country of the Prester, who were also there prisoners, stole two
brigantines, and fled to go in search of the said fleet. Not being able
to fetch Camaran, they made Masua, which is close to Arquico, the
country of the Prester. They landed at the said port and abandoned
the brigantines, and went to the court of the Prester, where they were
doing them great honour, more than to us up to the present time,
and they had given them lands, and vassals who provide them with
food. These are the Franks, and most men of these nationalities are
Genoese, two Catalans, one of Scios, another a Basque, another a
German; all these say that they have already been in Portugal, and
they speak Portuguese and Castilian very well. They call us also
Franks, and all other white people, that is to say, Syrians, which is
Chaldea and Jerusalem; and the people of Cairo they call Gabetes.

*

On Sunday, the 29th of October, there came to us two of the said Franks, saying that they came in consequence of an agreement amongst themselves with respect to what they had heard say about us, namely, that the people of the court said that the pepper and all the goods that we brought belonged to the Prester John, and that the captain-major had sent it to him, and that since we would not give it him, so we should not find favour with him: and they were of opinion that it would be well to give this pepper that we had brought and all the other goods, because otherwise we should not have leave to return, because this was their custom, never to allow anyone to return who came to their kingdoms: and that they would sooner have pieces and stuffs than cities or kingdoms: and that this was their opinion. Upon this we held council, and, with the opinion of the ambassador and of ourselves, we all agreed to give to the Prester four out of the five bales of pepper that we still had, and to keep one for our expenses. We also decided to send him four chests covered with hide, which were among the company, in which came clothes, and this because we thought that he would be pleased with them, and that we should obtain favour. Then, on Monday, the 30th of October, the Franks came to us very early with many mules and men-servants of theirs to carry our baggage. The ambassador, with all of us, determined to send the said present of pepper and chests, and that I, with the clerk and factor, should convey it, and that the ambassador, with the other people, should go later in the afternoon. We set out with the said pepper and chests, and going along the road we met a messenger, who said he was bringing us the words of the Prester; and he dismounted to give them to us, and we dismounted to receive them, because such is their custom to give the King's words on foot and for them to be heard on foot. He told us that the Prester John ordered that we should come at once to the camp. We said that the ambassador was coming presently after us, and that he should return with us in order to give us the means of being able to present a service which we were conveying to his highness. He said he would do so, and moreover asked what we would give him for himself; because this is their custom always to beg. We contented him with words, with the intention of giving him nothing. He conducted us before a great enclosure of a high hedge, within which were many tents pitched, and a large long house of one storey thatched with straw, in which they said the Prester sometimes remained, and this man said that he was there. Before the entrance of this hedge there were a very great many people, and these likewise said that the Prester was there. We dismounted a space further off (according to their custom) and thence we sent to say that we wished to present a service to his highness. There came to us an honourable man saying, almost with ill-humour, how was it the ambassador had not come. We answered him that it was because he had not got mules or people to carry his goods, and that now he would come because the Franks had gone for him. We asked this man to tell us how we could present this pepper and chests to his highness; he told us not to take care for anything, that anyhow the ambassador should come, and when he had come and when he was summoned he would take the present. This man then ordered us to be shown where our tent should be pitched when he came, and the ambassador delayed very little.

Francisco Alvarez (*c*.1465, Coimbra–1541, Rome). Alvarez' *True Relation of the Lands of Prester John*, or *Verdadeira Informação das Terras do Preste João das Indias*, is indeed truthful enough – bar one important element, the fact that Alvarez probably well knew that Lebna Dengel (the Ethiopian emperor of the time, whose court he had visited) was not Prester John. But everything else in Alvarez' account is just that, the plain truth. His story of tribulation and hardship, and one cultural misunderstanding after another, is never short of humour nor of trepidation, though he sometimes seems to veer towards a self-serving attitude as, for instance, when downplaying the importance of the long-lost ambassador Pero da Covilha. Without da Covilha's presence, it seems sure that not only would Rodrigo da Lima's embassy have been a failure, but one doubts they would have been allowed to leave. But for all this, Alvarez lays events down simply and refreshingly as they happen, and has no compunction in exposing the silliness of his compatriots as they squabble amongst themselves. The passage where Alvarez, deeming all lost (news, false as it will turn out, that the Portuguese Indian possessions have been lost to the Moors has been received), walks up a river to 'cry lying down in the sand' is poignant. His testimony of an unscathed Abyssinia, before the invasion of Ahmad ibn Ibrahim al-Ghazi ('Gragn'), is full of information that would otherwise have been lost for ever.

MIGUEL DE CASTANHOSO

FROM *The Campaign of Cristóvão da Gama*, 1543

Aethiopia is Saved by
Four Hundred and Fifty Portuguese

Of how the Moors following Don Cristóvão,
found him, and seized him, and of how he died.

Don Cristóvão and the fourteen Portuguese with him, marching all
that night, travelled with heavy labour, for they were all wounded and
very weary. They had therefore to leave the road they followed, and
enter a shady valley, with a very thick growth of trees, to take some
rest. As the morning was near, and there was great fear of discovery by
the enemy who were in pursuit, having, as I say, left the path, they
entered the bottom of the valley in the most solitary possible place,
where they found a little water that flowed from a water-fall. They
got D. Cristóvão off his mule to dress his wounds, which up to now
they had not had time to do; his companions, not having wherewith to
do it, killed the mule D. Cristóvão rode, and taking the fat, dressed
with it his wounds, and also the wounds of those among them that
needed it. When the Moors captured the camp some would not halt,
but followed us relentlessly; on the road by which D. Cristóvão
escaped there went twelve Turks on foot and twenty Arabs on horseback, eager to capture him; at dawn they were beyond where he lay,
and not finding him, they returned. Reaching the point where D.
Cristóvão turned into the thicket, an old woman came out of the
wood, looking as if she could hardly stand, and ran across the road;
the Moors, to learn her news, tried to catch her, and followed her into
the wood, without capturing her, as she ran from one thicket to
another. When she got to the valley she crossed it, running fast, and
entered among the trees where D. Cristóvão and the Portuguese lay.

As the Moors followed with pertinacity, they would not abandon the pursuit, and thus came on D. Cristóvão, and taking him by surprise, with loud cries of 'Mafamede', captured him. One of these [D. Christóvão's companions] who was but slightly wounded, hid in the thicket and escaped, and from him we heard the story of the capture. It is impossible that old woman can have been anyone save the devil, as she vanished from among them and was never seen again. This astonished the Moors greatly, who, from what they told us afterwards, considered that 'Mafamede' had sent her to direct them; they returned contented with their prize, as they at once recognised D. Cristóvão by the arms he bore; thus they went with him, making him many mocks by the way, and giving him but evil treatment. Thus they brought them before the King, who was very pleased with the victory, with more than one hundred and sixty Portuguese heads before his tent: for he had offered a reward to any Moor who would cut off the head of a Portuguese, and his men, to gain it, brought him those they found on the field. When D. Cristóvão reached his tent, that dog ordered the heads of the Portuguese to be shown him, to grieve him; telling him whose they were, and that here were those with whom he had designed to conquer his country, and that his madness was clear in his design; and that for this boldness he would do him a great honour. This was to order him to be stripped, with his hands tied behind him, and then cruelly scourged, and his face buffeted with his negroes' shoes; of his beard he made wicks, and covering them with wax lighted them; with the tweezers that he had sent him, he ordered his eyebrows and eyelashes to be pulled out: saying that he had always kept them for him, as he and his followers did not use them. After this, he sent him to all his tents and his Captains for his refreshment, where many insults were heaped on him, all of which he bore with much patience: giving many thanks to God for bringing him to this, after allowing him to reconquer one hundred leagues of Christian country. After they had diverted themselves with him they returned to the King's tent, who with his own hand cut off his head, it not satisfying him to order it to be cut off. After it had been cut off, in that very place where his blood was spilt, there started a spring of water which gave health to the sick, who bathed in it, which they understood the wrong way.

That very day and moment, in a monastery of friars, a very large tree which stood in the cloisters was uprooted, and remained with its roots in the air and its branches underneath, the day being very calm and still; and as it appeared to them that this event was not without mystery, they noted the day and the hour, and that they were all present to give witness. Afterwards, when they heard of the defeat and death of D. Cristóvão, they found that the tree was uprooted on the very day and hour that he was killed. After it had died, the friars cut up part for use in the monastery; six months later, the very day we gave battle to the King of Zeila and defeated him – in which battle he was slain and the kingdom freed – that very day the tree raised itself, planted its roots in the earth whence they had been drawn, and at the same moment threw out green leaves. The friars, seeing this great mystery, with great wonder, noted the day and hour it happened, knowing nothing of what was passing in the kingdom. When they heard of what had taken place, they found that it was the very day, as I say, that was the signal of freedom for so many Christian people. When they told us this, as the monastery lay on the road to Massowa, whither after the freeing of the country we were travelling, we all went to the monastery to see the tree and to bear witness. I saw it, with many of its roots exposed, all cut as the friars said, and it had only recently become green. As it was a great tree, it was wonderful that it could stand on the ground with so few roots below the earth. When, after the King of Zeila had cut off D. Cristóvão's head, that fact became known in the tents of the Turks, they were very enraged, and went angrily to the King, and asked him why he had thus killed the Portuguese Captain without telling them: because, as the Grand Turk had heard of his bravery, they could have taken him nothing from that country which would have pleased him more, that they would have taken him as a proof of their great victory to receive a reward from the Turk. They were so offended that they quitted him, taking the Portuguese to carry with them. The next day, when they started, there was one Portuguese, who had escaped, the less; he afterwards joined us, so that they went back with twelve and D. Cristóvão's head. They embarked for Azebide, where was the Governor of all the Straits, with three thousand Turks, of which body they formed a part.

Two hundred were left with the King of Zeila, because they filled up
the vacancies of those who were killed in the battle from among the
others, as this number was granted by the Grand Turk in exchange
for his tribute. The King stayed three days at that place, with great
content at the victory, for such is their custom, making great festival;
and as it appeared to him that we were entirely destroyed, and that
those who remained of us would be lost in that country, among those
mountains, where we could not find our way, he determined to visit
his wife and sons, whom he had not seen for a long time, who were in
his city on the shores of the lake whence the Nile flows, the most rich
and fertile country that ever was seen. This he did, leaving in that
country his Captains, with troops to retake possession of the land he
had lost; for of us he took no count, bad or good, but the Lord God
chose to show His great pity.

Miguel de Castanhoso (d. *c.*1565) was a soldier in the 400-strong
force that landed on the Red Sea shore in answer to an appeal sent to
Lisbon by Empress Eleni of Ethiopia shortly after the Portuguese
expedition led by Rodrigo da Lima (as recounted by Francisco Alvarez)
had left. Little, if anything, is known of his life and circumstances
other than what can be found in his testimonial on the expedition of
Cristóvão da Gama, which is a precious first-hand account of the
tribulations and eventual success of the expedition to save Christian
Abyssinia.

SIHAB AD-DIN AHMAD BIN 'ABD AL-QADER,
also known as Arab Faqih
FROM *The Conquest of Abyssinia, c.*1550

Mine Will be a Takeaway

On the third day, the Imam left for Bet-Amhara and spent the night in a place called Lalibala. The water there was frozen by the cold that killed many Muslims. When one wanted to drink, one had to strike the ice with a pick and break it. Then they left Lalibala; then appeared in front of them the royal church that is Bet-Amhara. Seeing it, the guide stopped and said to the Imam: 'It is this church that you see; you have arrived.' Ahmad asked them: 'Shall we stay here until our soldiers have rejoined us or not?' He answered: 'We will wait to enter all together and shall ready ourselves for war.' The Imam stopped until the Muslim army was complete, then he said to the guide: 'How many churches are there here?' He enumerated a great number, amongst which the one called Makana-Selase; that of Atronsa-Maryam, built by king Zarea-Yaqob, son of king Dawit; that of Dabra-Naguadguad, that of Beta-Samayat. The Imam sent Muslims against each of them, to the exception of Makana-Selase where he went himself. He had the vizir Nour ben Ibrahim march on that of Atronsa-Maryam, Sidi Mohammed with his army against that of Dabra-Naguadguad; Becharah ben Djouchou against Beta-Samayat. He himself arrived at Makana-Selase, stopped near its perimeter wall with his soldiers and penetrated inside with admiration. He entered with his entourage: the mere contemplation of which nearly caused them to lose their sight: it was embellished with gold and silver plaques, where had been placed incrustations of pearls: a wooden door was ten cubits long and four large; it had been covered in gold and silver leaf and above the gold had been placed incrustations of different colours. The length of the church was 100 cubits; its width likewise and its height was more than 150 cubits; its roofs and interior courtyards were covered in gold plaques and decorated with golden statues. The Muslims were much surprised by this work; those that had not yet entered began crying to the Imam: 'Open the door for us so we can enter and see.' He opened for them, they surged inside and he told them: 'What each shall take will be for himself, with the exception of the plaques.' They set to work with a thousand axes, tearing out the gold and jewels that were in the church, from the middle of the afternoon till the evening: each took as much gold as he needed and became rich for ever after; more than a third of its gold was burnt in the church. The Imam spent the night nearby; he asked the Arabs that were with him: 'Have you seen in the country of the Roum, in India or elsewhere a church like this one with its statues and its gold?' – 'Nor in the country of the Roum, nor in India,' they said, 'we have not seen or heard mentioned anything similar: there is no such thing in the world.' There were near the church three dwellings for the king who resided there: they were filled with marvels for the eyes. The Imam went into one of them and set himself up there; he gave the second to the emir Ahmouchouh and to the emir Abou Bekr Qatin; both entered with their troops and they were large enough to contain them; the third, the Imam made into a mosque. The vizir Nour arrived with his people at Atronsa-Maryam; they entered and marvelled at the work, but they did not find gold; the polytheists had removed all it contained. They met four monks and the vizir told them: 'Where is the treasure of the church?' They answered: 'We shall not indicate it to you, even if we were to die for the religion of Mary.' The Muslims killed them. Then one of ours, called the Farachaham Ali, glimpsed a house closed by iron bars; he broke one of them and put his head inside to see what was there: he saw chests piled up from the floor to the roof. He came back to find the vizir and told him about it. Nour went with him, stopped near the door and counted about a hundred soldiers to which he said: 'Enter and pull out the riches from there.' Each one started to load brocades and brought several out; but the house kept its aspect; they had tired themselves carrying them and they sat down. The vizir told them: 'Why do you sit, is nothing left in the house?' They answered:

'Despite what we have taken out, it still has the same appearance and we are tired.' He said again: 'You only removed some brocades, some satin and silk; is there no gold?' – 'The gold is in a corner of the dwelling and we began by the side where are the chests containing the brocades.' He said to others: 'You, take out the gold and leave the precious clothes.' They went in and carried out the gold, silver, and golden artifacts such as censers, cups, all in gold; there was a load for ten vigorous men; they brought it to him. The vizir sent his companions that were one thousand in number and told them : 'Here is my share and that of the Imam; go into this house and take for yourselves what is inside; what each will remove will be his.' They went in, and each carried off red gold, silver and silk; there were those who took three loads; others four; they did not stop their pillage from noon until dusk, and from this time till the morning. The vizir told them: 'Now, you are satisfied; you do not have camels to carry your treasure; you have carried it on your necks and on your mules; the house is still full of riches and silks; let us not leave this abundance of silk to the polytheists, but let us burn it.' Then he added: 'Set fire to the house.' It was set alight with the brocades it contained, and also the church that was burnt to ashes. They returned to the Imam and when they arrived he was in the king's dwelling. He received his share of gold and brocades; there was an incredible quantity of gold, amongst which, a calf with four legs and called in their language *tabot*; its weight was one thousand ounces and more; a book of gold with a human figure; figures of birds and ferocious beasts; and gold plates where four could eat. The Imam gave four to Sid ech-Cherif, a combatant for the faith, Djemal ed-din Mohammed Marzouq – may God give us favour by him – and one to the Sid Mohammed Handoul; he had the rest placed in the Muslim's treasure. As for Sidi Mohammed and Becharah, they left him the church of Beta-Samayat, built by the mother of king Ouanag-Sagad; they went in and saw marvels, but found no riches. They met there four monks that they interrogated on the gold and treasures. They answered: 'The mother of the king was buried in a coffin in the church. When we heard of your arrival, we removed the king's mother and the gold that was with her and took everything off to the amba.' The Muslims set the church on fire;

the monks cried, went inside and were burnt, may God fight them! Becharah, together with Sidi Mohammed, left for the church of Dabra-Naguadguad. It was a large church built by king Admas [Baeda-Maryam], son of Zarea-Yaqob; they arrived there, went inside and found considerable riches. King Admas was buried there in a coffin, in the middle of the church. Our people seized the treasures, amongst which a golden calf, as long as a man, and carried off all of the riches, in gold [. . .] In loads of which they did not know the weight; they burnt the church and returned to the Imam who was in the same place. He gave to each his share in gold and silk and had the rest placed in the treasury of the Muslims. For his part, Abd en-Naser arrived at a church called Ganata-Giyorgis, built by king Eskender. The Imam had been informed by two prisoners, treasurers of the king, who had told him, the day when he had been put to flight: 'Do not kill us: we will guide you there to the riches of the king, in gold, in silver and in silk; there is a load for 500 men.' – 'In which country?' – 'In that of Oualaqah; they are in a church above a mountain.' Therefore the Imam sent Abd en-Naser with the two prisoners to guide him. Arriving at the church, the Muslims found nothing and burnt it. They went to the place of the treasure in the country of Oualaqah, preceded by the guide. To all the Christians they met they said: 'We are Christians, from the army of the king; we are going to Godjam.' The prince, indeed, had taken that direction on the day of his defeat. In this fashion they arrived to the designated place. The guide went to tell Abd en-Naser: 'We have reached the treasure; you see that mountain and the church that is atop it; that is where the riches of the king and those of his fathers and ancestors are.' Those that were in charge of guarding the path of the mountain numbered 50 slaves of the king with a chief. It happened that day that the mother of this chief died in a hamlet at the foot of the mountain. He left with his companions to bury his mother; the Muslims had already replaced them on the mountain. There were only four monks and three eunuchs in the church. When our people arrived at the base, Abd en-Naser took his shield and sabre, his companions did the same and they went up. When they were in the church, they stopped above the door where stood the eunuchs and the monks and told them: 'Bring out the treasures,' and they killed the monks. The eunuchs brought out the treasures: about 500 loads of brocade with gold thread, red gold with vases, and, amongst the treasures of the church, many crowns that belonged to the king or to his predecessors; the coats with which the kings drape themselves, and, on the fore part, gold plates encrusted with gemstones; golden belts, golden bracelets, golden daggers of which the sheath and the handle were in gold; golden maces, golden calves with feet encrusted with gemstones. The calf's neck was two cubits long; there were golden bridles, plates and drinking vessels all in gold. Abd en-Naser collected all this, as he was the treasurer of the Imam, and wrote it down in the ledger; he distributed the riches between his companions to carry it; they were 3000; each troop had a chief; he sent for the chiefs and shared out the riches; there were those that carried 2000 ounces of gold, others 1,500, others 1000 and others 500. They came back to the Imam who they found in his first encampment. He was astonished, him and his companions, of such a thing that they had never seen. He shared the brocade in three parts; one he had placed in the treasury of the Muslims and gave the other two to Abd en-Naser. As to the gold, all that was decoration and objects of art he took for presents. The rest of the gold, that was abundant and that is called *sambarah*, that couldn't be weighed, he shared it between the Muslims and they stayed in Bet-Amhara [. . .]

The Samen is a difficult country, furnished with castles and high mountains; there is no route for cavalries and in all of Abyssinia, there does not exist a more difficult country. When the Imam said: 'We shall pursue those that escaped,' some people from Balaou, that is to say the choum Mohammed and his companions came to tell him: 'Do not enter into the Samen, for you will have no success there, even if you remain for long.' Ahmed answered them: 'We shall not abandon the Samen until we have converted it, for it is the head of the country; if it believes, the whole country will believe.' He named as governor of this province, until his entry, Ganzai, brother of the Patrice Saoul, who left his wife as hostage with the Imam. Ahmed gave him back his freedom. He left and began to convert the country, then he betrayed and fled alone, abandoning his wife. There was in the Samen a great quantity of castles and strongholds, a precipitous mountain whose summit was a half day's march; there were harvests and ploughed land. One sole man, occupying the road, could, because of the narrowness of the path prevent a considerable army from ascending. The Imam sent there Absama-Nour. The latter departed and climbed it, putting to advantage the enemies' negligence, seized it and returned. Then he took the captives of Bahr Amba, numbering forty, and cut off their heads. The Samen was occupied by the Abyssinian Jews who call themselves in their language, 'Falachas'. They recognise one sole God, but that is all they have in faith; they have nor prophets, nor saints. The people of Bahr Amba had reduced them to servitude since forty years ago, forcing them to serve them and plough for them. After the victory of the Imam over the Patrice Saoul, they all came to find him, arriving by deep gorges, from the bottom of caves, for they do not live in the plains, but in the mountains and caverns. They told him: 'There is between us and the people of Bahr Amba an animosity which goes back forty years; now, we shall kill those that remain and take their fortresses after you have vanquished them; we will suffice against them. As to you, remain in your residence; we shall take care of them in a fashion that will please you.' The Imam gave them soldiers to support them and they went in the direction of that mountain. They climbed it, tied up the inhabitants of Bahr Amba with chains and brought them to Ahmed. He himself remained in the Samen until he had conquered it. He had all of the inhabitants of Bahr Amba taken out and killed them. The people of the Samen made peace with the Falachas; they paid tribute without exception and were humiliated.

Translated by YVES-MARIE STRANGER

Arab Faqih (d. *c.*1559) was a Yemeni volunteer who joined the army of Ahmad ibn Ibrahim al-Ghazi ('Gragn'). He was a direct witness to many of the events he relates, and at other times transcribes what is related to him by direct witnesses. His *Conquest of Abyssinia*, though an incomplete text, is an important testimonial, firstly of Abyssinia as it was before the utterly destructive war waged on it by the Imam Ahmad (one only needs to read the stomach-churning depictions of massacres retold in the book itself), but it is also a vital document to understand the Muslim point of view.

EMPEROR GELAWDEWOS

FROM *Confession of Faith*

A Jesuitical Answer to the Jesuits

In the Name of the Father, the Son and the Holy Spirit, One God. This is my faith, as it is the faith of my fathers, the kings which descend from Israel, and of all of the Christians that dwell in my Kingdom.

We believe in one God and in His only son Jesus Christ. He is the word, the power, and the wisdom of the Father. Before the beginning of the world, he was with the Father. In the fullness of time even while still on his heavenly throne, he descended from heaven and was incarnated by the Holy Spirit and the Virgin Mary and became truly a man. When he was 30 years old he was baptised in the River Jordan. He was ill treated, then crucified, died and was then buried in the time of Pontius Pilate. On the third day he rose again. And on the fortieth day he ascended in full glory to heaven to sit on the right hand of the Father. He will come again in glory to judge the living and the dead and His Kingdom shall have no end. And we believe in the Holy Spirit, the Lord and Giver of Life who emanates from the Father. We believe in one sole baptism for the forgiveness of sins. We look forward to the resurrection of the dead, and the life of the age to come.

AMEN

In this manner we walk in the righteous path in the Orthodox Way and will not stray from the teachings of our fathers neither to the left nor to the right!

> The twelve apostles
> The fount of wisdom of Saint Paul
> The 72 disciples
> The 318 Orthodox assembled in Nicaea

The 150 that came to Constantinople
The 200 assembled in Ephesus

I the son of Naod, the son of Wenag Seged, who is known by my throne name as Asnaf Saged Emperor of Ethiopia, this Faith I confess and thus this Faith I bear witness to.

We do not honour the first Sabbath for the same reasons as the Jews, for they do not fetch water, nor do they light fires, cook or bake, nor do they come together in one another's house. We do however honour the day as the apostles commanded us to in the Didache: by way of the Divine Liturgy and in sharing our meals together. We do not observe or honour this day in the same fashion as the Sunday Sabbath. For this Day is the Day that David prophesied on, stating that it was a New Day that the Lord God had created and that we should rejoice and be glad upon it. For on this day our Lord was resurrected; it is on this day that the Holy Spirit descended on the Apostles on Mount Zion. As it is on this day and in the womb of the very pure and Holy Virgin Mary that he was incarnated as a man. And it is also on this day that, for the glory of the Saints, and for the condemnation of the evil, that he shall return.

When it comes to circumcision, we do not circumcise in the manner of the Jews. For we know the teachings of the Fount of Wisdom Paul in Galatians 5:6 'for in Christ neither circumcision nor uncircumcision counts for anything but only faith working through love'; and in Galatians 6:15 'for neither circumcision counts for anything, nor uncircumcision, but a new creation'. We have all of the epistles of Paul here by our side, and he teaches us about circumcision and being uncircumcised. The circumcision that we practise here is similar to the custom of scarring faces in Ethiopia and Nubia or ear piercing in India. That is to say that we do not do this to follow Jewish law but rather because it is the people's custom.

As to the practice of eating pork, it is not done here. However, we do not abstain from this food to comply with Jewish law. We do not have hatred for those who partake of it nor do we do oblige those who do not eat it to partake of it. As our father St Paul wrote in Romans 14:3–17 'the man who eats of everything must not look askance on he who does not do so and the man who refrains from partaking of everything must not condemn the man who does so, for God has accepted him . . . I know and am persuaded by the Lord Jesus, that there is nothing unclean in itself: but to he who esteems a thing to be unclean, to him it is unclean . . . For the kingdom of God is not meat and drink; but righteousness, and peace and joy in the Holy Spirit.' Similarly we also can find in the Lord's Gospel, in Matthew 15:11–20, it is written 'it is not what goes into the mouth that defile a person but what comes out of the mouth; this defiles a person . . . everything that goes into the mouth transits through the stomach and is done with but the things that come out of the mouth proceed from the heart and those will defile the man . . . ' These teachings of our Lord rendered obsolete all the teachings of the Jews that erred by professing the Mosaic Law.

This is my faith and the faith of those who propagate it on my command within my kingdom, the priests' faith. From the path of The Gospel, and from the teaching of Saint Paul, they will neither stray to the right nor to the left. In the Church's History book that we possess, we read that during his reign Emperor Constantine commanded that newly baptised Jews should eat pork on the very day of the resurrection of our Lord Jesus Christ. However, persons can abstain from eating various kinds of flesh because of their preferences. This one might like to eat fish, while another gives preference to chicken; while another might choose to abstain from partaking of mutton. All this can be carried out to the contentment of one's own heart. On these matters people can follow their own preferences. On the subject of dietary consumption of animal flesh there is no law, no canon in the New Testament. To the pure all things are pure; he also says the believer can eat anything 1 Corinthians 10:25. I strived to set all this down in writing so that you may know the faith I confess.

Gelawdewos (1522–1559) became emperor of Ethiopia upon the death of his father Lebna Dengel (Dawitt II), who had spent the last years of his reign harried around his own kingdom by Ahmad ibn Ibrahim al-Ghazi. After the Imam was shot down at the battle of Weyna Dega by a Portuguese matchlock man's bullet, Gelawdewos turned to shoring up his fragile kingdom's defences. He was now wary of his erstwhile Portuguese allies, and especially of the self-proclaimed Patriarch of Abyssinia, João Bermudez. Gelawdewos held the Jesuits at arm's length, for they had brought a new discord to his kingdom with their claims to setting the Ethiopians right on matters of religious doctrine. It is to refute the Jesuits that Gelawdewos wrote his *Confession of Faith*.

FROM *The History of Ethiopia*, 1681

A Historical Collaboration

Being entertained at Rome in the college of the Habessins [Abyssinians], he [Gregorius], with three others were maintained at the Pope's Charge: amongst whom Antonius de Andrade, whose father was a Portuguese, and his mother an Habessinian, was wont to say mass, which he did always hear standing, according to the custom of his own country, as he did it also in other places. For the ancient Popes disprudently allowed the liberty of their own rites to foreign Christians, that by this means they might draw them more to Rome.

Going all over the city to no purpose, I enquired for the Habessins, whom I had heard lived at Rome whom I at last found in their college before-mentioned. I addressed to them, and acquainted them how desirous I was to learn the Ethiopick language: They surround me, and wonder, and at length demand the reasons; to which, being heard, they return this answer: 'That that could not be done out of Ethiopia, for it was a thing of great labour, and much time: That there was indeed one Gregorius there, a very learned man (whom he shewed me) but that he neither understood Latin or Italian.' I desired they would only resolve some doubt, and satisfy my difficulties, for that I had already acquired the rudiments of that language. Gregorius understanding from his companions what I desired, immediately runs in, and fetches a great parchment book, curiously writ, and bids me read, (it was the book of the councils, which I describe in my history).

But when I went about to interpret, they turned their laughter into admiration, scarce believing that that language which seemed so difficult, (as they said) to the fathers of the society who abode so long in Ethiopia could be learned without a master. For afterwards Gregorius writ thus to me: 'The fathers (meaning the Jesuits) who came from Italy and Portugal were many years in our country, and we find none amongst them able to perform what you do, in writing and interpreting epistles in our language, notwithstanding they were learned in books, and divines.'

I daily visited Gregorius. But at the beginning we did not converse in discourse, for he understood no European language besides the Portuguese, and that not very perfectly which then I had not learned. He was then beginning to learn Italian: So that we did a long time confer by an interpreter, Antonius d'Andare, and at last began to discourse imperfectly ourselves. Afterwards we conversed in the Ethiopick, which neither of us had ever spoke before; for amongst the Habessins the Amharick language is used in speaking throughout the whole kingdoms, the Ethiopick only in writing. Concerning speaking the Ethiopick, I had not so much as dreamed. So we were forced, that we might understand each other, to use a tongue to which neither of us had been accustomed. Gregorius was very knowing in the affairs of his own country; for he had followed the court very long, first in a private capacity, and later as a domestic of the patriarch. He was well acquainted with the royal family, the nobility and several affairs which had been acted in this age. Besides this, he was eloquent, and witty, and behaved himself courteously and affably to all, and did not conceal from me anything I asked him and communicated to me as many books as he had there. In requital, I gave him an account of the affairs of Europe, he desired to know.

From the letters of Gregorius

As to my origins do not imagine, my friend, that they are humble, for I am of the house of Amhara which is a respected tribe; from it come the heads of the Ethiopian people, the governors, the military commanders, the judges and the advisers of the king of Ethiopia who appoint and dismiss, command and rule in the name of the king. I, too, have always spent my time with the king, his governors and grandees.

The emperor of Ethiopia has a big army and possesses three times as many horses as his father did. The rebels have given themselves up and have thrown themselves at his feet. The king of Enariya who in his fear brought much gold came all the way to the Emperor's camp to kiss his feet. The Emperor received him with great joy and presented him with many costly gifts and then sent him back to his country. Robbers and thieves have disappeared in the face of the Emperor's might.

The Emperor of Ethiopia, together with his governors, advisers, counsellors and monks, has firmly resolved that no Portuguese should set foot in Ethiopian soil, least of all a bishop or priest. All inhabitants of the land were informed through herald of that if one of these people appeared he would be brought to justice and put to death by hanging, and that anyone who sheltered him would die with him. This is why six priests and the bishop of the Jesuits were hanged when their wicked intention was discovered. I will tell you the story later when we meet. And subsequently when two Franciscan monks came they too were hung. And, thirdly, when three Franciscans reached Suakin island the Turks killed all three of them on the order of the Emperor of Ethiopia.

The strip of land behind Suakin is called Tigre. This is a country in which there is a Dejazmach under whom there are 44 high prefects who move about heralded by trumpeteers and hornblowers. Then Semien must be mentioned and then Dambea, the province in which the King's camp is situated, then Begemder, and then the province of Amhara, the birth place of the kings and high officers and the residence of previous rulers. The learned men, the writers, the judges and the government officials come from there.

The head of Amhara is near Gedem and Angote is towards the east; one of the feet of Amhara, the left, treads on the country of Walaga in the west, and the right foot would tread in Gojam were it not hindered by the Abay. These later provinces face each other on either side of the river. One of the sides of Amhara, towards the north, touches Begemder, from which it is divided only by a big river called Bishalo, and the other side borders on the kingdom of Shoa in the south from which it is separated by the river Wanchit. Amhara rises above all these provinces and towers above them. This is in brief the position of Amhara.

There are pagans in our land, but they live far from us; we fight them and make them prisoners for they are our enemies. Mohamedans live in small numbers among us; they have no mosque for they are our servants for trade and commerce, and they are weavers of our clothes.

Dwellings, called *saqala* in Ethiopia, are made of wood and stone, not of skin, for they are not movable houses. The tents, sedan chairs and barracks of the king are made of cotton. It is these which move from place to place with the king. At court, however, one does not put up tents for there one lives in *saqalas*; the tents are rolled up and put aside together with the tent poles and stakes.

You must allow me to return in peace to my fatherland because I have made up my mind and am full of longing to return. My dear fatherland Ethiopia is like an earthly paradise, the land of peace and love, the land of health and happiness, the land of law and justice, the beautiful, godly mother of orphans, refuge of the persecuted, food of the poor, rest of the wanderer, for Christ's sake.

I had invited him to Erfurt, in to my country, where my mother did then live; but I had not writ the name of Erfurt plain enough in Ethiopick character, so that he read it Erfart, which in German language is pronounced Erhfahrt, that his friends whom he consulted, told him they knew no such place, and it might be, that I, being casually asked, had so answered. So that one letter of point, not rightly placed or read, occasioned the mistake. For the same reason Acalexus, an Habessinian young man, following Gregorius, without any recommendation, enquired of the city of Erfart in Germany, and losing his labour at last returned to Italy.

The most serene prince, Ernestus Duke of Saxony, to whom I had given an account of the matter, commanded that I should bring him to Gota, to his court, for that he was very desirous to understand the truth of the affairs of the Habessins, whom he had heard to have been ancient Christians, and that he would bear all the expense of his journey. I was not unwilling, by this means, to be freed from the burden of his expenses, and so I wrote to Gregorius, who was already come to Germany. He being wholly ignorant which way he went, or which way he should return or by whom he was sent for, answered, 'That he was at my disposal, that I might do what seemed to me just and right.' I went therefore as far as Nurnberg to meet him; there as soon as I saw him, he fell into ecstasies of joy, most affectionately embracing me, that he almost drew tears from me, reflecting that I, but a private person, and a young man not settled in the world, nor as yet knowing the charitable intention of the prince of Gota, had prevailed with that good man, being more than fifty years old, and also lame in his feet, to come from foreign countries, into the heart of Germany.

Duke Ernestus commanded him first to be carried to his castle of Heldburg in Franconia, and after that to that of Tenneberg in Thuringia, that his qualities being found out, he might the better know how to entertain and treat him. When therefore nothing that was disagreeable was related of his person, manners, and inclinations, being clothed in the German fashion, he was brought to the castle of Gota, called Friedenstein, and there placed in a convenient apartment with me. Afterwards, on the appointed day, being called to the prince, the Chancellor, and the rest of his counsellors, both secular and ecclesiastical, being present, after he made his obeisance, he said, 'That he gave thanks to the immortal God, that had granted him the good fortune both to behold and speak to a Christian prince, beyond his hope and expectation, in the remote countries of the north, whose piety and prudence, since his coming to these parts, he had heard highly spoke of; neither could he hope less from his clemency and benevolence, who had entertained him, who was a stranger, and unknown, so charitably, and had admitted him to kiss his hand.' To which the prince replied, 'That it was not less acceptable to him, to see a Christian from such remote parts, in his court. That the divine providence was to be adored with the greatest praise, that had preserved the Ethiopick church in Africa, through so many ages, amongst so many barbarous people, amongst so many persecutions; and commanded him not at all to doubt of his benevolence.' Which when I was about to interpret in Italian, which bystanders might understand what I said, he cried out in the Amharican dialect, 'Metzhafena, Metzhafena; in Ethiopick, in Ethiopick.' All admiring what he meant, he told them, 'Whereas he had to do with a prince, he ought to understand most accurately what he spoke, that he might know what to answer him; and therefore he did desire, that I would discourse with him in the Ethiopick tongue.' Which I did as well as I could. Then he replied, 'That it was true, that the Christian religion had been miraculously preserved in his country for so many ages, and did wonderfully extol the antiquity of it.'

[. . .]

When he heard so many vain and fabulous stories to be reported concerning Habessins, by our writers, he did with indignation say, 'That the Europeans were sick of a certain itch of writing, and did both write and publish whatsoever they heard, whether true or false; that his countrymen were wholly heretofore ignorant of this their humour, otherwise they would have answered more cautiously to their questions, so that our interpreters would have understood them rightly; that when he first saw the famous library of Alphonsus, the Portuguese patriarch, and the books put out with the royal privilege, and the licence and approbation of a great man, he looked on printing as some sacred invention, to be reckoned amongst the regalia of princes, and supposed that nothing was printed, but was true, and good, and useful to the publick; but that he was amazed when he found that many fictitious, vain and trifling things, and indeed hurtful to the public, were daily sent to the press.'

In composing my Ethiopick lexicon he willingly assisted me, and with a great deal of readiness did explain the more difficult places of authors and words more rarely used; and this he did with much exactness [. . .] But he was wholly ignorant of how to compose a dictionary or grammar, and he did not understand how to place words according to their primitives; and at first was much against it. But when he observed me to set in order both what I read and heard from him, and to refer the derivatives to their primitives, he frequently repeated his 'O wonderful'! And when he discoursed concerning the different signification of any word, he would add, 'Now do you dispose of that according to your art.' I did also explain to him the mysteries (as he called them) of the Latin grammar, and by this means he became more ready in answering my questions. When I had explained to him the terms of art, viz. The declensions, conjugations, cases, tenses, and the like, with much labour, in the Ethiopick tongue, as soon as he understood the end and use of them, it is *revealed*, says he, 'To God be praise.'

He was so desirous to learn the Latin tongue, that in my absence from him for two days, this hopeful scholar proposed to himself for his task, to learn by heart, by frequent reading and repeating, the whole etymologie, the declensions, and all the conjugations. Therefore beginning in the morning, by constantly reciting till late at night, and endeavouring by himself, none molesting him, he had so disturbed his heart, that at my return I found him ill of a vertigo or dizziness. A physician was called, who enquiring diligently into the cause of his unwonted distemper, at last we found that it proceeded from too much attention to studying.

[...]

In this country, horses are by nature generous and solid, as they are only ridden on the battle field, or in fantasias; so it is that their hooves go unshod; when on rough and abrupt terrain, they lead them, while riding mules. They are of diverse coats, as are ours, bay-brown, grey, dappled, dark and especially black (...) Gregorius held our horses in pity when he saw them harnessed pulling heavy chariots and was surprised by their endurance and our cruelty; as if we were abusing this noble war animal by putting it to work in servile occupations. In Ethiopia therefore, they use more usually mules and hinnies; they carry heavy loads through steep mountains: they go for long marches; as no other beast of burden can walk in a more assured manner next to precipices. In order to better transport travellers, they train them to be saddle animals. When Gregorius would travel (in Europe), the trip on horseback always seemed to him too hard as for most of the time horses trot: and because of this allure they tire their riders [while Abyssinian mules amble comfortably]: and he complained to have made the experience many times as he travelled in Germany.

[...]

A surprising breed of sheep, quite well known in the Orient and in Africa, is here common. Their tails are so voluminous that the small ones weigh ten or even twelve pounds, the biggest sometimes more than forty pounds. A chariot therefore has to be placed under so that they can pull more easily such a heavy load and that the tail not be wounded or torn by dragging on the ground.

[...]

We finally have to speak of the Portuguese in Abyssinia, who are neither Africans, nor foreigners as they have submitted themselves to Abyssinian law for some time now. For, of the four hundred men that Christopher de Gama had brought to the succour of the Abyssinians during the war with the Adal, some one hundred and seventy survived, of which the numbers increased over a century to the point that during the epoch of the fathers of the Society they were one thousand four hundred warriors, a small force no doubt, but of no small importance for the party they gave support to, as they possessed from their fathers the knowledge of fire arms, superior to the musquets of the Abyssinians. Later on, once finished the war against the Adal and Gragn killed, they had received, to raise their children, lands from Claudius (Galawdewos) and had married; wealthy, as is the usage of the country, in horses, mules, slaves and all the necessary. As long as was conserved the memory of their support to the country, they lived at ease, they were famous and admitted, and could practise their Latin rite at liberty; but the successor of Claudius, Minas, forbad them. These people ill supported to be the object of hatred as the mentality of soldiers is better suited to inflict damage than receive it. That said, the fields came to be closer to the enemy so that the kings of Portugal saw themselves obliged to alleviate their misery by the means of an annual subsidy of one thousand two hundred pataques. It is only in the past century, when the fathers of the Society were in favour, that they experienced great prosperity, but upon their fall they came to know extreme poverty. It is therefore not without reason that Alphonse Mendez feared that now, lacking in everything, they should forget their country language as well as their ancestors, and that in the future they shall be distinguished less and less from the Abyssinians by their mores and religion, as has been the case for skin colour and physical aspect.

Job Ludolf (1624–1704) is often called the 'father of Ethiopian studies'. His *History of Ethiopia*, published in 1681, remains the cornerstone of serious Ethiopian study – a work that addressed all matters of Ethiopian interest; from the genealogy of the ruling families, to the dress, mores, languages and habits of Ethiopians to the crops and

animals of their farms and the animals that roamed in the wild, to
matters of faith and its differences from the Apostolic Roman Church.
All this was addressed with the help and active collaboration of Abba
Gregorius (1595–1658) an Ethiopian monk, a Catholic convert, who
had made his way to Rome after the expulsion of the Portuguese
Jesuits in 1633. So it is that Ludolf and Gregorius' work is the first
'scientific' writing on the country, in that it both seeks to be encyclo-
paedic in its scope, and also seeks to address misconceptions about
the so-called Prester John.

JERONIMO LOBO

FROM *The Itinerario: a relation of travels in Abyssinia in the years 1622–1640, 1660*; first English edition translated by Samuel Johnson in 1735

The Land of Honey and Butter Turns Sour

The animals of Abyssinia; the elephant, unicorn, their horses and cows; with a particular account of the moroc

There are so great numbers of elephants in Abyssinia that in one evening we met three hundred of them in three troops: as they filled up the whole way, we were in great perplexity a long time what measures to take; at length, having implored the protection of that Providence that superintends the whole creation, we went forwards through the midst of them without any injury. Once we met four young elephants, and an old one that played with them, lifting them up with her trunk; they grew enraged on a sudden, and ran upon us: we had no way of securing ourselves but by flight, which, however, would have been fruitless, had not our pursuers been stopped by a deep ditch. The elephants of Aethiopia are of so stupendous a size, that when I was mounted on a large mule I could not reach with my hand within two spans of the top of their backs. In Abyssinia is likewise found the rhinoceros, a mortal enemy to the elephant. In the province of Agaus has been seen the unicorn, that beast so much talked of, and so little known: the prodigious swiftness with which this creature runs from one wood into another has given me no opportunity of examining it particularly, yet I have had so near a sight of it as to be able to give some description of it. The shape is the same with that of a beautiful horse, exact and nicely proportioned, of a bay colour, with a black tail, which in some provinces is long, in others very short: some have long manes hanging to the ground. They are so timorous that they never feed but surrounded with other beasts that defend them. Deer and other defenceless animals often herd about the elephant, which, contenting himself with roots and leaves, preserves those beasts that place themselves, as it were, under his protection, from the rage and fierceness of others that would devour them. The horses of Abyssinia are excellent; their mules, oxen, and cows are without number, and in these principally consists the wealth of this country. They have a very particular custom, which obliges every man that has a thousand cows to save every year one day's milk of all his herd, and make a bath with it for his relations, entertaining them afterwards with a splendid feast. This they do so many days each year, as they have thousands of cattle, so that to express how rich any man is, they tell you he bathes so many times. The tribute paid out of their herds to the King, which is not the most inconsiderable of his revenues, is one cow in ten every three years. The oxen are of several kinds; one sort they have without horns, which are of no other use than to carry burdens, and serve instead of mules. Another twice as big as ours which they breed to kill, fattening them with the milk of three or four cows. Their horns are so large, the inhabitants use them for pitchers, and each will hold about five gallons. One of these oxen, fat and ready to be killed, may be bought at most for two crowns. I have purchased five sheep, or five goats with nine kids, for a piece of calico worth about a crown. The Abyssins have many sort of fowls both wild and tame; some of the former we are yet unacquainted with: there is one of wonderful beauty, which I have seen in no other place except Peru: it has instead of a comb, a short horn upon its head, which is thick and round, and open at the top. The *feitan favez*, or devil's horse, looks at a distance like a man dressed in feathers; it walks with abundance of majesty, till it finds itself pursued, and then takes wing, and flies away. But amongst all their birds there is none more remarkable than the moroc, or honey-bird, which is furnished by nature with a peculiar instinct or faculty for discovering honey. They have here multitudes of bees of various kinds; some are tame, like ours, and form their combs in hives. Of the wild ones, some place their honey in hollow trees, others hide it in holes in the ground, which they cover so carefully, that though they are commonly in the highway, they are seldom found, unless by the moroc's help, which, when he has discovered any honey, repairs immediately to the road side, and when he sees a traveller, sings, and claps his wings, making many motions to invite him to follow him, and when he perceives him coming, flies before him from tree to tree, till he comes to the place where the bees have stored their treasure, and then begins to sing melodiously. The Abyssin takes the honey, without failing to leave part of it for the bird, to reward him for his information. This kind of honey I have often tasted, and do not find that it differs from the other sorts in anything but colour; it is somewhat blacker. The great quantity of honey that is gathered, and a prodigious number of cows that is kept here, have often made me call Abyssinia a land of honey and butter.

The manner of eating in Abyssinia, their dress, their hospitality, and traffic

The great lords, and even the Emperor himself, maintain their tables with no great expense. The vessels they make use of are black earthenware, which, the older it is, they set a greater value on. Their way of dressing their meat, an European, till he has been long accustomed to it, can hardly be persuaded to like; everything they eat smells strong and swims with butter. They make no use of either linen or plates. The persons of rank never touch what they eat, but have their meat cut by their pages, and put into their mouths. When they feast a friend they kill an ox, and set immediately a quarter of him raw upon the table (for their most elegant treat is raw beef newly killed) with pepper and salt; the gall of the ox serves them for oil and vinegar; some, to heighten the delicacy of the entertainment, add a kind of sauce, which they call *manta*, made of what they take out of the guts of the ox; this they set on the fire, with butter, salt, pepper, and onion. Raw beef, thus relished, is their nicest dish, and is eaten by them with the same appetite and pleasure as we eat the best partridges. They have often done me the favour of helping me to some of this sauce, and I had no way to decline eating it besides telling them it was too good for a missionary. The common drink of the Abyssins is beer and mead, which they drink to excess when they visit one another; nor can there be a greater offence against good manners than to let the guests go away sober: their liquor is always presented by a servant, who drinks first himself, and then gives the cup to the company, in the order of their quality. The meaner sort of people here dress themselves very plain; they only wear drawers, and a thick garment of cotton, that covers the rest of their bodies: the people of quality, especially those that frequent the court, run into the contrary extreme, and ruin themselves with costly habits. They wear all sorts of silks, and particularly the fine velvets of Turkey. They love bright and glaring colours, and dress themselves much in the Turkish manner, except that their clothes are wider, and their drawers cover their legs. Their robes are always full of gold and silver embroidery. They are most exact about their hair, which is long and twisted, and their care of it is such that they go bare-headed whilst they are young for fear of spoiling it, but afterwards wear red caps, and sometimes turbans after the Turkish fashion. The ladies' dress is yet more magnificent and expensive; their robes are as large as those of the religious, of the order of St Bernard. They have various ways of dressing their heads, and spare no expense in ear-rings, necklaces, or anything that may contribute to set them off to advantage. They are not much reserved or confined, and have so much liberty in visiting one another that their husbands often suffer by it; but for this evil there is no remedy, especially when a man marries a princess, or one of the royal family. Besides their clothes, the Abyssins have no movables or furniture of much value, nor does their manner of living admit of them. One custom of this country deserves to be remarked: when a stranger comes to a village, or to the camp, the people are obliged to entertain him and his company according to his rank. As soon as he enters a house (for they have no inns in this nation), the master informs his neighbours that he has a guest; immediately they bring in bread and all kinds of provisions; and there is great care taken to provide enough, because, if the guest complains, the town is obliged to pay double the value of what they ought to have furnished. This practice is so well established that a stranger goes into a house of one he never saw with the same familiarity and assurance of welcome as into that of an intimate friend or near relation; a custom very convenient, but which gives encouragement to great numbers of vagabonds throughout the kingdom. There is no money in Abyssinia, except in the eastern

provinces, where they have iron coin: but in the chief provinces all
commerce is managed by exchange. Their chief trade consists in
provisions, cows, sheep, goats, fowls, pepper, and gold, which is
weighed out to the purchaser, and principally in salt, which is properly
the money of this country. When the Abyssins are engaged in a law-
suit, the two parties make choice of a judge, and plead their own cause
before him; and if they cannot agree in their choice, the governor of
the place appoints them one, from whom there lies an appeal to the
viceroy and to the Emperor himself. All causes are determined on the
spot; no writings are produced. The judge sits down on the ground in
the midst of the high road, where all that please may be present: the
two persons concerned stand before him, with their friends about
them, who serve as their attorneys. The plaintiff speaks first, the
defendant answers him; each is permitted to rejoin three or four times,
then silence is commanded, and the judge takes the opinions of those
that are about him. If the evidence be deemed sufficient, he pro-
nounces sentence, which in some cases is decisive and without appeal.
He then takes the criminal into custody till he has made satisfaction;
but if it be a crime punishable with death he is delivered over to the
prosecutor, who may put him to death at his own discretion. They
have here a particular way of punishing adultery; a woman convicted
of that crime is condemned to forfeit all her fortune, is turned out of
her husband's house, in a mean dress, and is forbid ever to enter it
again; she has only a needle given her to get her living with. Sometimes her head is shaved, except one lock of hair, which is left her, and
even that depends on the will of her husband, who has it likewise in
his choice whether he will receive her again or not; if he resolves
never to admit her they are both at liberty to marry whom they will.
There is another custom amongst them yet more extraordinary,
which is, that the wife is punished whenever the husband proves false
to the marriage contract; this punishment indeed extends no farther
than a pecuniary fine, and what seems more equitable, the husband is
obliged to pay a sum of money to his wife. When the husband
prosecutes his wife's gallant, if he can produce any proofs of a criminal
conversation, he recovers for damages forty cows, forty horses, and
forty suits of clothes, and the same number of other things. If the

gallant be unable to pay him, he is committed to prison, and continues there during the husband's pleasure, who, if he sets him at liberty before the whole fine be paid, obliges him to take an oath that he is going to procure the rest, that he may be able to make full satisfaction. Then the criminal orders meat and drink to be brought out, they eat and drink together, he asks a formal pardon, which is not granted at first; however, the husband forgives first one part of the debt, and then another, till at length the whole is remitted. A husband that does not like his wife may easily find means to make the marriage void, and, what is worse, may dismiss the second wife with less difficulty than he took her, and return to the first; so that marriages in this country are only for a term of years, and last no longer than both parties are pleased with each other, which is one instance how far distant these people are from the purity of the primitive believers, which they pretend to have preserved with so great strictness. The marriages are in short no more than bargains, made with this proviso, that when any discontent shall arise on either side, they may separate, and marry whom they please, each taking back what they brought with them [. . .]

As we could not go to court before November, we resolved, that we might not be idle, to preach and instruct the people in the country; in pursuance of this resolution I was sent to a mountain, two days' journey distant from Maigoga. The lord or governor of the place was a Catholic, and had desired missionaries, but his wife had conceived an implacable aversion both for us and the Roman Church, and almost all the inhabitants of that mountain were infected with the same prejudices as she. They had been persuaded that the hosts which we consecrated and gave to the communicants were mixed with juices strained from the flesh of a camel, a dog, a hare, and a swine; all creatures which the Abyssins look upon with abhorrence, believing them unclean, and forbidden to them, as they were to the Jews. We had no way of undeceiving them, and they fled from us whenever we approached. We carried with us our tent, our chalices, and ornaments, and all that was necessary for saying mass. The lord of the village, who, like other persons of quality throughout Aethiopia, lived on the top of a mountain, received us with very great civility. All that depended upon him had built their huts round about him; so that this place compared with the other towns of Abyssinia seemed considerable; as soon as we arrived he sent us his compliments, with a present of a cow, which, among them, is a token of high respect. We had no way of returning this favour but by killing the cow, and sending a quarter smoking, with the gall, which amongst them is esteemed the most delicate part. I imagined for some time that the gall of animals was less bitter in this country than elsewhere, but upon tasting it, I found it more; and yet have frequently seen our servants drink large glasses of it with the same pleasure that we drink the most delicious wines. We chose to begin our mission with the lady of the village, and hoped that her prejudice and obstinacy, however great, would in time yield to the advice and example of her husband, and that her conversion would have a great influence on the whole village, but having lost several days without being able to prevail upon her to hear us on any one point, we left the place, and went to another mountain, higher and better peopled. When we came to the village on the top of it, where the lord lived, we were surprised with the cries and lamentations of men that seemed to suffer or apprehend some dreadful calamity; and were told, upon inquiring the cause, that the inhabitants had been persuaded that we were the devil's missionaries, who came to seduce them from the true religion, that foreseeing some of their neighbours would be ruined by the temptation, they were lamenting the misfortune which was coming upon them. When we began to apply ourselves to the work of the mission we could not by any means persuade any but the lord and the priest to receive us into their houses; the rest were rough and intractable to that degree that, after having converted six, we despaired of making any farther progress, and thought it best to remove to other towns where we might be better received. We found, however, a more unpleasing treatment at the next place, and had certainly ended our lives there had we not been protected by the governor and the priest, who, though not reconciled to the Roman Church, yet showed us the utmost civility; the governor informed us of a design against our lives, and advised us not to go out after sunset, and gave us guards to protect us from the insults of the populace. We made no long stay in a place where they stopped their

ears against the voice of God, but returned to the foot of that
mountain which we had left some days before; we were surrounded,
as soon as we began to preach, with a multitude of auditors, who came
either in expectation of being instructed, or from a desire of gratifying
their curiosity, and God bestowed such a blessing upon our apostolic
labours that the whole village was converted in a short time. We then
removed to another at the middle of the mountain, situated in a kind
of natural parterre, or garden; the soil was fruitful, and the trees that
shaded it from the scorching heat of the sun gave it an agreeable and
refreshing coolness. We had here the convenience of improving the
ardour and piety of our new converts, and, at the same time, of leading
more into the way of the true religion: and indeed our success exceeded
the utmost of our hopes; we had in a short time great numbers whom
we thought capable of being admitted to the sacraments of baptism
and the mass. We erected our tent, and placed our altar under some
great trees, for the benefit of the shade; and every day before sun-
rising my companion and I began to catechise and instruct these new
Catholics, and used our utmost endeavours to make them abjure their
errors. When we were weary with speaking, we placed in ranks those
who were sufficiently instructed, and passing through them with great
vessels of water, baptised them according to the form prescribed by
the Church. As their number was very great, we cried aloud, those of
this rank are named Peter, those of that rank Anthony. And did the
same amongst the women, whom we separated from the men. We
then confessed them, and admitted them to the communion.

Jeronimo Lobo (1595–1678), son of the Portuguese governor of the
Cape Verde Islands, entered the Company of Jesus at age fourteen
and became a priest at twenty-one, before travelling to Goa, India
where he was chosen to accompany a mission sent to further the
'evangelisation' of Ethiopia – a work well under way with the successful conversion of Emperor Susneyos by Pero Paes. Civil strife
followed by an internal succession struggle in which Susneyos
abdicated in favour of his son Fassilides soon ensued, however, and
the modest gains that had been made by the Jesuits were first reversed,
before being completely lost when Emperor Fassilides ordered them

to leave the country. But not before Lobo had enjoyed several fruitful years in Ethiopia, first at Fremona (the Jesuits' headquarters in Tigray, near Adua), then travelling far and wide throughout the Lake Tana basin, Agew Meder and Gojjam. His book, besides a few fanciful departures on the unicorn, 'abundant in the forests of Agew Meder', is accurate and full of useful information. Its translation was Samuel Johnson's first literary endeavour – and thus it provides the kernel for *Rasselas* as well.

EDWARD GIBBON

FROM *The History of the Decline and Fall*
of the Roman Empire, 1776–1788

Do Not Disturb

Encompassed on all sides by the enemies of their religion, the Aethiopians slept near a thousand years, forgetful of the world, by whom they were forgotten. They were awakened by the Portuguese, who, turning the southern promontory of Africa, appeared in India and the Red Sea, as if they had descended through the air from a distant planet. In the first moments of their interview, the subjects of Rome and Alexandria observed the resemblance, rather than the difference, of their faith; and each nation expected the most important benefits from an alliance with their Christian brethren. In their lonely situation, the Aethiopians had almost relapsed into the savage life. Their vessels, which had traded to Ceylon, scarcely presumed to navigate the rivers of Africa; the ruins of Axum were deserted, the nation was scattered in villages, and the emperor, a pompous name, was content, both in peace and war, with the immovable residence of a camp. Conscious of their own indigence, the Abyssinians had formed the rational project of importing the arts and ingenuity of Europe; and their ambassadors at Rome and Lisbon were instructed to solicit a colony of smiths, carpenters, tilers, masons, printers, surgeons, and physicians, for the use of their country. But the public danger soon called for the instant and effectual aid of arms and soldiers, to defend an unwarlike people from the Barbarians who ravaged the inland country and the Turks and Arabs who advanced from the sea-coast in more formidable array. Aethiopia was saved by four hundred and fifty Portuguese, who displayed in the field the native valour of Europeans, and the artificial power of the musket and cannon. In a moment of terror, the emperor had promised to

reconcile himself and his subjects to the Catholic faith; a Latin
patriarch represented the supremacy of the pope: the empire,
enlarged in a tenfold proportion, was supposed to contain more
gold than the mines of America; and the wildest hopes of avarice
and zeal were built on the willing submission of the Christians of
Africa.

But the vows which pain had extorted were forsworn on the return
of health. The Abyssinians still adhered with unshaken constancy
to the Monophysite faith; their languid belief was inflamed by the
exercise of dispute; they branded the Latins with the names of Arians
and Nestorians, and imputed the adoration of four gods to those who
separated the two natures of Christ. Fremona, a place of worship, or
rather of exile, was assigned to the Jesuit missionaries. Their skill in
the liberal and mechanic arts, their theological learning, and the
decency of their manners, inspired a barren esteem; but they were
not endowed with the gift of miracles, and they vainly solicited a
reinforcement of European troops. The patience and dexterity of
forty years at length obtained a more favourable audience, and two
emperors of Abyssinia were persuaded that Rome could ensure the
temporal and everlasting happiness of her votaries. The first of these
royal converts lost his crown and his life; and the rebel army was
sanctified by the abuna, who hurled an anathema at the apostate, and
absolved his subjects from their oath of fidelity. The fate of Za-
Denghel was revenged by the courage and fortune of Susneus, who
ascended the throne under the name of Segued, and more vigorously
prosecuted the pious enterprise of his kinsman. After the amusement
of some unequal combats between the Jesuits and his illiterate priests,
the emperor declared himself a proselyte to the synod of Chalcedon,
presuming that his clergy and people would embrace without delay
the religion of their prince. The liberty of choice was succeeded by a
law, which imposed, under pain of death, the belief of the two natures
of Christ: the Abyssinians were enjoined to work and to play on the
Sabbath; and Segued, in the face of Europe and Africa, renounced his
connection with the Alexandrian church. A Jesuit, Alphonso Mendez,
the Catholic patriarch of Aethiopia, accepted, in the name of Urban
VIII, the homage and abjuration of the penitent. 'I confess,' said the

emperor on his knees, 'I confess that the pope is the vicar of Christ, the successor of St Peter, and the sovereign of the world. To him I swear true obedience, and at his feet I offer my person and kingdom.' A similar oath was repeated by his son, his brother, the clergy, the nobles, and even the ladies of the court: the Latin patriarch was invested with honours and wealth; and his missionaries erected their churches or citadels in the most convenient stations of the empire. The Jesuits themselves deplore the fatal indiscretion of their chief, who forgot the mildness of the gospel and the policy of his order, to introduce with hasty violence the liturgy of Rome and the inquisition of Portugal. He condemned the ancient practice of circumcision, which health, rather than superstition, had first invented in the climate of Aethiopia. A new baptism, a new ordination, was inflicted on the natives; and they trembled with horror when the most holy of the dead were torn from their graves, when the most illustrious of the living were excommunicated by a foreign priest. In the defence of their religion and liberty, the Abyssinians rose in arms, with desperate but unsuccessful zeal. Five rebellions were extinguished in the blood of the insurgents: two abunas were slain in battle, whole legions were slaughtered in the field, or suffocated in their caverns; and neither merit, nor rank, nor sex, could save from an ignominious death the enemies of Rome. But the victorious monarch was finally subdued by the constancy of the nation, of his mother, of his son, and of his most faithful friends. Segued listened to the voice of pity, of reason, perhaps of fear: and his edict of liberty of conscience instantly revealed the tyranny and weakness of the Jesuits. On the death of his father, Basilides expelled the Latin patriarch, and restored to the wishes of the nation the faith and the discipline of Egypt. The Monophysite churches resounded with a song of triumph, 'that the sheep of Aethiopia were now delivered from the hyenas of the West'; and the gates of that solitary realm were forever shut against the arts, the science, and the fanaticism of Europe.

Edward Gibbon's (1737–1794). See page 59.

3

ERA OF THE PRINCES (1700–1855)

Introduction

We are travellers from curiosity, and our native country
is Abyssinia.

Dinarbas; A Tale: being a Continuation of Rasellas,
Cornelia Knight

The Era of the Princes, or Era of Judges, was named after the biblical
Book of Judges which tells of a time in Israel when 'every man fought
for himself and the lineage of David was forsaken'. It starts with
decadence in the capital, Gondar, when Abyssinian imperial power
waned as Muslim Oromo chieftains from Wollo (the Wollo Imams)
made a puppet of the emperor, first from behind the throne, then
by marrying into the sacred line itself. To the shock and horror
of staunch Christian Abyssinians – for whom nothing short of the
coming of Gog and Magog could have been worse – the Oromo
language, long practised in the atriums and guardrooms of the palace,
became the language of choice of an emperor whose mother was a
Wollo warlord's daughter.

And why not? The Oromo language is ascribed, after all, to the
Cushitic group (together with Somali, Afar, Agaw and many other
languages in the Horn of Africa), which links it back to the biblical
Cush, grandson of Noah, and the thorny deserts of Judea. Amharic
itself, oft described as 'semitic', is in reality a medley of influences,
though much of the language's vocabulary, syntax and grammar is
grafted on the vigorous rootstock of Cushitic language and culture.

If the Oromo did not have the benefit of a written script until the twentieth century, their oral history, storytelling and poetry is as rich as any 'semitic' Song of Songs:

Ox

If I were an ox, an ox, a beautiful ox!
beautiful and stubborn,
a rich merchant would buy me,
buy me and slaughter me,
spread out my skin and take me to the market.
An ugly woman would bid for me,
but a beautiful girl would buy me!
She would crush perfumes for me.
I would spend the night rolled up around her,
I would spend the afternoon rolled up around her.
Her husband would say, 'It's just a dead skin'.
But I would have my love!

Translation by ENRICO CERULLI

Today Oromo uses a Latin-based alphabet, but early texts, such as *The Chronicle of the Imams of Wollo* (included here), were written down using Geez symbols but never really dented the all-encompassing Abyssinian narrative – Menelik I, the Queen of Sheba, the Ark of the Covenant and Israel – which had the benefit of being etched on to skin in script, as if on stone, and was wedded to the Bible itself. This proved to be a robust cultural model, which swallowed one after the other the cultures it encountered in its path.

This perceived decadence in Gondar was but one aspect of the beginning of the sombre days of the Era of Princes which, for many Ethiopians, marks the point when Abyssinia's long natural march of progress was halted and the country broke up into a number of rival regions with no effective central authority. Even under the strong fist of Menelik II in the late nineteenth century, when reunification of the country was well underway, the lords of Gojjam, Wollo, Tigray and Adal were vassals in name, but kings at home.

It often seems that the only thing that distinguished the Kings of Gondar from their regional counterparts was a good story of a manifest destiny, which they possessed by dint of their lineage from Solomon and Sheba – imaginary or otherwise it does not matter – as not only they themselves, but also others, came to believe in it. Only very gradually over the nineteenth and twentieth centuries did the country edge towards a unitary state – rather than a complex of sometimes warring, sometimes tributary, nations. During that time, perhaps, Gondar could have been called *primus inter pares* – a situation that the Ethiopian Emperor's traditional title of *King of Kings* seems to recognise. Today, the idea of the Ethiopian state is alive and kicking – but the Era of the Princes was its nadir.

James Bruce, Earl of Kinnaird, is the best chronicler of the early period of the Era of Princes, while later, Arnaud d'Abbadie, a dashing Basque-Irish aristocrat, gives one a real flavour of the mid-nineteenth century and, importantly, a sympathetic view of the Oromo with whom he lived and fought – against and side by side – while criss-crossing the Nile and collecting rare manuscripts. D'Abbadie spends a lot of time in Wollo, a province of north-central Ethiopia that many see as being quintessentially Ethiopian for its mix of ethnicities, languages and religions. It later became infamous as the site of late-twentieth-century famines, but d'Abbadie describes it as fertile, lush and salubrious and, visibly enamoured of the locals, he describes the Ilmorma Oromo – or Galla, a term that has since become derogatory – as noble, trustworthy and fine horsemen. He goes on to point out that the only reason they have not conquered all of the neighbouring lands is their permanent internal dissensions.

James Bruce was a swashbuckling adventurer, standing nearly two metres tall. He possessed none of d'Abbadie's endearing, effortless panache and indeed had a rather grating manner that was not appreciated back in England. However, he must have been more diplomatic in Ethiopia, to not only survive but also to get the Queen's ear. Inevitably, there is gossip about the Scot's relationship with Queen Mentewab (a name signifying *How-Beautiful-She-Is*), a woman, if we are to believe Bruce's testimony, who was wont to comment on her pale skin and 'Portuguese ancestors'.

The Scottish explorer's abrupt ways made him many enemies back in the salons of London, and none more terrible than the formidable Doctor Johnson, who owned everything Abyssinian since he had translated Jeronimo Lobo's book. Bruce told tall tales in a haughty, take-it-or-leave-it manner. He spoke of cows eaten alive and the satirist Peter Pindar's phrase 'Nor have I been where men (what loss alas!)/ Kill half a cow, then send the rest to grass' was, for a time, all the rage in London. Boorishly, Bruce cut his Italian employee out of the scene in which he 'discovers' the source of the Nile alone – the 'papist' Portuguese of course made it there a full one hundred and fifty years beforehand, a fact Bruce simply brushes aside. Questioned at a London dinner party on Ethiopian musical instruments, Bruce hesitated before venturing that he thought he remembered a 'lyre', at which point one of the guests famously whispered 'Yes, and there is one less since he left the country.'

I rather like the Abyssinian Liar myself. Over the years, all his fanciful stories have been verified as being either true, or, if not, highly plausible. He died of a broken neck in a fall at his home in Scotland, but not before he was immortalised by a dedicatory – and somewhat bellicose – book title:

A Sequel to the Adventures of Baron Munchausen humbly dedicated to Mr Bruce the Abyssinian Traveller, as the Baron conceives that it may be of some service to him making another expedition into Abyssinia; but if this advice does not delight Mr Bruce, the Baron is willing to fight him on any terms he pleases.

HASAN BEN AHMED EL HAIMI

FROM *A Yemeni Embassy to Gondar in the year 1648*

A Visit to Habestan

Know that these Galla are a people of violent courage, firm endurance, great number and wide frontiers; when they march to fight one of the peoples, be it the unbelievers or others like the Muslims of Aussa and thereabouts, their numbers swell sometimes to about 100,000. To this may be added the fact that they are a people who are strongly built and of endurance on long journeys and while supporting hardships. And it was told to me by one informed in their ways that when one of them cried out with a mighty voice during battle, and this was heard by one of the unbelievers, namely the Christians, the latter's heart split so that he died of the noise alone. And on the whole I have observed that the characteristics of these people are similar to those of the Tartars according to what the chronicles and historian recount of them.

Every month ten men are relieved on a mountain called Kuhl. When these guards notice that the Gallas are coming they rush back to their own people and raise the alarm. Then all flee to the mountain tops and abandon their homes and what is heavy among their possessions.

The Falashas

We came to the country of the Falashas, the first part of which is a mighty valley at the foot of an extraordinary high gigantic mountain [. . .] It is the mightiest mountain in Abyssinia. And if I were to say the mightiest of the mountains on earth, I would not be far from the truth because it is visible from every side of Abyssinia. It also has severe frost the like of which I know not in severity; water does not cease to be frozen on it both winter and summer. And the country is an

administrative district the government of which is entrusted to one of
the viziers of the King who belongs to his court . . .

And this tribe which is called Falasha, is a numerous tribe [. . .] it
persists in the Jewish faith and the religion of the Torah. And formerly
they used to refuse obedience to the King because of difference
in religion, as they were a brave, very warlike and heroic people.
However, the King did not cease to war against them from all sides of
their territory, because the lands of the Christians surrounded them,
until he had defeated them and driven them from their strongholds.
And they entered into obedience to him and obeyed his word. Their
country he made into a province of this vizier. And most of them went
over to the religion of Christendom, and only a few kept back. This
was not because the King had forced them in regard to religion, but
only because he had demanded from them obedience to himself.

Gondar

We went to the King's stronghold and climbed a high building, a
stately edifice which ranks among the most wonderful of wonderful
buildings and among the most beautiful of exceptional wonders, constructed of stone and lime. And there is in that town, indeed in the
whole of Abyssinia, no other but it (as it is of very pleasing appearance
and handsome design), because all other dwellings in these localities
are only nests of grass. The builder of the edifice was an Indian and the
characteristics of his design correspond to the method of his country.
And this stronghold, which partakes of the characteristics of the King's
houses, is situated beside the town and at the highest point there; and
it comprises many courtyards and long halls. Around these quarters
are some other buildings made of earth, stretching in length, breadth
and height to an extent which no eye has beheld any other building.
And these apartments are furnished as the King is wont to stay there,
and there is in each apartment manifold Byzantine beds and Italian
mattresses, which are embellished with gold, and magnificent sofas
which are studded with precious stones and gems. And these palaces
are unsurpassed as a wonder for the visitor and as a pride for this
unbeliever king.

When we came to the King, his court had already assembled, and the courtiers, namely the viziers etc., had assumed the highest and most splendid magnificence. They wore mantles of gold-bordered brocade and embroidered silk robes which completely dumbfounded the observer by the strangeness of their decoration and their unusual design. And the courtiers were girt about their loins with golden sashes adorned with precious stones and costly jewels, which are theirs in this world and ours, God willing, in the next. In addition the nobles held in their hands swords of Sennar which were similarly adorned with the best and purest gold [. . .] The courtiers had arranged themselves for this occasion in the most handsome order corresponding to the comeliness of their appearance and according to their stature as God had made them. And their exterior appearance did not seem marred by their coal-black skin. And their heads were bare, with magnificent frizzly hair; and on their hands were gold rings, and in their ears, flaming like fire, earrings of shimmering pearls.

He has descended from his throne and had set himself on the ground to honour us and to show respect for our Imam. And his custom, as is well known, is only to descend from his throne upon the arrival of someone who occupies the highest rank or is worthy of the greatest show of honour. Furthermore, no one sits down before him except with his permission and he permits it only to whose rank is worthy thereof. And now our audience got under way; the King received us as he had already provided himself with an excellent interpreter, saying that the latter was of the family of Hussein, the son of Ali, whom God preserve, from the land of Buhara. And he belonged to the King's most intimate circle as Satan had robbed him of his faith and had been victorious over him. And he drew on himself the displeasure of the all merciful [. . .] And this sheriff understood the speech of the Arabs excellently and translated from it fluently. Now he stood before the King interpreting us and him. And the King asked us about the Imam's health, and he repeated this question and took great trouble to ascertain the condition of the Imam and of his nephews with expressions of the greatest sympathy.

Hasan Ben Ahmed El Haimi (1608–1659) is known for his embassy to Ethiopia as well as his poetry and polemic in defence of the Zaydi Imam al-Mutawakkil. We know the embassy was sent by Imam al-Muayyad billah from Yemen and that, if conditions were apparently peaceful enough at the time to contemplate such a mission, we also know that nothing tangible came of it and that no treaty of peace or trade was made (it seems the Iman had misconstrued Fassilides' letters as perhaps being a desire to convert to Islam). El Haimi's account remains an extremely valuable description of the country during a period of great isolation from the West. It is also a first-hand account of Gondar, the capital city that had been completed some twelve years previously, and that El Haimi admires greatly and says is the work of an Indian architect. Haimi is also a first source for the Oromo populations (that he calls 'Galla') – they have rendered certain areas of the country 'extremely dangerous' he says, before adding 'May God annihilate them and sever their roots'. Also interestingly, he speaks of the Falasha (Beta Israel) of whom many 'have converted to Christianity'.

CHARLES-JACQUES PONCET

FROM *A Voyage to Ethiopia in the years 1698, 1699 and 1700*

The African Camelot

After having conducted me thro' more than twenty apartments, I enter'd into a hall, where the Emperor was seated upon his throne. It was a sort of couch, cover'd with a carpet of red damask flower'd with gold. There were round about great cushions wrought with gold. This throne, of which the feet were of massy silver was plac'd at the bottom of a hall, in an alcove cover'd with a dome all shining with gold and azure. The Emperor was cloth'd with a vest of silk, embroider'd with gold and with very long sleeves. The scarf with which he was girt was embroider'd after the same manner. He was bareheaded and his hair braided very neatly. A great emerald glitter'd on his forehead and added majesty to him. He was alone in the alcove I mention'd; seated upon his couch, with his legs across, after the manner of the Orientals. The great lords were on each side of him, standing in their ranks, having their hands cross'd one upon the other, and observing an awful silence.

When I was come to the foot of the throne, I made three profound reverences to the Emperor and kiss'd his hand. 'Tis an honour which he allows to none but such as he has a mind to distinguish; for as to others he permits them not to kiss his hands till after thrice prostrating on the ground and kissing his feet. I presented to him a letter of Monsieur Maillet, the French Consul at Cairo. He caus'd it immediately to be interpreted to him and seem'd well pleas'd with it. He ask'd me several questions concerning the king (of whom he spoke to me as the greatest and most powerful prince of Europe), of the state of his royal family, (and) of the greatness and strength of France. As soon as I had answer'd all these questions I made him my presents, which consist of pictures, looking-glasses, crystals, and other glass works finely wrought . . .

The Emperor was upon that occasion clad with a vest of blue velvet, flower'd with gold, which trail'd upon the ground. His head was cover'd with a muslin, strip'd gold. Which fram'd a sort of crown after the manner of the ancients, and which left the middle of his head bare. His shoes were wrought, after the Indian fashion, with flowers beset with pearls. Two princes of the blood, richly cloath'd, waited for him at the palace gate with a magnificent canopy, under which the Emperor march'd, with his trumpets, kettle-drums, flutes, hautboys, and other instruments going before him, which made a good agreeable harmony. He was follow'd by the seven chief ministers of the empire, supporting each other under the arms and with their hands with their heads cover'd almost like the Emperor; having each a lance in his hand. He that walk'd in the middle carry'd the imperial crown, with his head uncover'd, and seemed to rest it, with some difficulty, against his breast. This crown, which is clos'd with a cross of precious stones on the top, is very magnificent. I march'd in the same line with the ministers; habited after the Turkish manner and conducted by an officer who held me under the arm. The officers of the crown, supported in the same manner, follow'd singing the priests of the Emperor and answering as it were in choirs. Then came the muskeeters, in their closebody'd coats of different colours; and were followed by the archers, carrying their bows and arrows. Last of all, this procession was closed by the Emperor's led horses, richly harness'd and cover'd with costly stuffs of gold hanging down to the ground, over which were the skins of tygers, extremely beautiful.

The Patriarch, in his pontifical habits, wrought with crosses of gold, waited for him at the entrance of the chapel, accompany'd with near a hundred religious persons clad in white. They made a lane on both sides, and holding an iron cross in their hands; some within the chapel, and some without. The patriarch took the Emperor by the right hand at his entering the chapel (which is call'd *Tensa Christos,* that is to say 'the Church of the Resurrection') and led him up thro' the middle of the monks, each holding a lighted flambeau in their hands. They carry'd the canopy over the Emperor's head up to his praying-place, which was cover'd with a rich carpet and is almost like the praying-desks of the prelates in Italy. The Emperor remain'd standing almost all the while, unto the time of communion, which the patriarch gave him under both species. The ceremonies of the Mass are very fine and majestic; but I have not so exact a remembrance as to give a relation of them.

The ceremony being ended, they discharged two pieces of cannon, as they had done at the entrance, and so the Emperor withdrew, and return'd back to the palace in the same order he came.

The Emperor has great qualities – a quick and piercing wit, a sweet and affable humour, and the stature of a hero. He is the handsomest man I have seen in Aethiopia. He is a lover of curious arts and sciences; but his chief passion is for war. He is brave and undaunted in battles, and always at the head of his troops. He has an extraordinary love for justice, which he administers to his subjects with great exactness; but whereas he is averse to blood, 'tis not without reluctance that he condemns a criminal (to death). Such eminent qualities make him equally fear'd and belov'd by his subjects, who respect him even to adoration. I have heard him say that 'tis not lawful for one Christian to shed the blood of another (without weighty reason); hence it comes that he will have exact and ample informations before he condemns a criminal to death. The punishment of the guilty is hanging, or losing their head. Some are punish'd with the loss of their goods; with a strict prohibition to all persons whatsoever to assist them, under severe penalties, or even to give them to eat or drink; which makes those miserable wretches to wander about like wild beast. The Emperor being very merciful, is not difficult in granting favour to those un-fortunate creatures. 'Tis somewhat surprising that, the Aethiopians being so lively and passionate as they are, we scarce ever hear of murder or of those enormous crimes which fill us with horror. Besides religion, I am persuaded that the exact justice which is perform'd in that empire, and the great order that is kept there, contributes much to the innocence and integrity of their manners.

Charles-Jacques Poncet (d. *c.*1706) was a physician and pharmacist who had somehow made it to Cairo, where he plied his trade at the end of the seventeenth century. His *A Voyage to Ethiopia in the years 1698, 1699 and 1700*, where he was summoned to treat the Emperor

Iyasu I and his son – perhaps for leprosy – was met with great curiosity,
all the more so as Ethiopia and its capital city Gondar had been
inaccessible to most Western travellers since the expulsion of the
Jesuits in 1632. The account does not disappoint with tales of riches
and African Camelots – although it does seem, from other contemporary accounts, that the intrepid pharmacist was quite truthful.
And he must have been a good doctor as well, for, a rarity until then,
Poncet was allowed to leave and not only tell the tale but continue his
adventures all the way to Persia, where he died in 1706. The French
writer Jean-Christophe Rufin has written a fictionalised account of
his life in *The Abyssinian*.

JAMES BRUCE

FROM *Travels to Discover the Source of the Nile, in the Years 1768, 1769, 1770, 1771, 1772 and 1773*, G. G. J. and J. Robinson, London, 1790

A Scotsman at the Nile

It is easier to guess than to describe the situation of my mind at that moment – standing in that spot which had baffled the genius, industry and inquiry of both ancients and moderns, for the course of near three thousand years. Kings had attempted this discovery at the head of armies, and each expedition was distinguished from the last, only by the difference of the numbers which had perished, and agreed alone in the disappointment which had uniformly, and without exception, followed them all. Fame, riches and honour, had been held out for a series of ages to every individual of those myriads these princes commanded, without having produced one man capable of gratifying the curiosity of his sovereign, or wiping off this stain upon the enterprise and abilities of mankind, or adding this desideratum for the encouragement of geography. Though a mere private Briton, I triumphed here, in my own mind, over kings and their armies; and every comparison was leading nearer and nearer to presumption, when the place itself where I stood, the object of my vainglory, suggested what depressed my short-lived triumphs. I was but a few minutes arrived at the sources of the Nile, through numberless dangers and sufferings, the least of which would have overwhelmed me but for the continual goodness and protection of providence; I was, however, but then half through my journey, and all those dangers which I had already passed, awaited me again on my return. I found a despondency gaining ground fast upon me, and blasting the crown of laurels I had too rashly woven for myself. I resolved therefore to divert, till I could on more solid reflection overcome, its progress.

I saw Strates expecting me on the side of the hill. 'Strates,' said I,

'faithful squire, come and triumph with your Don Quixote at that
island of Barataria where we have wisely and fortunately brought
ourselves; come and triumph with me over all the kings of the earth,
all their armies, all their philosophers, and all their heroes.' 'Sir,' says
Strates, 'I do not understand a word of what you say, and as little what
you mean: you very well know I am no scholar; but you had much
better leave that bog, come in to the house, and look after Woldo; I
fear he has something further to seek than your sash, for he has been
talking with old devil-worshipper ever since we arrived.' 'Did they
speak secretly together said I.' 'Yes, sir, they did, I assure you.' 'And
in whispers, Strates!' 'As for that,' replied he, 'they need not have
been at the pains; they understand one another, I suppose, and the
devil their master understands them both; but as for me I compre-
hend their discourse no more than if it was Greek, *as they say*. Greek!'
Says he, 'I am an ass; I should know well enough what they said if they
spoke Greek.' 'Come,' said I, 'take a draught of this excellent water,
and drink with me a health to his majesty king George and a long line
of princes.' I had in my hand a large cup made of a cocoa-nut shell,
which I procured in Arabia, and which was brim-full. He drunk to the
king speedily and cheerfully, with the addition of, 'Confusion to his
enemies,' and tossed up his cap with a loud huzza. 'Now friend,' said
I, 'here is to a more humble, but still a sacred name, here is to –
Maria!' He asked if that was the Virgin Mary? I answered, 'In faith, I
believe so, Strates.' He did not speak, but only gave a humph of
disapprobation.

James Bruce (1730–1794) of Kinnaird was one of Scotland's greatest
explorers and travel writers – though was better known upon his
return from Africa as 'the Abyssinian Liar'. A main point of con-
tention was (and remains) that James Bruce was adamant he had
discovered the springs of the Blue Nile – when even he must have
known this was patently untrue – the Portuguese travellers and Jesuits
of the sixteenth and seventeenth centuries had 'discovered' them more
than a hundred years beforehand – but the Scottish traveller dismissed
them himself as 'Papist liars . . . ' Other aspects of Bruce's *Travels* have
been largely corroborated by subsequent travellers and Ethiopian

records. Besides extensive details of new plants and animal species and Ethiopian history and anthropology, Bruce brought back a large number of manuscripts – amongst them a copy of the long-lost Book of Enoch. The wealth of detail in the book, and Bruce's success in navigating extremely treacherous times in Ethiopia, are laudable and remain one of the greatest feats of the later age of exploration.

RICHARD BURTON

FROM *First Footsteps in East Africa*, 1856

The Forbidden City of Harar

After waiting half an hour at the gate, we were told by the returned warder to pass the threshold, and remounting guided our mules along the main street, a narrow uphill lane, with rocks cropping out from a surface more irregular than a Perote pavement. Long Guled had given his animal into the hands of our two Bedouins: they did not appear till after our audience, when they informed us that the people at the entrance had advised them to escape with the beasts, an evil fate having been prepared for the proprietors.

Arrived within a hundred yards of the gate of holcus-stalks, which opens into the courtyard of this African St James, our guide, a blear-eyed, surly-faced, angry-voiced fellow, made signs – none of us understanding his Harari – to dismount. We did so. He then began to trot, and roared out apparently that we must do the same. We looked at one another, the Hammal swore that he would perish foully rather than obey, and – conceive, dear L., the idea of a petticoated pilgrim venerable as to beard and turban breaking into a long 'double!' – I expressed much the same sentiment. Leading our mules leisurely, in spite of the guide's wrath, we entered the gate, strode down the yard, and were placed under a tree in its left corner, close to a low building of rough stone, which the clanking of frequent fetters argued to be a state-prison.

This part of the court was crowded with Gallas, some lounging about, others squatting in the shade under the palace walls. The chiefs were known by their zinc armlets, composed of thin spiral circlets, closely joined, and extending in mass from the wrist almost to the elbow: all appeared to enjoy peculiar privileges – they carried their long spears, wore their sandals, and walked leisurely about the royal precincts. A delay of half an hour, during which state-affairs were being transacted within, gave me time to inspect a place of which so many and such different accounts are current. The palace itself is, as Clapperton describes the Fellatah Sultan's state-hall, a mere shed, a long, single-storeyed, windowless barn of rough stone and reddish clay, with no other insignia but a thin coat of whitewash over the door. This is the royal and vizierial distinction at Harar, where no lesser man may stucco the walls of his house. The courtyard was about eighty yards long by thirty in breadth, irregularly shaped, and surrounded by low buildings: in the centre, opposite the outer entrance, was a circle of masonry against which were propped divers doors.

Presently the blear-eyed guide with the angry voice returned from within, released us from the importunities of certain forward and inquisitive youth, and motioned us to doff our slippers at a stone step, or rather line, about twelve feet distant from the palace-wall. We grumbled that we were not entering a mosque, but in vain. Then ensued a long dispute, in tongues mutually unintelligible, about giving up our weapons: by dint of obstinacy we retained our daggers and my revolver. The guide raised a door curtain, suggested a bow, and I stood in the presence of the dreaded chief.

The Amir, or, as he styles himself, the Sultan Ahmad bin Sultan Abu-bakr, sat in a dark room with whitewashed walls, to which hung – significant decorations – rusty matchlocks and polished fetters. His appearance was that of a little Indian Rajah, an etiolated youth twenty-four or twenty-five years old, plain and thin-bearded, with a yellow complexion, wrinkled brows and protruding eyes. His dress was a flowing robe of crimson cloth, edged with snowy fur, and a narrow white turban tightly twisted round a tall conical cap of red velvet, like the old Turkish headgear of our painters. His throne was a common Indian Kursi, or raised cot, about five feet long, with back and sides supported by a dwarf railing: being an invalid he rested his elbow upon a pillow, under which appeared the hilt of a Cutch sabre. Ranged in double line, perpendicular to the Amir, stood the 'court', his cousins and nearest relations, with right arms bared after the fashion of Abyssinia.

I entered the room with a loud 'Peace be upon ye!' to which H. H.

replying graciously, and extending a hand, bony and yellow as a kite's claw, snapped his thumb and middle finger. Two chamberlains stepping forward, held my forearms, and assisted me to bend low over the fingers, which however I did not kiss, being naturally averse to performing that operation upon any but a woman's hand. My two servants then took their turn: in this case, after the back was saluted, the palm was presented for a repetition. These preliminaries concluded, we were led to and seated upon a mat in front of the Amir, who directed towards us a frowning brow and an inquisitive eye.

Some inquiries were made about the chief's health: he shook his head captiously, and inquired our errand. I drew from my pocket my own letter: it was carried by a chamberlain, with hands veiled in his *tobe*, to the Amir, who after a brief glance laid it upon the couch, and demanded further explanation. I then represented in Arabic that we had come from Aden, bearing the compliments of our Daulah or governor, and that we had entered Harar to see the light of H. H.'s countenance: this information concluded with a little speech, describing the changes of Political Agents in Arabia, and alluding to the friendship formerly existing between the English and the deceased chief Abu-Bakr.

The Amir smiled graciously.

This smile I must own, dear L., was a relief. We had been prepared for the worst, and the aspect of affairs in the palace was by no means reassuring.

Whispering to his Treasurer, a little ugly man with a badly shaven head, coarse features, pug nose, angry eyes, and stubby beard, the Amir made a sign for us to retire. The *baise main* was repeated, and we backed out of the audience-shed in high favour. According to grandiloquent Bruce, 'the Court of London and that of Abyssinia are, in their principles, one': the loiterers in the Harar palace yard, who had before regarded us with cut-throat looks, now smiled as though they loved us. Marshalled by the guard, we issued from the precincts, and after walking a hundred yards entered the Amir's second palace, which we were told to consider our home. There we found the Bedouins, who, scarcely believing that we had escaped alive, grinned in the joy of their hearts, and we were at once provided from the chief's kitchen with a dish of Shabta, holcus cakes soaked in sour milk, and thickly powdered with red pepper, the salt of this inland region. When we had eaten, the treasurer reappeared, bearing the Amir's command, that we should call upon his Wazir, the Gerad Mohammed. Resuming our peregrinations, we entered an abode distinguished by its external streak of chunam, and in a small room on the ground floor, cleanly whitewashed and adorned, like an old English kitchen, with varnished wooden porringers of various sizes, we found a venerable old man whose benevolent countenance belied the reports current about him in Somali-land. Half rising, although his wrinkled brow showed suffering, he seated me by his side upon the carpeted masonry-bench, where lay the implements of his craft, reeds, inkstands and whitewashed boards for paper, politely welcomed me, and gravely stroking his cotton-coloured beard, desired my object in good Arabic.

I replied almost in the words used to the Amir, adding however some details how in the old day one Madar Farih had been charged by the late Sultan Abu-Bakr with a present to the governor of Aden, and that it was the wish of our people to re-establish friendly relations and commercial intercourse with Harar.

'Khayr inshallah! – it is well if Allah please!' ejaculated the Gerad: I then bent over his hand, and took leave.

Returning we inquired anxiously of the Treasurer about my servants' arms which had not been returned, and were assured that they had been placed in the safest of store-houses, the palace. I then sent a common six-barrelled revolver as a present to the Amir, explaining its use to the bearer, and we prepared to make ourselves as comfortable as possible. The interior of our new house was a clean room, with plain walls, and a floor of tamped earth; opposite the entrance were two broad steps of masonry, raised about two feet, and a yard above the ground, and covered with hard matting. I contrived to make upon the higher ledge a bed with the cushions which my companions used as shabracques, and, after seeing the mules fed and tethered, lay down to rest worn out by fatigue and profoundly impressed with the *poesie* of our position. I was under the roof of a bigoted prince whose least word was death; amongst a people who detest foreigners; the only European that had ever passed over their inhospitable threshold, and the fated instrument of their future downfall.

I now proceed to a description of unknown Harar.

The ancient capital of Hadiyah, called by the citizens 'Harar Gay', by the Somal 'Adari', by the Gallas 'Adaray' and by the Arabs and ourselves 'Harar', lies, according to my dead reckoning, 220° S.W. of, and 175 statute miles from, Zayla – 257° W. of, and 219 miles distant from, Berberah. This would place it in 9° 20' N. lat. and 42° 17' E. long. The thermometer showed an altitude of about 5,500 feet above the level of the sea. Its site is the slope of a hill which falls gently from west to east. On the eastern side are cultivated fields; westwards a terraced ridge is laid out in orchards; northwards is a detached eminence covered with tombs; and to the south, the city declines into a low valley bisected by a mountain burn. This irregular position is well sheltered from high winds, especially on the northern side, by the range of which Kondura is the lofty apex; hence, as the Persian poet sings of a heaven-favoured city – 'Its heat is not hot, nor its cold, cold.'

During my short residence the air reminded me of Tuscany. On the afternoon of the 11th January there was thunder accompanied by rain: frequent showers fell on the 12th, and the morning of the 13th was clear; but, as we crossed the mountains, black clouds obscured the heavens. The monsoon is heavy during one summer month; before it begins the crops are planted, and they are reaped in December and January. At other seasons the air is dry, mild, and equable.

Richard Burton (1821–1890) was an Arabist, erudite explorer, myth builder, polyglot and pornographer – but not the discoverer of the source of the Nile, the accolade he perhaps most sought. Burton's early days in India and his famed knack for picking up languages and studying the native's mores – a little too closely for the comfort of his superiors sometimes, as in his report on the male brothels of Calcutta – are the stuff of legend. Likewise, his rumoured mastery of twenty-five languages – although, to be fair, he did speak a huge variety of them, and really quite well, enough so to make it in disguise to Mecca and back. He was later accused of having killed a boy who had caught him urinating in the desert standing up – a sure sign of being in reality a *kaffir*. But stories like these were to hound Burton his whole life, and rather than the glory he felt was his due, he finished his life as a minor functionary in a series of remote postings.

WILLIAM CORNWALLIS HARRIS

FROM *The Highlands of Ethiopia*, 1844

A Military Expedition

Thus far the greatest irregularity and confusion had prevailed among the Amhára troops, alike during the march and the encampment. A council of war was daily convened, when each leader made his report and received verbal instructions for his guidance; but no order of any sort was promulgated until the moment before it was to be carried into effect, and all depended rather upon the whim and caprice of the monarch than upon the exigencies of the service. The first intimation of intended march was conveyed by the royal drums sounding suddenly to saddle a quarter of an hour before the advance, which, as the state pavilion went down, was announced by a flourish of horns.

But notwithstanding that the strictest silence had been observed on the subject by the Negoos, as well as by all who might have been unavoidably admitted to his confidence, strong surmises were entertained that a foray from Karábarek was to be the order of the following day; and about two hours after midnight, the sudden and unusual cessation of the psalm singing, followed by the heavy tramp past our tents of Ayto Shishigo's detachment of Shoa-Meda horse, confirming the opinion, the hum of the surrounding body, like that of a disturbed hive of bees, continued until dawn. No sooner was it light than His Majesty rode silently forth from his enclosure without beat of the *nugáreet*, and thousands instantly flocked towards the royal person. The state umbrellas were encased in white bags, and the usual cumbrous Abyssinian robe, which effectually impedes all rapid movement, was on this occasion cast aside. Short wide trousers of various hues hung loosely to the knee. A thick white cloth girded up the loins. The skins of wild beasts, the lion, the panther, and the ocelot, alone hung over the brawny shoulder of the warrior; and, with the exception of about two hundred musqueteers with bayonets fixed, every man-at-arms was equipped with spear, sword, and buckler, a mounted henchman behind many leading a spare charger.

At first starting the crush and confusion was truly terrific. Horses and mules rearing, kicking, and plunging, with lances bristling, and shields thumping in every direction, threatened instant destruction to each component member of the dense mass, which, crowded and locked fast together, streamed at a rapid trot after the king without the slightest order or regularity, save such as was preserved by the exertions of the shield-bearers who rode immediately behind. The occasional passage of ploughed land, producing a suffocating cloud of dust, served still more to increase the confusion, which had reached its climax when a rivulet intersected the line of march. Steep perpendicular banks and treacherous channels opposing the extended front of the legion, and checking advance, a simultaneous exertion was made to gain the only practicable fords, which were in an instant filled to choking. The fiercest struggle for extrication ensued. Numbers floundering in the soft mud, or borne out of their saddles by the pressure of the crowd, were trampled underfoot, whilst those who bestrode the stoutest steeds, clearing the way before them by sheer strength, forced their weaker neighbours to incline to the right and to the left, like frail reeds before the rush of the mountain deer.

The morning was bitterly cold. The hoar-frost lay thick and white upon the meadows; and as the rabble host trampled over the crisp grass towards the high range of Garra Gorphoo, which, at the distance of a few miles, rose to the height of twelve or fifteen hundred feet, the breath arose heavy from the nostril of man and beast, like a cloud of smoke, mixing with the dark columns of dust which followed the clattering hoofs of neighing war-steeds. During the first hour's advance up the valley, reports were continually being brought in, and messenger after messenger galloping off in every direction; and as the foot of the mountain was gained, Ayto Berkie, with a large detachment of the men of Bulga, leaving the main body, moved upon the left, whilst the king struck up the steep face of the range in the centre of an extended line of men, who scoured every hill and hollow, and beat every nook and corner at a rapid pace.

Stretching thirty miles in length by about twelve or fifteen in breadth, the mountains of Garra Gorphoo, covered throughout with one sheet of rich cultivation, form the water-shed between the Nile and the Háwash. The various rivulets that on either side wind down towards the parent streams, intersect it into hundreds of verdant valleys, on the swelling slopes of which the white-roofed houses of secluded Galla hamlets peep forth among dark green groves of juniper and acacia, that add beauty to the fair prospect. These tropical high-lands are inhabited by the Sertie tribe, who, long in a state of open rebellion, had rendered themselves doubly obnoxious to the despot, by attacking a detachment of Amhára the preceding year, of whom, whilst entangled in a morass near the foot of the range, eight hundred men were slain. The day of retribution had at length arrived. The object of the expedition, hitherto so carefully concealed, was now fully developed; and the military dispositions for sweeping destruction appeared to be right skilfully made.

Hurrying onward with ominous rapidity, slaughtering all who fell in their path, and with their weapons goading forward the herds of sleek cattle which teemed in every valley, the wild host now poured like an overwhelming torrent down the flowery slopes – now breasted the steep sunny acclivity like flames driven before the wind – and now wound in Indian file along the edges of cliffs affording scanty footing for a wild cat, where the loose soil, crumbling at every step, left the naked precipitous rock as the only available passage. Far and wide the crops were laid prostrate, as if beaten down under the violence of the hurricane; and before ten o'clock, the highest pinnacle of the green range having been crowned, a wide prospect burst upon the eye. A succession of richly cultivated plains dotted over with clusters of conical white houses, in parts surrounded by clumps of tall junipers, stretched away from the foot, the very picture of peace and plenty. Embosomed between the isolated peaks of Yerrur, Sequala, and the far-famed Entótto, lay the wide plain of Germáma, thickly peopled by the Ekka and Finfinni Galla, upon whose doomed heads the thunder-bolt was next to fall; and full in its centre two placid silver lakes, like great mirrors, reflected back the rays of the morning sun across sheets of luxuriant cultivation, extending for miles, nearly ready for the sickle. Far beyond, the long wooded line of the Háwash, rolling its troubled waters towards the plain of the Adaïel, loomed indistinctly through the haze; and in the extreme distance, the lofty blue range of the Aroosi and Ittoo Galla, skirting the mysterious regions of Guráguê, bounded the almost interminable prospect.

The morning mist, loaded with dust raised by the tramp of the Amhára steeds over acres of ploughed land, hung heavy on the slopes, and partially screening the approach of the locust army, conspired to enhance its success. Twenty thousand brawny warriors, in three divisions, covering many miles of country, and linked by detachments in every direction, pressed on towards the inviting goal – their hearts burning with the implacable hatred of hostile barbarians, and panting to consummate their bloody revenge. Taken entirely by surprise, their devoted victims lay helplessly before them, indulging in fatal dreams of happiness and security, alas! too speedily to be dispelled. Hundreds of cattle grazed in tempting herds over the flowery meads. Unconscious of danger, the unarmed husbandman pursued his peaceful occupation in the field; his wife and children carolled blithely over their ordinary household avocations; and the ascending sun shone bright on smiling valleys, which, long before his going down, were left tenanted only by the wolf and the vulture.

Preceded by the holy ark of Saint Michael, veiled under its scarlet canopy, the king still led the van, closely attended by the father confessor, and by a band of priests, with whom having briefly conferred, he turned towards the expectant army, and pronounced the ominous words which were the well-known signal for carrying fire and sword through the land, 'May the God who is the God of my forefathers strengthen and absolve!' Rolling on like the waves of the mighty ocean, down poured the Amhára host among the rich glades and rural hamlets, at the heels of the flying inhabitants – trampling underfoot the fields of ripening corn, in parts half reaped, and sweeping before them the vast herds of cattle which grazed untended in every direction. In the extreme distance their destructive progress was still marked by the red flames that burst forth in turn from the thatched roofs of each invaded village; and the havoc committed many miles to the right by the division of Abogáz Maretch, who was advancing parallel to the main body, and had been reinforced by the detachment under Ayto Shishigo, became equally manifest in numerous columns of white smoke, towering upwards to the azure firmament in rapid succession.

We followed close in the train of the Negoos, who halted for a few minutes on the eastern face of the range; and the eye of the despot gleamed bright with inward satisfaction, whilst watching through a telescope the progress of the flanking detachments, as they poured impetuously down the steep side of the mountain, and swept across the level plain with the fury of the blast of the Sirocco. A rapid détour to the westward in an hour disclosed the beautifully secluded valley of Finfinni, which, in addition to the artificial advantage of high cultivation, and snug hamlets, boasted a large share of natural beauty. Meadows of the richest green turf, sparkling clear rivulets leaping down in sequestered cascades, with shady groves of the most magnificent juniper lining the slopes, and waving their moss-grown branches above cheerful groups of circular wigwams, surrounded by implements of agriculture, proclaimed a district which had long escaped the hand of wrath. This had been selected as the spot for the royal plunder and spoliation; and the troops, animated by the presence of the monarch, now performed their bloody work with a sharp and unsparing knife – firing village after village, until the air was dark with smoke, mingled with the dust raised by the impetuous rush of man and horse.

The luckless inhabitants, taken quite by surprise, had barely time to abandon their property, and fly for their lives to the fastness of Entótto, which reared its protecting form at the distance of a few miles. The spear of the warrior searched every bush for the hunted foe. Women and girls were torn from their hiding places to be hurried into hopeless captivity – old men and young were indiscriminately slain among the fields and groves; flocks and herds were driven off in triumph, and house after house was sacked and consigned to the flames. Each grim Amhára warrior vied with his comrade in the work of retributive destruction amongst the execrated Galla. Whole groups and families were surrounded and speared within the walled courtyards, which were soon strewed with the bodies of the slain. Wretches who betook themselves to the open plain, were pursued and hunted down like wild beasts; and children of three and four years of age, who had been placed in the trees with a hope that they might escape observation, were included in the inexorable massacre, and pitilessly shot among the branches. In the course of two hours the division left the desolated valley laden with spoil, and carrying with them numbers of wailing females and orphan children, together with the barbarous trophies that had been stripped from the mangled bodies of their victims.

The hoarse scream of the vulture as she wheeled in funereal circles over this appalling scene of carnage and devastation, and the crackling of falling roofs and rafters from the consuming houses, alone disturbed the grave-like silence of the dreary and devoted spot, so lately resounding to the fiendish shouts and war-whoops of the excited warriors, and to the unpitied groans of their helpless captives. And as the exulting barbarians, followed by the curses of many homeless fugitives in Entótto, crossed the last range, gloomy columns of smoke, rising thick and dense to the darkened heavens, for miles in every direction, proclaimed that this recently so flourishing and beautiful location had, in a few brief hours, been utterly ruined, pillaged, and despoiled, as far as the means of ruthless man could affect its destruction.

William Cornwallis Harris (1807–1848), English military engineer, artist, hunter. Harris spent most of his career in India in the armed forces of the East India Company, with two important exceptions. He took a long trip to southern Africa, in which he first showed his tenacity as a traveller and hunter, and initiated his career as a painter, initially as a means to archive his trophies, though it became a way to scientifically portray new animals and sights. Nowhere was this more important than in his second expedition (1841–43) to Ethiopia and the court of Sahle Selassie, the King of Showa, where Harris drew up a commercial treaty with the king. Besides his lively and highly critical written account, Harris left us very detailed and colourful depictions of life in Ancober, the capital of Showa, and of proceedings at court.

MANSFIELD PARKYNS

FROM *Life in Abyssinia*, 1853

Glimpses of Life in Abyssinia

Before starting on any expedition, the Abyssinians, like the ancient Romans, listen for the voice of certain birds; and according to whether their notes are heard on the right hand or on the left so do they anticipate a prosperous or unfavourable journey. I have known many expeditions for the purpose of war or hunting postponed at the moment when, if undertaken, success seemed nearly certain, simply because a little bird called from the left-hand side at starting. Similarly, many a wife has been kept for several days anxiously expecting her husband, because the bird chose to perch on the right hand; the right-hand omen being propitious for setting out from home, the left for returning. The black and white falcon, called here 'gaddy gaddy', is considered a bird of omen in some parts of Tigre. If this bird flies away at the approach of travellers, the sign is unfavourable; while, on the contrary, if it remain perched and looking at them, they count upon a most prosperous journey. Hunters on the Mareb follow much the warning of a small bird as to the direction they should take; and I have known parties turn back from pursuing the fresh trail of a herd of buffaloes, and take an opposite direction, merely because its chirp was heard on the wrong side. Once, a party of about thirty Barea having been reported to be in the neighbourhood, a large force collected, perhaps a hundred and fifty men; but after arriving in sight of the enemy the gallant army returned peaceably home, and considered such a course not only justifiable but right, because, when halting to reconnoitre, the omen had been heard on the side favourable to their adversaries. On another occasion I had started on a hunting and foraying expedition, with some fifteen tried and picked men. We had remained a fortnight in the frontier woods, and had seen nothing of the Barea: one day, however, a bird gave us an omen of success, and the night following we discovered their fires on a hill scarce a mile distant from where we lay. Our party was in a moment on the *qui vive*: primings were looked to, edge of knives felt and rubbed on a stone, and each one anticipated the glory he was to gain for himself in butchering a few of the enemy. Some were even so much excited, that they began to strut about and count their deeds of valour, in expectancy of what they would have to do on their return home; and, to use a Yankee expression, the whole felt themselves 'half froze for hair', or rather for the still more cruel trophies which Abyssinians take from their slaughtered enemies. But a night-bird's voice settled the whole business; and instead of waiting, as had been our intention, for a few hours before sunrise to strike the *coup*, we all sneaked off homeward, like so many whipped dogs; for the vainglory of the warriors had oozed out of their finger-ends at this intimation of the beaked augur that their bones would be safest in the bosoms of their family circles. In advance, signs of the Barea were eagerly sought for; in retreating, so great was the panic caused by the unwitting bird, that we kept the sharpest look-out lest they should come upon us unawares.

There is nothing so agreeably exciting as this sort of expedition, or even as scouting in these countries; though the latter is rather lonely work, especially when, as is often the case, it is undertaken by a single man. Still I have often been a week or more alone on this sort of errand for my own amusement, without even saying where I was going, or indeed without so much as knowing it myself. It is a most independent life. My dress on these occasions consisted of a short kilt of nicely tanned antelope's hide, a piece of coarse cotton cloth wrapped round my waist by day as a belt and used as a covering at night, and a small wild cat's or jackal's skin thrown over the left shoulder. Add to these a kid-skin filled with flour, a little horn of cayenne pepper and salt mixed, and a small piece of thin leather for a bed, and you have all the wardrobe, kitchen, and furniture which an Abyssinian frontier-man thinks necessary for a fortnight's outlying. A flint and steel, slow match, an awl, nippers for extracting thorns, and arms and ammunition, are of course added: and with such means for procuring comforts, and some luck with his rifle, if a man cannot be happy in a dry climate, I wonder what he would wish for! Even if you have no spot with game, there are always small birds, snakes, fish, lizards etc, to be had; so that you need never want. Besides, the branches of the dima-tree furnish a kind of fruit, which, though not very solid as food, yet aids much to the flavour of the *cuisine*. It has a large greenish shell (as it may be called): inside of it are a number of seeds, attached to which by fibres is a quantity of yellowish white cakey powder, having a sweetish acid taste, and when mixed with water forming an agreeable beverage, something resembling lemonade. The Abyssinians make a paste of this, mixing it with red pepper and salt, and eat it with the 'gogo' bread. When the dima reaches a certain size its trunk almost always becomes hollow; and then it often contains wild honey, which may easily be obtained with the help of a small axe and fire. St John the Baptist's living on locust and wild honey is easily understood by anyone who has been in these countries. The Abyssinians refuse to eat the locust, and deny that it was the insect which was the Saint's food, asserting that it was the fruit of a tree called by the same name (ambatta). The niggers and inhabitants of Sennar, however, eat the locusts willingly. I have often tasted them; and though there is nothing disagreeable in their flavour, still I cannot say that they are a particularly delicious food. The natives prepare them by pulling off their legs and wings, and roasting them on an iron dish, like coffee.

The usual spot chosen by a scout for passing the night is on some small hill, which, being a little elevated above water, places the sleeper, in a measure, out of danger of miasma and of being run over by a herd of buffaloes or elephants. There is a very convenient spot for this purpose nor far below Rohabaita: a hollow in the top of the hillock prevents the fire from being seen either by man or beast, and the canes below are often chosen by buffaloes as lodging for the night. Far from keeping up great fires, as a protection from wild beasts, hunters on the Mareb usually make theirs either in a natural hole in the ground, or dig one on purpose, if such should not be found in a convenient spot, and pile boughs of trees all around to prevent the glare from being seen. These precautions are necessary, partly that the blaze may not keep away the buffalo, and partly lest it should attract the Barea. As for the lions, they almost always prowled about us during the night; but our only prayer was that they might stop near us and not disturb other game. I fancy that the attacks from which travellers have suffered must have been induced by their having animals with them. I remember one night being especially annoyed by lions. We were anxiously waiting for morning to attack a herd of buffaloes that we had watched into some canes not many hundred yards distant. Two lions had been prowling round us for some hours. At last, tired of us, they descended and fell upon our horned neighbours; and we had the mortification of hearing them gallop away with the lions after them. Even if the pursuers had had luck, we might have profited by it; for we should surely have killed a gorged lion next day, besides getting the horns, and perhaps part of the skin, of its victim.

I never killed a lion single-handed during all my stay in Abyssinia; it is not an easy thing to accomplish. In the plain country they are almost unknown. In the 'quollas' they are plentiful, but no one knows where to find them in the day-time: in fact, from the nature of the country, to discover them is almost impossible. I never once heard a native hunter of these parts say that he had seen or heard of a lion's den. The opinion of the natives was, that these animals lived during the day among the inaccessible rocks and jungle, but at no fixed place. A few are killed; but these are either met by accident, or are found sleeping after having gorged themselves on some animal. At night I have often watched for them, but generally without success; a stream is very different from a single pool; you station yourself at a spot where by their trails you see they have been before, watch all night, and in the morning find that, either by accident or being aware of your presence, they have selected another drinking-place half a mile off; and when they did come it was next to impossible to shoot them.

You hear a lion roar in the distance; presently a little nearer; then you start up hearing a short bark close by; and if there be a fire of moonlight, perhaps you may see a light-coloured object gliding quickly past from one bush to another: before you are sure whether or not you saw anything, it is gone. You sit watching for a moment, rifle in hand, expecting him to appear again, when (how he got there you know not) his roar is heard at a considerable distance off in an opposite direction: and thus you go on for an hour or two, when, getting sleepy, you politely request him to take himself off to a certain warm place, and, returning your rifle between your legs, roll over and go to sleep. Some people may think that this is a queer place for a rifle; but, on the contrary, it is the position of all others wherein utility and comfort are most combined. The butt rests on the arm, and serves as a pillow for the head; the muzzle points between the knees, and the arms encircle the lock and breech; so that, besides having a smooth pillow, the butter from your hair is beneficially employed in toughening the wood, instead of being lost on a stone, while you are always prepared to start up armed at a moment's notice.

A propos of sleeping on hills. A party of fourteen men once rested for the night on an eminence near the river, and at no great distance from the road between Addy Harisho, where I lived, and Davra Mariam, a village of Serawi, to which they belonged. Early in the morning three of them went down to fetch water, leaving the remainder to prepare the breakfast. After a short time, as they did not return, some of their comrades set out to see what had become of them; and, cautiously advancing, saw a party of nine Barea leaving the spot; so they returned in haste, and told their companions what they conjectured had been the probable fate of their brethren. Now, although the survivors were eleven in number, all armed, and according to their own account (and in these matters Abyssinians always exaggerate) the Barea were inferior to them in numbers by two persons, still they had not the courage to attempt to punish the murderers, or even to ascertain for certain the fate of their victims, but sneaked away among the grass, and returned homeward to Serawi, bearing the sad news. The three sufferers were relations of my host, and the news was sent across to us with all speed, that we might join the force which was to be raised to pursue the enemy. Accordingly, though we all foresaw that, from so much time having been lost, we had little chance of succeeding in our enterprise, still disgusted with the cowardice and lethargy of our neighbours of Serawi, we determined to set them a better example, and immediately started down the river in hopes of cutting off the retreat of the enemy, without heeding the meeting place which had been assigned to us. But it was of no use: the Barea, after striking a *coup*, are too wise to remain long in the same spot, and being more active, and quite as well acquainted with the country as the Abyssinians, they had no doubt arrived near their own frontier long before we even started in pursuit of them. Returning after a hard day's work, we found the people of Serawi dawdling about, taking the bodies to be buried, while some of them had even the impudence to upbraid us for having started without them, and for not having attended the place of meeting agreed upon. A few of our party were desirous of forming a strong force, in order to avenge our lost friends, but we could not collect a dozen who would consent to join us: some pleaded that it was better to stay at home and guard their property and families; others, that although that sort of foray would have been well enough in better times, yet now they were a poor and oppressed race, and had therefore more inclination to remain at home and try to make money. It is a well-known fact, that, if you feed an Abyssinian well, and clothe him smartly, he will, as he becomes fat and proud, be not only tolerably courageous, but even often horribly quarrelsome; while, if thin and ragged, he is as meek as a half-weaned lamb. An Abyssinian's courage, indeed, chiefly depends either on personal vanity or interested hopes; there are, of course, many exceptions to this rather too general rule; and while I speak of them thus severely on this point, I cannot but pity rather than blame them. Before the oppression of the Amhara they were truly brave; but when a nation is reduced to a state of slavery, it is rare that it does not become demoralised in every way, the people losing their former energy and that feeling of pride which, after all, is mostly the inducement to great deeds. Until the Tigreans were subdued they had had for centuries the prestige of victory on their side, and this is always a great encouragement even to brave men: now they have nothing, being scarcely to be considered as a nation, trodden under foot and oppressed as they are by the stranger. The Barea, moreover, are enemies not at all despised even by the bravest. Equal in every respect, as regards cunning and agility, to the Red Indians of North America, they are superior to them in point of stature and physical strength. When they lie out near a road, in wait for passers-by, they will follow a strong party for days, gliding unperceived and noiselessly, like so many snakes in the grass, and waiting till an opportunity occurs when the party, fatigued or hungry, should put aside their weapons and seek for repose at a halting-place; at other times they will lie concealed near a road with scouts in every direction on the look-out, yet no one venturing to speak, but only making known by signs what he may have to communicate to his companions or leader. Thus he will point to his ear and foot on hearing footsteps, to his eyes on seeing persons approach, or to his tongue if voices be audible; and will indicate on his fingers the numbers of those coming, describing also any particulars as to how many porters, beasts of burden or for riding, there may be with the party. This was told me by a man who had been taken prisoner by them, and lived for some time among them.

Their attack is made on a sign from their leader, by a volley of stones and clubs being discharged at once on the comers; and before they have recovered from the disagreeable start which this rattle about their ears may have caused them, the Barea rush at them with the fury of so many devils, armed with lance and sword. Their lances are very poor tools, and seldom much esteemed by them for fighting, being more often employed for digging holes in the ground; the formidable two-edged, cross-handled broadsword, used by all the Arabs and Nubians, is their favourite weapon, and one which they generally wield with considerable vigour, if not skill. Like most people acting on the offensive in a bad cause, it has frequently been remarked of these savages that, if their opponent, undismayed by their first attack, stand firm, or rise boldly to meet them, they will retire as fast as they came on; whereas, if the attacked party be taken by surprise, they will most assuredly butcher every man of them. It is of no use running away, for they have longer legs than their neighbours, both when pursing and fleeing. In their flight they are quite as much cunning as in their attacks. As I before said, they are in general both stronger and lighter of foot than the Abyssinians; but if by chance an old or clumsy Barea should find himself pursued by an Abyssinian, and perceive that his pursuer gains on him, he will first drop his garment, then his lance, then his shield, retaining always to the last his trusty sword. The Barea, in doing this, shows his knowledge of the character of his enemy. An Abyssinian is always most anxious for a trophy, and would never think of passing by anything thus cast away by the foe, lest some one of his comrades should pick it up, and gain the credit which he more deservedly aspires to; so he takes up each successive article as it is thrown down, and in the end the Barea usually succeeds in effecting his escape; for his pursuer not only encumbers himself with what he has to carry, but also, by frequently stopping to collect his trophies, allows the fugitive a considerable advantage. Moreover, to speak the truth, many an Abyssinian would prefer letting a Barea get away to forcing him to stand and fight for his life.

Mansfield Parkyns (1823–1894) was from a well-known family in Nottinghamshire, from a marriage between the landed gentry and the new commercial class – and had he not lost both parents by a young age, his life would certainly have been very different. A steady income and little restraint meant Parkyns could indulge in the whims he chose to pursue and this he did, first engaging in a sort of extended Grand Tour of Europe and the Levant, before taking off, apparently on the spur of the moment as well, to 'find the spring of the White Nile and reach the Atlantic by the interior of Africa'. In fact, Parkyns, beyond some wanderings in Nubia and Egypt on his way home, would give the next three years to Abyssinia, where he took to dressing in the local style, even going barefoot, and engaging in hunting expeditions. Upon his return to Europe, and apart from a couple of years working in the British embassy in Istanbul, Parkyns resolutely returned to type, buying an estate in Nottinghamshire and fathering eight daughters with his wife. *Life in Abyssinia* was a great success – and rightly so. For the second edition, published shortly after the Napier expedition, Parkyns wrote that he hoped to offer the Victorian reader 'a tolerably accurate idea of Abyssinia and Abyssinians'. What he forgot to mention was that when the mountain redoubt of Magdala was stormed by Napier's troops, one 'Parkyns junior', an interpreter by profession, was also freed. It seems that Mansfield Parkyns had failed to be totally accurate in his record of his own life in Abyssinia.

ARNAUD D'ABBADIE

FROM *Douze Années dans la Haute Ethiopie*, 1868

Chivalry on the Nile

We were on the borders of Wollo, a country which, before the Ilm Orma conquest, was known as Kolo. The population of Wollo is composed of conquered natives and of Ilm Orma families called Galas, the latest arrivals of this conquering race which, arriving from the eastern lowlands at the beginning of the eighteenth century, penetrated the empire between Lake Haik and Mount Efrata, and seized the highlands now known as Wollo. Before pushing on southwards, they passed between Shewa and Abbay and are now in the vast area bounded by the River Abbay to the north, the kingdom of Kaffa to the south, Shewa and the Gurage countries to the east and the kingdom of the Siddamos to the west. The territory of Wollo mainly consists of large and flat highlands, which are cool, salubrious and fertile. It is divided into several small states which are either hostile or united, depending on the interests of the moment. The constitution of these states is based on patriarchal-feudal habits. Inside the family, in domestic society, power follows the natural order: it is self-regulating. In civil and political society, power vests spontaneously, and is confirmed and held with the consent of those that are governed. Heredity establishes a right to possession, but, in Wollo as in the other parts of the old empire, the tradition relative to the government of the family and of the state is that of primogeniture, which only constitutes a presumption in favour of the heredity of power, which, in all cases, must go to the most capable and the most honourable, whatever the gender, and one sometimes sees a woman at the head of a family, a commune, a district or a whole province. Depending on circumstances, power is temporary, for life or hereditary.

The Ilm Orma conquerors of Wollo, even though vastly inferior in numbers to the natives, keep them in a state of serfdom. They normally leave all agricultural work to them and reserve near exclusively to themselves the undertaking of defending themselves against the enemy, whoever he may be. With the exception of a few districts where the Galla language, or better said Oromo, is the only language, the inhabitants speak both Oromo and a slightly corrupted Amarigna. In less than a century, Muslim missionaries from the kingdom of Harar to the north-east have completed the conversion of the Ilm Orma who, having adopted Islam, have nevertheless conserved some of their previous habits quite opposite to the Law of Mahomet, notably the use of fermented beverages and the taurobolium [bull sacrifice] practice. As for the natives, Christian in origin, having long resisted the pressure of their rulers, they are also now abandoning their religion to adopt Islam. The Ilm Orma themselves will often take a native wife, but seldom give their own daughters in marriage to the natives. The most active centre for Muslim propaganda in oriental Africa is now amongst the Ilm Orma of Wollo, who show high disdain for Christians and a desire to conquer them as is characteristic of true Muslims. Bar a few exceptions, imposed by the Muslim religion, they have adopted the customs and even the dress of their Christian neighbours of Begamdir and Shewa, and they despise their blood brothers farther south, because of the relative simplicity of their mores, and especially because they have remained faithful to paganism, the religion of their common ancestors. They are said to be intelligent and to observe quite faithfully, between themselves especially, their given word. They put on naïve airs, that are risible, but they are astute and are recognised as being born politicians. They are excellent warriors, although, like the people of Agaw Medir, they lose a part of their valour when they fight outside their country. The Rases of Begamdir and the governors of Shewa, who are the sovereigns who maintain the most frequent relations with Wollo, have as constant policy to foment and feed among its chiefs dissensions to occupy them at home, and a widely held opinion in Ethiopia is that, if all these chiefs just got on, they would complete the conquest of the old empire. Their country is, with the province of Idjou, a few pagan Ilm Orma districts of the south of Gojjam and the small province of Amhara, the part of the old empire where citizens enjoy the most liberty and initiative, and it is often cited as an example of how much prosperity and cohesion can be given to a country by the old ways and customs. These Ilm Orma, in effect, while penetrating the empire, made theirs what remained of the antique free communal regime that the Dedjazmatchs of the other provinces were destroying in the name of the unity and centralisation of imperial power. But today the conquerors seem to be losing these advantages. They are letting themselves be contaminated little by little by the byzantine and servile spirit of the old populations that neighbour them. The troubadours, coming from Gojjam, Semen and Begamdir, entertain them with the power of the Dedjazmatchs, the relative splendour of their courts, titles and the honorific distinctions that are given there to the most brave, and several of them have gone to serve in Begamdir, amongst the Rases of Gouksa's family, of Ilm Orma origin. Some of them, returning to their country after occupying high posts in Begamdir, in the Semen, at first did not dare adorn themselves with the titles and decorations they had won abroad, but they have begun to wear them today, and a few chiefs from the western borders willingly recognise Ras Ali's nominal sovereignty since it offers them subsidies and sometimes support in the quarrels they have with their neighbours. The true patriots of Wollo still speak out against these innovations and these corrupting influences, but their voices are more and more drowned out and Wollo seems to be losing its conquering spirit and to be accustoming itself progressively to servitude.

[. . .]

Wollo is a sparsely wooded highland, but cool, green and fertile. Its population is relatively dense and, with the exception of a few uninhabited plains, the ground under plough nearly everywhere. The huts and the houses have that discreet air, well organised and clean, that distinguishes the houses of the Ilm Orma. Herds of oxen are rare; conversely, sheep abound. In certain districts where there are pastures without the bushes or thorny shrubs against which sheep like to scratch themselves, which damages their fleece, the Ilm Orma raise a particular breed, with long wool, of which the pelt, with the wool, cut into the form of a cape, like the fawn skin or the leopard skin of Bacchus, is sought after by all Ethiopians. These lambs become the object of particular care. They are shorn once or twice and subjected to an invariable regime, which is followed until they are slaughtered. If the regime is grass, no other food will be given. Some breeders think that it is better to limit the grass, which, in their opinion, makes the wool harder and causes kemp and a lot of matting, and they feed them exclusively on grain and salted asslis flour. This last diet fattens and produces, they say, a finer wool. The sheep that are fed grass go to pasture; those fed grain remain tethered; they are walked for an hour or two in the day. The rest of the time, they are kept on an elevated platform and care is taken to hobble their back feet and to saw off their horns to prevent them from scratching, because the mass of wool and the heat produced by the abundance of the fleece and the lack of sufficient ventilation, means that the animal suffers a constant pruritus. The Dedjadj Birro gave me one of these sheep that Aly Wadadj had sent him as a curio, while we were still in Gojjam. This sheep did the whole campaign with us. He was black, with long thin legs and, so that he could walk more freely, we were obliged to tie up the locks of his fleece, which measured a cubit and four fingers in length and swept the floor. The plateau of Wollo is also particularly favourable to the equine species and, like all the Ilm Orma, the inhabitants pay much attention to the care of horses. As is the practice in Nejd in Arabia, the horse is the object of the solicitude of the whole family. The women in particular see to it that it lacks for nothing, when it is a part of the household; the children play with it; finally it is subjected to a domestication of an intimate nature, that makes it as close as possible to man and causes it to work with an intelligence that is sometimes surprising. This intimacy with horses bestows upon the people of Wollo a virile and decisive bearing, though a little wooden, abrupt and somewhat taciturn. As open and free grazing is very rare, in many neighbourhoods horses find little to feed on, and for at least nine months of the year they are fed solely with straw and barley, whereas those of other Ethiopian provinces, where depopulation is severe and where unploughed pastures or empty lands are common,

are fed on grass for most of the year, which means they are unable to
stand much work. When the chiefs of Wollo are at peace with their
neighbours from Wora Himano, Amhara, Begamdir and Shewa, they
seize the opportunity to solve their own differences with the weapons
at hand. Their cavalry is thus constantly exercised, and is said to be the
best in Ethiopia. When circumstances allow for a few days' rest, they
are careful to turn their horses out during the day. The horses rarely
find pasture and group together, inhaling the air, chasing each other
and playing in all sorts of fashions. But if the alarm is sounded, they
stop suddenly, snorting and, carrying their heads high with pointed
ears, they form themselves into squads, along neighbourhood lines,
and each horse returns at a gallop to the door of his master, whose
wife awaits him, saddle in hand, while the rider is arming himself and
girding his loins.

[...]

It was at the end of June: this therefore meant that it was only a few
days before the winter flood of the Abbay. We could not therefore
remain where we were, and the army resumed its march. As, despite
his desperate circumstances, Teumro Hailo fought off death, we
carried him on an alga with all possible precautions and, upon his
request, we agreed to leave him in a highland district of Wollo, called
Galle, with a local notable, an old friend of his, who was known as Aly
Wadadj. He asked that I stay with him, but Monseigneur would not
consent to this. On the second leg, a few friends and I left the army
with a strong escort and we went to establish him in Galle, where a
large and very clean hut in the middle of a small elevated plain, fertile
and cool, awaited him. Here he had first fought during the lifetime of
his father, Dedjadj Teumro. We knew that the dignitaries of central
Wollo, our enemies of yesterday, would pay him a visit as soon as we
departed and would fulfil all his needs. Two young women of the
family came to assure us that they would take care of our friend, as if
they were his sisters. Hailo told us in quite a steady voice: 'Come, now
is the time of my real death to start as you are to leave me.' Each of us
stepped up to his resting place, pronouncing the customary words for
such an occasion: 'Brother, may God bring forgiveness upon you,
may we find each other in propitious circumstances.' Lying on his

back, tears ran down his temples, and to each of us he answered: 'Amen!' His dear Mahmed himself did not obtain one word more; and we left him without hope of ever seeing him again. It was 28th June 1843.

Five days later, our two armies had reached the bank of the Abbay. The swollen river was a mass of muddy waters and would not allow us to ford at the place where we had crossed it at the beginning of the campaign. We followed its bank for several hours, looking for a ford, and our anxiety was all the greater, as it was 3rd July and eight days later, during the feast of Hamle Abbo, which coincided that year, 1843, with the 11th July of our calendar, all of Ethiopia's waterways are said to reach their highest level, which they then maintain for the rest of the winter. Our swimmers discovered a ford. Twenty-one riders immediately went forward, but only five reached the other bank: the others drowned in front of our eyes with their mounts. Amongst these unfortunates was an already aged dignitary, who had served under the Dedjadj Zaoude, the father of Dedjadj Guoscho. Birro began to laugh looking at him appear and disappear in the river, similar to an empty brille, he said, which, before filling and sinking, jerks around at the waters' command. Those present were shocked by his behaviour. Further on, we at last found a serviceable ford, but the sun was setting, and we put off crossing til the morrow. As soon as it exits Lake Tsana, the Abbay digs itself a deeper and deeper bed and flows around Gojjam, protecting it from Begamdir to the Ilm Orma country of Amourou against its neighbours, who all want to conquer it, as it is called the garden of Ethiopia. The low lying land by the river is beset annually by fevers, often deadly. The terraces become healthier and healthier, the higher they are, and here the traveller, thirsty from the heat of the lowlands, finds greenery that soothes his eyes and cool air that soon makes him forget the aridity of his travels. The troops set us up as best they could for the night on the narrow riverbank, all trying to sleep on the shingles next to the water, for the fevers run especially high at the end of autumn, when we were there, as well as at the beginning of spring, when the waters recede, and the natives believe that in all seasons one can sleep without harm on the shingles, while only an hour's sleep taken a few yards from there,

upon the earth, exposes one to illness. As is customary, most of our
people drew a cross on their forehead with a mixture of gunpowder
and water and, to keep the evil spirits and djinns at bay, the apparent
conveyors of the epidemic, the troops simultaneously fired off great
discharges with their rifles. The wisest who, as in all countries, are the
less numerous, made fumigations of sulphur, believed to be the best
prophylactic. The army slept little: there was anxiety about crossing
the ford tomorrow. A cry of 'God, forgive us, Christ!' uttered loudly
up-river, floated down to us, taking on a supernatural potency in the
sonorous gorge in which we were encamped. It briefly eclipsed the
noise of the waters, reached a last meander downstream and in the
distance, echoing from cliff to cliff, lost itself in the crests of the high
country. A little before daybreak, I was awoken by piercing cries:
crocodiles, which most often attacked at this hour, had taken two
sleeping men and cruelly bitten several others. Shortly after, we began
to cross. Monseigneur, surrounded by an escort of numerous swimmers
and riding his horse, set foot on the other side. The Waizero Oubdar,
Birro's wife, was placed upon an alga that men of high stature carried
on their shoulders and, in the middle of the river, out of superstition,
unveiled her face, for it is thought that water spirits are curious and
that they sometimes, to wreak vengeance on beautiful girls who hide
their faces, pull them down to the bottom of the river. From the bank,
Birro watched this favourite daughter of the Waizero Mannan carefully, partly out of the superstitious belief that she had an influence on
his good fortunes and especially because she would be a valuable
hostage if she were to fall into Ali's hands. It is difficult to give an idea
of the disorder that reigns in these undisciplined armies when they
ford a great watercourse: horses, riding and pack mules, donkeys, oxen,
sheep, hunting dogs, poultry, maids, concubines, pages, infants, the
wounded, the ill, the lame, high and lowly lords, poets, priests and
clerics, foot soldiers, cavalry, boors embarrassed by their loads, by
their horses, by their weapons; musicians noisily safeguarding their
instruments; marksmen holding high their bullet belts and shouting:
'Make way cannon fodder! Beware of my powder!'; stubborn beasts,
insolent packhorse and kettledrum players and, what is worse, problem
makers, idle bystanders and opportunists, all pressing down, shoving,

shouting as loud as they can, laughing or complaining at each vicissitude. At the place where we crossed the Abbay, it was about one hundred and thirty to one hundred and fifty metres wide. Towards the middle of the ford and for about twenty metres, the water reached the eye-level of a man of medium height. To cross fords of this depth, the men come together in groups of sixty to one hundred and fifty, each carrying a heavy load, or a woman or a companion whose weight gives anchorage to his feet on the bottom; when it becomes deep, they proceed by little hops, in order to take a breath each time. A few yards below the ford the water deepened and formed rapids that rendered the passage very dangerous, so a few swimmers on each bank downstream were ready to help men or animals carried away by the current. After a whole day, the army had almost all crossed, when I was warned that my long-haired sheep had been forgotten and that my swimmers were exhausted. For the fourteenth time I reforded the river with a few men of good will, and we pushed the precious four-legged animal into the water, as some Ilm Orma, having crawled undetected from bush to bush, ran us down. With only stones for weapons, we bravely ran along the bank. Luckily a few opportune rifle shots by our people on the other side of the river intimidated the enemy, and we threw ourselves into the Abbay, pulling our sheep in with us, and set foot on the opposite bank to great acclamation. I was all the happier for not having lost a single man, unlike the occasion when we had to cross the rapids. It was estimated that eighty men were drowned in that passage.

Translated by Yves-Marie Stranger

Arnaud d'Abbadie (1815–1893). Arnaud's well-written, extensively researched and lively account of his twelve years in Ethiopia in the 1840s – no doubt because he chose to publish it in French rather than in his mother's English (she was Irish) – is today unjustly forgotten. His first act in the country was to change his name – Arnaud, sounded like *ArNo* in Amharic, which translates very handily into 'He is sh*t', an altogether inauspicious name under which to travel in Ethiopia.

His royalist and conservative tendencies are plain to see in his cultural interpretations, but Arnaud – or Mikael as he was then known for twelve years – is never less than a sympathetic observer and even an active participant in the skirmishes and historical happenings of these times, and, to use a modern turn of phrase, is refreshingly unjudgemental in his descriptions and observations.

Chronicle of a Death Foretold

His father Abba Djibo, a man from Worai Haimanot. His mother Alco, a daughter of the land of Ambassel. They were Muslims, and gave birth, excluding several girls, to three boys: Batto, Adam, and Ahemedie. The latter grew up with his father who had influence in the Worai Haimanot, tending cows. At 20, he took the fancy of Ras Guosho who baptised him and gave him the daughter of his paternal aunt, named Sihin, as wife; the name of Ahemedie was changed to Wolde Gabriel. He came into the service of Guosho where he stayed for about nine years. When the latter died he abandoned his wife who refused to follow him into Muslim lands; she had given birth to a son named Liben. He took himself to Worai Haimanot, where his brother Adam held part of the country and was fighting against the son of his uncle. Ahemedie became Muslim again and joined the troops of his brother. Atie Tekla Georgis came campaigning in Worai Haimanot. The two cousins joined up and established themselves in the hill fort of Ligouot.

The emperor entered Wollo, but his rear was harried by the cousins. Upon his return from Wollo, the Atie decided to climb the hill and entrusted Wolde Gabriel with this task. He took the hill and seized Adam, whom he beheaded. Ahemedie managed to escape, and went into exile where he stayed three years, in Wollo. He then came back and engaged in banditry in the Worai Haimanot. He fought against Djanterar Barou, a Galla, chief of Ambassel, beat him, then was able to beat a strong party from Wollo come to expel him. He then claimed his wife though her parents refused him on grounds of religion; in any case she had remarried. She fled with her husband and with Liben, his son, to Begemder, where she died eight years later. Meanwhile, Ahemedie moved and kept Worai Haimanot more or less under his sway. Soon after, Tallaq Aly, Ras of Begemder, died and Aly Gaaz succeeded him. The latter declared war upon Ahemedie, to make him accept his suzerainty. Ahemedie refused and a few months later came to Begemder to wage war upon him. Ras Aly Gaaz had wed the sister of Ras Haylo, the former Ras of Begemder and currently the master of Wag and Lasta.

This brother-in-law came to his succour, and the two of them united and fought with Ahemedie at Gouna (in Begemder), where they were beaten. They were able to escape, the one to Lasta, and Aly Gaaz to Idjou. Ahemedie returned to Worai Haimanot, having given Begemder to Ras Wolde Gabriel, the uncle of Ras Haylo. Two years then passed in gentle negotiation. During this time, Aly Gaaz rearmed and came to attack Ahemedie at Kai Afer in Worai Haimanot, with his faithful brother-in law Haylo. Three whole days were spent fighting. Ahemedie had about 11,000 horses, no foot soldiers, 400 guns. Aly Gaaz's troops were much more numerous, but he had few horses, lots of foot soldiers and plenty of guns, but he was defeated, fled from the defeat as did his brother-in-law. Ahemedie carved up Idjou between several strongmen of the country itself. By his victory in Kai Afer, Ahemedie won Wadla, Ambassel and Idjou. Aly Gaaz died in exile at his brother-in-law's in Lasta two years later. Ahemedie did not dare pursue Haylo in Lasta, where there were several hill forts, and little terrain suitable for his cavalry. While his father was dying in exile, Godjee, his son by a first marriage, campaigned in Idjou and was mastering it. After the battle of Gouna, Ahemedie again saw Liben his son, whose mother had died. He was Christian and refused to pray, but he did after his father tricked him into eating Muslim mutton. He then gave him Ambassel which includes the title of Djanterar. After the victory of Kai Afer, Ahemedie hurried to Gondar where he made the call to prayer from the top of the highest tower of the imperial palace. Atie Goualo was but a fleeting shadow of the emperors and their power. On the imam's approach, he fled to Woguera. His camp was at Kaa, where he stayed thirteen days. He sent a message to Ras Guebre of the Semene to send him the Gibre, which was done. He was asked to take the title of ras, but he refused, saying that it was a kafir's title, and that that of Iman suited him better. But, he said, Liben, this bastard who has something of the kafir, can take the title of Dedjazmach, and I give him the lands beyond the Nile, that is to say Gaent, Negala, Meket, Wadla, Waro, Dawount, Delanta. He made his general of the vanguard Abbe Negasi: Qegnazmatch le Abren Abba Woddai, Dejazmatch le Asseni . . . etc . . . etc. He gave them lands in Worai Haimanot. He then stayed six weeks in Fouoguera and Begemder, having the Guebre given to all the Asylums. Then took place the scene of Lac Tsana and Asseni became the gulagi for the fish. From there he returned to Worai Haimanot. Two months later, he left to wage war in Godjam, where Ras Mered had given asylum to Dedjaj Gobesi, the son of his paternal uncle and his alter ego (bale ante). Mered and Ahemedie made peace and met in Ahio, where the coward Mered bought his reconciliation handing over his guest. Ahemedie made his way back to Worai Haimanot, put his alter ego in the hill fort of Mukudula from where a few days later he had him thrown from the cliff. When Ahemedie and his brother Adam were fighting Gobesi, the latter, who was harrying them, made his entrance upon the appearance of Atie Tekla Georgis and caused the fall of the stronghold of Liguot where Adam was killed. For this he had him thrown from the cliff of Djib Godo where there are always numerous hyenas. Gobesi had two brothers named Aly and Youssoufe. Upon hearing this, they fled. Aly, stomping on the blood of his brother, made peace. After a while, he was bound, and on a day of drunkenness Ahemedie said 'This brother of Gobesi cannot be my parent after the death of his brother, have him thrown from the same cliff'. Two years later, he took off for Ambassel, where he stormed the stronghold of Guichen, which had resisted until then. He found the tefou, and having consulted it, not finding mention of his race, out of fury dealt it a blow with his sword that can still be seen.

Ahemedie Kolassi is the founder of the Wollo Imam dynasty – known as the Mammedoch. These Oromo Muslim chieftains ruled Wollo from the nineteenth century onwards, and not only leveraged their military prowess in the imperial seat of Gondar, but also expanded

their influence into surrounding – predominantly Christian – kingdoms, by way of alliances through marriage with these regional ruling
families. This does not prevent the Mammedoch from retaining their
Muslim faith, until Mohammed Ali, the father of the ill-fated Lidj
Yasu (deposed for apostasy by the future Haile Selassie), is converted
by force, relinquishing his Muslim title to become Ras Ali. The
Chronicle of the Imams of Wollo was first transcribed by Arnaud
d'Abbadie from an oral source. An in-depth scholarly analysis of
the chronicle can be found in *The Life and Times of Lij Iyasu of Ethiopia*
(E. Ficquet and W. Smidt).

HENRY AARON STERN

FROM *Wanderings Among the Falasha in Abyssinia*, 1863

A Stern Observation of Jewish Orthodoxy

From these vague traditions in which truth and fiction are inextricably jumbled together, the inquirer does not gain much trustworthy information on the history of Ethiopia, and the settlement of the Jews in that country. The most probable conjuncture is, that at a very early period – when Solomon's fleet navigated the Red Sea – some adventurous Jews, impelled by the love of gain, settled among the pleasant hills of Arabia Felix; whilst others of a more daring and enterprising spirit were induced to try their fortune in the more remote though not less salubrious mountain scenes of Ethiopia. The Queen of Sheba's visit to Solomon, whether she reigned over both or only one of those countries, is an incontestable proof that the wise King's fame had spread far beyond his own empire. To subjects of a monarch so renowned for wisdom, wealth and power, a gracious reception was, no doubt, everywhere accorded, and the new settlers, in their prosperity abroad, probably soon forgot the attractions of their home in Judaea. Subsequent troubles in Palestine and the final overthrow of the Jewish monarchy by Nebuchadnezzar increased the number of the emigrants, and within a few centuries the Jews formed a powerful State in Arabia, and a formidable and turbulent people in the Alpine regions between Tigré and Amhara in Ethiopia.

The legend of Menelik and the supposed descent of the Abyssinian sovereigns from the line of Solomon, unquestionably exercised a salutary influence in favour of the Jews, and contributed more than anything else towards the spread of those Mosaical rites and ceremonies, which to this day are still so extensively engrafted on the Christianity of the country. On the promulgation of the Gospel the Jews, who had now become scattered all over the western plains of

Tschelga and Dembea, retired again to their mountain fastnesses of
Semien and Bellesa, where under their own kings and queens, called
Gideon and Judith, they maintained till the beginning of the seventeenth century a chequered and independent existence. With the fall
of their last ruler, and the capture of their strongholds, the Falasha
were driven from their rocky homes, and forced to seek a refuge in the
midst of their enemies, the detested Amharas. The provinces where
they at present reside are Dembea, Quara, Woggera, Tschelga, and
Godjam, where their settlements are strikingly distinguished from
the Christian villages by the red earthen pot on the apex of their
mesquid, or place of worship, which towers from the centre of the
thatched huts by which it is invariably environed.

Claiming a lineal descent from Abraham, Isaac, and Jacob, the
Falasha pride themselves on the fame of their progenitors, and the
purity of the blood that circulates in their own veins. Intermarriages
with those of another tribe or creed are strictly interdicted, nay, even
the visit to an unbeliever's house is a sin, and subjects the transgressor
to the penance of a thorough lustration and a complete change of
dress before he can return to his own home. Their stern uncom-
promising sectarian spirit has been highly beneficial in excluding from
their community that licentious profligacy in which all the other
inhabitants of Ethiopia riot; and it is generally admitted that Falasha
men and women seldom, if ever, stray from the path of virtue, or
transgress the solemn law of the decalogue.

[. . .]

But, notwithstanding this apparent laxity in the observance of their
other festivals, they entertain the most rigid notions as to the sanctity
of the Sabbath. The preparations for the due celebration of this
sacred day commence on Friday at noon, when everyone, who is not
prevented by illness, repairs to an adjacent river to bathe and change
his garb. This task accomplished, the majority lazily saunter about
in the fields, or indolently recline on the grassy margin of some
sparkling stream till sunset summons to the *mesquid*. The service,
which consists in chanting Psalms and hymns relieved by allegorical
stories, and a few verses or a chapter of the book of Leviticus, lasts a
considerable time, and in some places, the plaintive notes of the

worshippers may even be heard across the quiet valley and around the lonely hill throughout the night. This extreme religious fervour the priests exclusively monopolise, nor do their flocks envy them a privilege, which would rob them after six days' toil of that very rest and physical health, which the Sabbath was designed to promote.

Early on the following morning, knots of figures enveloped in the graceful folds of a white cotton dress, are again seen trooping up the narrow lane and over the green sward towards the humble building dedicated to the worship of God. The service of the *mesquid* having been duly celebrated, the people again repair to their huts, where after a cold and frugal repast, they either indulge in a nap, or meet together for social intercourse. Most of the priests remain in the house of prayer from Friday night till Saturday evening, and no trifling circumstance could induce the few whom sickness or age forces to retire to transgress the misinterpreted command: 'Let no man go out of his place on the seventh day.'

Henry Aaron Stern (1820–1885) was born into a Jewish family in the Duchy of Hessen-Kassel. He converted to Christianity in London, where he then trained as a printer. He later entered the Hebrew College of the London Jews' Society (today known as The Church's Ministry Among Jewish People) in order to become a missionary among the Jews. He was ordained as an Anglican priest in 1849, sojourning three years in Baghdad before taking up residence in Istanbul. In 1860, he was sent by the London Jews' Society to preach Christianity to the Falasha (or Beta Israel as they are now known) of Ethiopia. Stern ended up as one of Emperor Theodoros' captives in Magdala, and was lucky to escape with his life since Theodoros had been made aware of his derogatory remark, reprinted in his book, that the emperor's mother was little more than a vendor of *kosso* (a strong local de-wormer).

4

EUCALYPTOPOLIS (1855–1974)

Introduction

L'Ethiopie, c'est moi.

HAILE SELASSIE (*apocryphal*)

Ethiopia's emergence from the Era of the Princes began in earnest during the reign of the ambitious Theodore II (1855–68), who came to embody the manifest destiny of the kings of Gondar. A young man of merit and valour, Kassa – as he was then known – managed to seize a few lands, win a couple of battles, and, perhaps to his own surprise, was soon the master of Gondar. His reigning name was a nod to prophecy, as the first Theodore, who only ruled for a few years in the 1400s, was said to have been such a good ruler that all awaited the coming of a second king of the same name. Soon there were ditties on everyone's lips about how he would conquer Jerusalem and restore Ethiopia to her lost glory:

> Tatek, Tatek! They call him,
> In Jerusalem they fear him,
> For next year they shall see him!

(Tatek was the name of his favourite horse, and Ethiopian warriors were often metonymically named after their steed.)

But Theodore was the subject of mood swings – he talked kindly and brilliantly one minute, and the next raged at slights real or imagined. He sent envoys to Queen Victoria and did not understand when nothing was forthcoming in return. He was a would-be moderniser but his soul was still located in the era of Prester John. He kidnapped diplomats and missionaries and had them make him a great big mortar that he christened Sebastopol. The gun was dragged over hill and vale from his regional base of Debre Tabor to the mountain redoubt of Magdala, where, besieged by Napier's Indian army, he shot himself with his own revolver – a present from Queen Victoria. His death was the signal for another free for all in which it seemed the Era of the Princes was back again – but in short order. Yohannes from Tigray prevailed, followed, after his death at the hand of dervishes on the borders of Sudan, by Menelik II, coincidentally once a royal hostage of Theodore, and even his son-in-law. And Menelik was also second of his name, a nod to Menelik I, son of Solomon and Sheba.

This time round Menelik, with an afflux of modern weapons, was able to integrate and centralise the kingdom somewhat, though the job was only properly finished by Haile Selassie, who put a definitive end to the feudalism and regional liberties of Auld Abyssinia with his creation of the modern state of Ethiopia after the Second World War. Ethiopians understand that the Kebra Negest, with its stories of Arks and Solomonic lines, is just a useful binding that stitches together disparate stories, regions and peoples, and keeps them on the same page. But when one looks at the Oromo origins in Wollo of Menelik, and of Haile Selassie himself, and their mixed Muslim/ Christian backgrounds, one understands that a manifest destiny is indeed a useful thing; that if blood is thicker than water, it stands to reason that ink is thicker still; and the story will supplant any putative bloodline, and in the end take on a life, a destiny, all of its own. Ethiopian kings came to believe in their heart of hearts that they indeed descended from Solomon, justification enough for the existence of this East African country with a Greek name, meaning the land of burnt faces, a country which turned its tanned face to Jerusalem, a city that undoubtedly one day an Ethiopian Emperor – Theodore III? – would conquer, and then all would be well.

When one sees what Menelik II managed to do, and Haile Selassie after him, as colonial appetites all around them sharpened their knives and later the centrifugal forces of nationalism and identity politics took root in Africa, it is a marvel that the country survived at all into the twentieth century.

To suit this new centralised state, the second half of the nineteenth century saw the emergence of a new capital, Addis Ababa. Entoto, the mountain range that today buffers the capital to the north, seemed an ideal position from which to defend Emperor Menelik II's reign – the thirty-kilometre range has precipitous slopes and cliffs facing the north, from which internal threats to the reign might emerge. It also had two auspicious omens for the founding of a major settlement in Ethiopia: there were the ancient ruins of a rock-hewn church at Yeka Mikael, and another rock-cave church at Entoto proper.

The foundation of the new capital began with the building of Raguel and Mariam Churches on Mount Entoto itself, together with a palace – a high wattle and daub two-storey building with an outside flight of stairs to access the upper floor – and a town of straw huts, soon containing close to fifty thousand souls. But, more auspiciously still, there was a legend that King Sahle Selassie, Menelik's grandfather, had once taken a rest in the shadow of one of the Entoto juniper trees, and, gazing down at the plains below, had declared that 'one day, my descendants shall build a town here'. There were other stone relics too: atop the crest of the mountain was a flat rock bed with what appear to be pillar bases, perhaps for a large rock-hewn church of the type of Medhanealem in Lalibela, and, a mere stone's throw away, hidden today in the eucalyptus groves next to a police station, are what appear to be the remains of a large medieval castle's foundations with certainly the best dry stone walls ever seen in the country. Strewn around this same hill are the scattered remains of what must once have been a large settlement – probably the remains of Menelik's first capital.

Some see in these carved rocks and dry stone walls the remains of the famed Barara, the medieval capital of Christian Abyssinia mentioned in Zorzi's *Itinerario*, but never conclusively found. Between the rock-hewn church of Yeka Mikael and that of Adadi Mariam, situated south-west of the modern capital, and a slew of medieval sites on the surrounding hills, there is concrete evidence of the site being occupied by the Ethiopian state since the late medieval period. To the south, where you can easily make out Mount Zukwala on a fair day – a landmark that features prominently in Fra Mauro's Venetian map of 1450 – and to the west, lie the trade routes whence came slaves, ivory, coffee and gold, and to the north-east are the exit points toward the Red Sea for these same goods. Entoto was thus the perfect tollgate and springboard for Menelik's land and goods acquisitions.

As soon as the Emperor's grasp on power was firmer, the capital made its way down to the plains underneath the Entoto ridge, where easy water access and the vast open meadows of Finfinne made for a more congenial setting. Legend has it that it was Menelik's Empress consort, Itegue Taitu, who built the first dwelling – a bath house at the Finfinne hot springs – and that she named the emerging settlement 'New Flower' after the blooms of the mimosa trees that grew in clumps around the muddy hot waters. Soon, *Addis Ababa*, the new flower, was indeed blooming. Menelik's 1886 victory at Adua against the posturing Italians cemented his power internationally. British, French, German, Russian and American envoys all made their way from the torrid coast to these salubrious highlands, to this land of opportunity where a just and mighty king ruled over a Christian highland kingdom – an *African Thibet* some called it. Adventurers, diplomats and engineers poured in, and the wily king used them well, and some say he learned from these Europeans how to rule his African state. Ethiopia and Addis Ababa captured the hearts and minds of the modern era, rekindling for the newspaper age the old legends, and adding a few more for good measure. In a matter of years, the capital had a telegraph, motor cars, telephones, piped water, a printing press and a newspaper in French. Menelik's legend, as the conqueror of Adua, and as a beacon of civilisation and independence in Africa, was securely founded.

However, due to an acute shortage of firewood and lumber, before long it was proposed to move the capital to another site fifty kilometres to the west of Addis – where there were still some forests to hack down – and rename it Addis Alem, New World. This transfer was rendered unnecessary thanks to the introduction of the fast-growing eucalyptus tree. Mondon-Vidaillet, a French musicologist and adventurer, is credited with bringing the first eucalyptus seedlings to the capital, and in a matter of a few years the tree spread from the low plains to the top of the Semien Mountains, thus saving the country and the capital from firewood and lumber shortages. Addis Ababa continued to develop, welcoming thousands of Greeks, Armenians, Yemenis and Indians, who were tailors, cobblers, photographers, mechanics and bakers. Today, their crumbling houses can be vaguely made out, emerging from a sea of rusty tin roofs in Serategna Sefer, the Neighbourhood of the Workers, in the vicinity of the Taitu Hotel. Their remains lie in the Cemetery for Foreigners and Catholics in the Gulele district, where the old tombstones of the Armenian corner are already too worn to be deciphered.

A new king emerged after the First World War, a certain Ras Tafari, who was crowned as *Haile Selassie*, Force-of-the-Trinity. A fresh palace was built, Swedish court protocol adopted, and a narrow-gauge railway, laid by the French, arrived in the capital from the coast, complete with provincial railway stations seemingly transported whole from the French countryside. There is something of *Babar the Elephant* in this Eucalyptopolis, with its relentless march towards progress under the aegis of a just African king. This would also have been the ideal time for Tintin to visit.

Tintin in Ethiopia would have the eponymous reporter at the coronation ceremony of Haile Selassie, preventing the doom of the country by thwarting Italian fascists' plans to steal the Ark of the Covenant – *hélas!* it was not to be. But Zig et Puce, the Franco-Belgian creation of Arthur Saint-Ogon, did get here (with their pet Great Auk). And Hugo Pratt's graphic novel, *The Ethiopiques*, sees his chiselled, foot-loose – and curiously, perennially boatless – mariner Corto Maltese wandering the deserts of Dankalia with his friendly foe, Cush. It puzzles me that Hugo Pratt (who knew Addis Ababa inside and out, having grown up there during the Italian occupation), chose the empty stretches of the Ogaden and Somaliland, rather than the cantilevered highlands he knew so well, to set such an epic. Nevertheless, Pratt's anarchist sailor and Cush, the stoical – and Kiplingesque ('the Fuzzy was the finest o' the lot') – Beni Amer tribesman, are a perfect match.

In the late 1930s, the African Thibet enters on to the international stage. The Italian invasion, with its use of gas and aerial strafing, is seen by many as a trigger for the Second World War, and the inability of the world and the Society of Nations to stand up to fascist Italy as a harbinger of things to come. The Emperor delivered a thoughtful speech at Geneva, and went into exile in Bath, whence he re-emerged to ride with the Gedeon Force and Orde Wingate back into Ethiopia in 1941. He made a triumphal entry into his capital city – but all was not well in the kingdom of Abyssinia. The ruler officially changed the name of the country to Ethiopia, to mark the ushering in of a new era, but from now on Haile Selassie's rule and hold on power were sclerotic.

There were a few years, perhaps, after the war, in which some of the initial energy with which he had initiated his rule were still manifest but, more and more, we see pomp, protocol and crony capitalism taking precedence over the reforms the country called for. This was *Babar in His Twilight Years* – another favourite book from my imaginary library. A failed coup in 1961 marked the beginning of the end, and one can only imagine what might have been if the coup had ushered in a parliamentary monarchy. Instead, the diminutive Emperor returned from his trip to Brazil, which was the moment the plotters had chosen for their uprising, and was handed back the reins of power. He retreated into his palace and let conservatives and young Turks battle it out in his name until things calmed down. A few years later, the eerie calm in Eucalyptopolis was shattered again, and a bloodline claiming descent from Sheba and Solomon was driven off into captivity by a coterie of army sergeants.

Was Haile Selassie, driven away in a maroon Volkswagen Beetle, a ruthless dictator getting his comeuppance, or a tragic figure, a beacon of African independence and black emancipation, ruthlessly disposed of by the winds of history? He was a complex man – an Ethiopian man of his times – used by many as a simplistic stooge to advance their agenda, as he used them too in a wily manner. When I think of him, I like to remember not the elderly statesman with a penchant for Rolls-Royces and photo opportunities with President Roosevelt or Marshal Tito, but rather a vignette from when Addis Ababa was still a makeshift bath house next to a muddy hot spring.

The French explorer and writer Henry de Monfreid chances upon a young Ras Tafari on his way to Harar – the prince must have been about fifteen – and the gushing French adventurer, who was yet to fall out with the ruler, describes a wide-eyed boy, with myriads of slaves filling water jars for his bath. And this fifteen-year-old, barefooted Abyssinian prince – it was considered unseemly to wear shoes at the time – the last representative of a three-thousand-year-old dynasty, was to jump through the all-encompassing hoop of history, and land in the Cold War, in the Non-Aligned Movement, and witness the first man on the moon. In this manner, Haile Selassie's life *is* truly emblematic of his country, and the grandiose title of his auto-biography, *My Life and Ethiopia's Progress* (two volumes, 1973–74), apt in conflating his personal life and the land he came to embody.

If de Monfreid had chanced upon the young princeling fifty years later, he would not have recognised the stooped old man in shoes from Savile Row who, like all old men who have outlived their time, is thought to be wise when nodding off to sleep. But in spite of all the imperial pomp, notwithstanding the numerous Rolls-Royces and the failure to step down in time, personally, I cannot help having some sympathy for this diminutive gentleman with wispy hair being ignominiously driven off in a maroon Volkswagen Beetle.

FROM *Travels in Abyssinia and the Galla Country*, 1868

A Dithyramb to Theodore

The King Theodorus is young in years, vigorous in all manly exercises, of a striking countenance, peculiarly polite and engaging when pleased, and mostly displaying great tact and delicacy. He is persuaded that he is destined to restore the glories of the Ethiopian Empire, and to achieve great conquest; of untiring energy, both mental and bodily, his personal and moral daring are boundless. The latter is well proved by his severity towards his soldiers, even when these, pressed by hunger, are mutinous, and he is in front of a powerful foe; more so even by his pressing reforms on a country so little used to any yoke, whilst engaged in unceasing hostilities; and his suppression of the power of the great feudal chiefs, at a moment when any inferior man would have sought to conciliate them as the stepping-stones to empire.

When aroused, his wrath is terrible, and all tremble; but at all moments he possesses a perfect self-command. Indefatigable in business, he takes little repose night or day: his ideas and language are clear and precise; hesitation is not known to him, and he has neither counsellors nor go-betweens. He is fond of splendour, and receives in state even on campaign. He is unsparing in punishment – very necessary to restrain disorder, and to restore order, in such wilderness as Abyssinia. He salutes his meanest subject with courtesy, is sincerely though often mistakenly religious, and will acknowledge a fault, committed towards his poorest follower in a moment of passion, with sincerity and grace.

He is generous to excess, and free from all cupidity, regarding nothing with pleasure or desire but munitions of war for his soldiers.

He has hitherto exercised the utmost clemency towards the vanquished, treating them rather as his friends than his enemies. His faith is signal. 'Without Christ,' he says, 'I am nothing; if he has destined me to purify and reform this distracted kingdom, with His aid who shall stay me?' Nay, sometimes he is on the point of not caring for human assistance at all, and this is one reason why he will not seek with much avidity for assistance from, or alliance with, any European power.

The worst points in his character are his violent anger at times, his unyielding pride as regards his kingly and divine right, and his fanatical religious zeal.

He had begun to reform even the dress of Abyssinia, all about his person wearing loose-flowing trousers, and upper and under vests, instead of the half-naked costume introduced by the Gallas. Married himself at the altar, and strictly continent, he has ordered or persuaded all who love him to follow his example, and exacts the greatest decency of manners and conversion: this system he hopes to extend to all classes.

He has suppressed the slave-trade in all his phases, save that the slaves already bought, may be sold to such Christians as shall buy them for charity: setting the example, he pays to the Mussulman dealers what price they please to ask for the slaves they bring to him, and then baptises them.

He has abolished the barbarous practice of delivering over murderers to the relatives of the deceased, handing over the offenders in public, to his own executioners, to be shot or decapitated.

The arduous task of breaking the power of the great feudal chiefs – a task achieved in Europe only during the reigns of many consecutive kings – he has commenced by chaining almost all who were dangerous, avowing his intention of liberating them when his power shall be consolidated. He has placed the soldiers of the different provinces under the command of his own trusty followers, to whom he has given high titles, but no power to judge or punish: thus, in fact, creating generals in place of feudal chieftains, more proud of their birth than of their monarch, and organising a new nobility – a legion of honour depending on himself, and chosen specially for their daring and fidelity.

To these he gives sums of money from time to time, accustoming them to his intention of establishing a regular pay; his matchlock men are numbered, under officers commanding, from 100 to 1000, and the king drills them in person. In the common soldiers he has effected a great reform, by paying them, and ordering them to purchase their food, but in no way to harass and plunder the peasant, as before; the peasantry he is gradually accustoming to live quiet, under the village judge, and to look no more to military rule. As regards commerce, he has put an end to a number of vexatious exactions, and has ordered that duties shall be levied only at three places in his dominions. All these matters cannot yet be perfected; but he intends also to disarm the people, and to establish a regular military force, armed with muskets only, having declared that he will convert swords and lances into ploughshares and reaping-hooks, and cause a plough-ox to be sold dearer than the noblest war-horse.

He has begun to substitute letters for verbal messages. After perusing the history of the Jesuits in Abyssinia, he has decided that no Roman Catholic priests shall teach in his dominions; and, insisting on his right divine over those born his subjects, has ordered the Abyssinians who have adopted that creed to recant. To foreigners of all classes, however, he permits the free exercise of their religion, but prohibits all preaching contrary to the doctrine of the Coptic Church. To the Mahomedans he has declared that he will first conquer the Gallas, who have seized on Christian lands, devastated churches, and, by force converted the inhabitants to Islamism; and, after that, the Mussulmans now residing in Abyssinia will have the option of being baptised or of leaving the country.

He is peculiarly jealous, as may be expected, of his sovereign rights, and of anything that appears to trench on them; he wishes, in a short time, to send embassies to the great European Powers, to treat with them on equal terms. The most difficult trait in his character is this jealousy, and the pride that, fed by ignorance, renders it impossible for him yet to believe that so great a monarch as himself exists in the world.

Some of his ideas may be imperfect, others impracticable; but a man, who rising from the clouds of Abyssinian ignorance and childishness, without assistance and without advice, has done so much, and contemplates such large designs, cannot be regarded as of an ordinary stamp.

Walter Plowden (1820–1860) was a British traveller and diplomat, remembered today for his impassioned portrait of Emperor Theodore II, whose close friend he had become. He became Britain's consul to Ethiopia and was an extremely valuable political asset because of the close relations he had cultivated with Theodore, who apparently adored him. Who knows what might have transpired if Plowden had remained by the Emperor's side? But Walter Plowden was murdered on the road near Lake Tana. In his grief Theodore massacred a few hundred men he held responsible for the Englishman's death and buried him inside the royal courtyard in Gondar, in a grave you can still visit today. And the Anglo-Ethiopian relationship deteriorated, eventually causing the British to send Napier to unseat him.

HENRY STANLEY

FROM *Coomassie and Magdala*, 1874

Emperor Theodoros, I Presume?

The Artillery then warmed into action; soon twenty guns of all calibres were thundering with might and main at the gates of Magdala, while a chorus of fierce hisses burst from the Rocket Battery.

During the energetic bombardment one of the correspondents asked me if I had seen Theodore's last handiwork. I replied in the negative. He then said that he could show it to me; leading me, at the same time, to the edge of the precipice, when he pointed downward, and looking in that direction, I saw a sight which forever beggars description.

Of a verity, reader, I am no lover of the horrible or the disgusting. But if you can conceive 308 dead people, piled one upon another, stripped naked, in a state of corruption, with gyves and fetters round their limbs, you will save me the unpleasant task of describing the scene!

The late captives said that they were present during the execution; that the prisoners were manacled hand and foot, and that they were sabred and shot by Theodore and his men as they lay helpless on the ground. Many of them, it is said struggled to their knees, and entreated in the wild 'fervour and passion of prayer' for mercy, but it was of no avail. They were butchered to the last soul. This took place the day we arrived upon the Dahonte Dalanta plateau, April 9.

Sir Robert Napier perceived during the bombardment, which lasted two hours, that the defenders were weak, and that his troops would suffer no great loss in the assault. He therefore ordered the Royal Engineers, the 33rd, the 45th and the 'King's Own', to prepare for the final work.

The musketry from the fortress had ceased soon after the British artillery had opened fire. The troops destined for the storming were drawn out in battalions at quarter distance, across Islamgee, facing Magdala. The Engineers, under the command of Major Gordon Pritchard, were in the front of the battalions deployed as skirmishers. Soon signals for rapid firing were made to the artillery, and under the furious cannonade which now commenced, the troops began their march along the plateau with trailed arms. Upon arriving within fifty yards of the base of Magdala the artillery ceased firing, and the Royal Engineers at once opened fire with their Sniders, which was taken up by the 33rd and 45th, who plied their breechloading rifles with admirable rapidity, raining a storm of leaden pellets, for ten minutes. The volleys of musketry were as continuous and rolling as ever an army of 20,000 men, armed with the ancient muzzle-loaders, produced.

Theodore and his faithful adherents had lain concealed during the artillery fire; but so soon as it ceased, up he sprang, sounding his war cry, and with his followers he hurried to the gates and defences, determined to give the advancing columns the benefit of a reception worthy of an Emperor who was about to conquer or die.

So long as Theodore was wedded to the idea that there was no forgiveness for him, so long would he have manifested the same implacable rancorous spirit towards the English had the siege lasted as many months as it did hours. Now, seeing no avenue open for him to escape, with his faithful men willing to shed their blood for him, nerved with the deepest courage born out of his extreme despair, he arrived at the barbican and lowest revetment, posted his men at the loopholes and along the wall topped with the wattled hurdles. As he saw the soldiers still firing while they faced right, and wheeled into columns of fours for the purpose of ascending the path that led up to the barbican, his signal was given, and their presence was known to the English by sharp shot falling amongst them, wounding several.

Instantly the British fire was concentrated on the barbican and the suspicious revetment, through the interstices of which wreaths of pearly smoke issued, indicating the presence of the dogged riflemen. At this time, as fit concomitants of a battle, the rain fell in large warm drops, splashing heavily on our heads. But through the pelting shower the soldiers, invincible seemingly, undreading certainly, advanced, making their Sniders keep fatal music to their steps, scrutinising suspiciously granite embrasures and natural basalt battlements that shot up here and there on the brow of the cliff of Magdala.

Still preceded by the Engineers, and still sowing the deadly missiles over every inch of the superjacent slope, they arrived at, and halted near the barbican.

For a minute there was a pause, and again a dozen shots hurtled amongst the more advanced of the Engineers; wounding Major Pritchard and three or four of the Engineers; but they were immediately replied to by a thousand directed at each spot from whence the reports came, and Major Pritchard and Lieutenant Morgan – the latter a most enthusiastic officer – made a dash upon the barbican to effect an entrance. They found the gate closed, and the inside of the square tower completely blocked up with stones to the depth of ten feet, so that a passage through was not readily available.

'Hasten up with the powder!' shouted the Major.

'Hasten up with the powder! Hasten up with the powder!' was passed along the contiguous columns. But who was to bring up the powder? Why were those canvas bags with fuses attached made? Were they not for the purpose of blowing up this place? Where were the heavy hammers and iron wedges for breaking open the barrier and knocking off the bolts or drawing the hinges? Where the hand–saws and the axes to cut the hurdle revetment down? Where the pickaxes to demolish or sap the wall? Where the escalading ladders, constructed for the purpose of sealing the walls and stockades or any raised defences there might be?

Echo answered, 'Where? Oh where?' No mortal Voice...Answered the eager question.

Private M'Guire of the 33rd thought he would climb up the cliff wall. Surmounting a ledge, without pause he ascended another in the same way, and then turned round and shouted aloud that he had found an opening. With a fierce cheer which was faintly heard on Islamgee, he faced the wall on the height hotly seconded by Private Bergin of the same regiment.

The whole regiment, now urged by the bold example of their darling comrades, scrambled up the almost perpendicular slope, and after a few minutes of breathless work they surmounted the ledges, and seeing men suspiciously moving about on the summit of Magdala they opened fire, at once sweeping them away as with a breath.

Intruding their rifles into the interstices of the hurdle fence which topped the wall, they lifted it up, and in a second had passed over the lower defences. Scattering themselves over the ground, they made simultaneously for the other defence which was seventy-five feet above them, passing over several ghastly relics of the battle.

Shortly we heard them firing quickly, eagerly, as they discovered their enemies moving about. Then were heard their clubbed muskets beating a fierce 'rat-tat-tat' upon the gates. Big rocks were thrown by them with a crashing force against the gates, and now and again they pertinaciously fired through every crevice and loophole. Neither gate, nor fence, nor stone wall, nor brush heap, nor even rocks and strong barriers could stop the excited Irishmen; and no sooner had their bayonets gleamed through the fence than it was laid prostrate, and a wild 'Huzza!' 'Hurrup! and 'Hoorah!' was shouted out as they leaped over. Forward before them they flung their bristling rifles, and fired volleys into the very faces of the Abyssinians!

But we must not forget the Icarian charge of Drummer M'Guire and Private Bergin upon Magdala. The two men were advancing onward, a few paces from each other, to the upper revetment, when they saw about a dozen fellows aiming at them. They instantly opened fire, and so quick and so well delivered was it that but few of their assailants escaped. Seeing a band of redcoats advancing upward, the others retreated precipitately. Over the upper revetment both men made their way, and at the same time they observed a man standing near a haystack with a revolver in his hand. When he saw them prepare to fire, he ran behind a haystack, and both men heard plainly a shot fired. Marching on with their Sniders on the present, they came to the haystack, and saw the man who had run behind lying prostrate on the ground, dying, with the revolver still convulsively clutched in his right hand. To their minds the revolver was but their proper loot, and without any ceremony they took up what they considered their own; but on a silver plate on the stock, during an examination of it, they perceived an inscription which read thus:

PRESENTED BY
VICTORIA QUEEN OF GREAT BRITAIN AND IRELAND
TO THEODORUS EMPEROR OF ABYSSINIA
AS A SLIGHT TOKEN OF HER GRATITUDE
FOR HIS KINDNESS TO HER SERVANT PLOWDEN
1854

'What d'ye think, Pat; can this be that unblessed devil of a Theodorus, the No-goose as they call him?' asked M'Guire. 'Mebbe, Mac; can't say; but we had better stay near him till the Sergeant shows his phiz inside Mag-da-la. Och here he comes!'

They saw a swaying line of Irish soldiers advancing, and at once these two heroes raised their sun helmets, and swinging them round their heads, they shouted the warlike cry of the Anglo-Saxons, 'Hurrah!' with the strength of unusual lungs, to greet their comrades.

With heads bent low, like charging bison, the 'Duke's Own' came surging up almost intact; the colour-bearer in the centre; officers cool and martial-like to the rear of their companies, all striding audaciously forward, alert, keen-eyed, and prompt as tinder, to burst into a white-heat blaze upon the slightest provocation. Near the spot where the dying man, who had been drawn out to the open, lay, the centre of the regiment halted.

At this moment the rain ceased, and the sun shone forth in the full power of his departing splendour.

Eagerly stepped out the standard-bearer at the word of command, and high and triumphant, in all its silken bravery, streamed the 'Wavy Cross' emblem of Britannia's majesty and power, above the surrounding world of mountains – an omen to all beholders that the tyrant Emperor had been humbled, and that his proudest stronghold, MAGDALA, had passed into the strangers' hands. As it fluttered and rippled in mid air, the 'Duke's Own' doffed helmets, and simultaneously, in the acme of enthusiasm, they raised their voices in cheers, which sounded to those on Islamgee, 500 feet below, like the deep roar of an ocean's tide. The cheers were recognised, caught up, and flung from Magdala to Selasse, thence to Fahla, and that grey crag sent it quivering far below; finally the British camp nearly two miles off caught the sounds, and strengthened the universal 'Hurrah' by their own exuberant voices. Strains of music burst from the martial bands. The National Anthem of England, 'God Save the Queen', was never played or sung with greater effect or vigour than when the hoary crags of Magdala responded to its notes in an overwhelming chorus of echoes!

A few unarmed Abyssinians, attracted by the clamour of music and shouting, mustered courage enough to approach the standard, which waved so gaily in the mountain gale; and, on beholding one of their countrymen on the ground, they bent over the body, but quickly recoiled with fearful dismay on their faces, exclaiming 'Todros! Todros!'

The words attracted the attention of every one and they strode towards the body, jostling each other eagerly in the endeavour to obtain a glimpse of him the natives styled 'Todros, Negus, Negashi of Itiopia!'

And what did they see? The body of a native seemingly half famished; clad in coarse upper garments, dingy with wear, and ragged with tear, covering under garments of clean linen!

The face of deep brown was the most remarkable one in Abyssinia; it bore the appearance of one who had passed through many anxious hours. His eyes, now overspread with a deathly film, gave evidence yet of the piercing power for which they were celebrated. The mouth was well defined and thin-lipped. The lower lip seemed well adapted to express scorn, and a trace of it was still visible. As he gasped his last, two rows of whitest teeth were disclosed. Over his mouth two strong lines arched to a high aquiline nose. The nostrils expanded widely as he struggled to retain the breath which was rapidly leaving him. The face was broad, high-cheek-boned with a high, prominent forehead, and overhanging eyebrows. The hair was divided into three large plaits extending from the forehead to the back of the neck, which latter appeared to be a very tower of strength. The body measured five feet and eight inches, and was very muscular and broad-chested. There was a character about the features denoting great firmness of obstinacy mingled with ferocity; but perhaps the latter idea was suggested upon remembering the many cruelties ascribed to him. And thus was it, that we saw the remains of him whom men called 'Theodorus, Emperor of Abyssinia. The Descendant of Menilek; Son of Solomon. King of Kings, Lord of Earth, Conqueror of Ethiopia, Regenerator of Africa and Saviour of Jerusalem', now dying – dead by his own hand!

Fitting punishment was it that the red right hand, which had bereft so many hapless once of their lives, should have deprived that of its outlawed owner! Fitting was it also that the banner of St George should first shadow his body, as it first proclaimed his downfall!

The Irish soldiers took hold of his legs, and roughly dragged him to a hammock, where, after two or three gasps, he breathed his last.

Curious remarks were passed upon the body by the dense groups which surrounded it. One man, with a spice of Latin in him, uttered sententiously, 'Sic semper tyrannis,' to which many a one responded heartily 'Amen and amen!' Another Celtic warrior hoped the scoundrel would 'trouble nobody no more'; and another with some regard for decency covered up the bared abdomen, evened the nether limbs, and folded the arms upon the breast.

Larger grew the crowds around the body. Officers and privates as they came up hastened to get a glimpse of it. The released captives hurried to obtain a farewell glance at their dead captor, and when they recognised him all doubts as to his identification were at an end. Theodore had been fighting in disguise, knowing that bright colours attracted England's marksmen. The Commander-in-Chief with his staff rode up to view the corpse, but not one kind word of sympathy for the dead Emperor's fate was uttered. He who had been merciless to others was not deserving of sympathy.

Not until the last moment, when on the threshold of certain defeat, did he surrender his life. Seeing speedy death in the levelled muskets of the advancing soldiers, he quickly retired behind the haystack, and with the revolver – the queen's gift – into his mouth the Imperial Suicide had fired, and died.

The advance was sounded, and the regiments with arms aslope filed off in columns through the narrow streets of Magdala, the

Commander-in-Chief and staff following. Passing through a long lane flanked on each side by store-houses with conical thatched roofs, they came to a large open space on the southern side, which was probably used by the Emperor as a parade or drill ground.

At the upper extremity of this open area, near a group of black tents, were seen several groups of armed natives, who fired two or three shots as they perceived the soldiers. The 33rd formed line, deploying across its whole width, and opened fire upon them, steadily advancing the while. Before the determined approach of the soldiers and their withering fire, the last remnants of Theodore's army incontinently fled down the cliffs, led by his illegitimate son Dajatchmatch Masheshai.

When the Irish regiment arrived at the eastern extremity, having traversed its whole length, another flag was raised to announce the complete capture of the fortress; and the Prince with his flying warriors must have heard the glorious cheers that greeted the flag as it was waved, as well as the martial strains of 'Rule Britannia'; the Gallas on the alert on the opposite mountains of the Walla Galla country must have heard it also.

When Sir Robert Napier appeared, the music was changed to 'See the Conquering Hero Comes'; and other rousing cheers and anthem chants, amid mutual congratulations, closed the 'Storming of Magdala'.

Sir Henry Morton Stanley (1841–1904) was better known for his no doubt fictitious 'Dr Livingstone, I presume?' than for his reporting and documentation of the Napier expedition to free the European hostages of Emperor Theodore. Sir Henry has a chequered reputation today due to his role in setting up – partly unwittingly he would later argue – King Leopold's Belgian Congo, under the guise of a scientific expedition. Conflicting accounts of his brutality or lack thereof to porters and natives in general – some said Stanley was fair in his treatment (a statement somewhat weakened by the follow-up explanation, that if Stanley had killed anyone, it would only be six or seven hundred, and 'only in self-defence'). Richard Burton's own damning comment was that 'Stanley shoots negroes like they were monkeys'. Different times no doubt, and today Sir Henry's poor and harsh origins would be invoked as attenuating circumstances: brought up in the poor house till the age of fifteen, he ran away to America where he served first in the Confederate army, before being conscripted as a galvanised Yankee for the north. He served in the Union navy – where he got his first taste of journalism – before setting up an expedition to the Ottoman Empire and being thrown into prison.

A LETTER TO VICTORIA

FROM Emperor Theodoros 1866 – Gregorian calendar

From a King to a Queen

In the name of the Father, of the Son and of the Holy Spirit – one God. God's creature and slave, David and Solomon's son, the King of Kings, Theodoros. May it reach who God placed on the throne after choosing and elevating her above all men, who loves the faith and charity and who lends protection to the downtrodden poor, Bictoria [sic], Queen of England. Ato Hormuzd Rassam, on that thing you told me about, that is that you had sent your servant, on the subject of Cameron – even if the lowest of your slaves, let alone you yourself, had sent me a message, would I have refused?

Very well then, in truth and by the power of God, I have set Mr Cameron free and given him to your servant, Ato Hormuzd Rassam. I have, by the power of God, released and handed over together all the Europeans who had been imprisoned and whom you had asked me to release for your sake. By the power of God, I have freed all the imprisoned Europeans and those that pine for their country may leave. It is my intention to send you Ato Hormuzd Rassam, your servant, whom I have kept with us, as soon as I have consulted with him in the manner in which you told me to 'advise with him about all matters you may wish'. Ethiopia's people are blind; so open our eyes for us. May God in heaven shed light on you.

Written in the year 7358 after the creation of the world; in the year 1858 after the birth of Christ (Julian calendar), in the year of Mark, in the month of Miyaziya, on the 10th day, at Zege.

Emperor Theodoros (*c.* 1818–1868) has become an emblematic figure in Ethiopia's resurgence from the decadence of the Era of the Princes. Considered by Emperor Haile Selassie to be little more than a blemish on the Solomonic line, Theodoros was made into an inspiring Robin Hood figure by the regime of Colonel Mengistu – a proto-socialist-anti-imperialist hero. The emperor's death from a wound inflicted by him with a pistol gifted by Victoria (the letter's *Bictoria* is due to the absence of the sound 'V' from the Geez syllabary at that time), only adds to the Shakespearian emperor's tragedy – for the whole story, read Philip Marsden's *Barefoot Emperor*. His son Alemayehu was 'kidnapped' and brought to Great Britain, where he became the ward of one Captain Speedy. The prince died at the early age of eighteen. A favourite of 'Bictoria' ('A pretty, polite, graceful boy,' she was to write in her diary), Alemayehu is buried in the St George's Chapel in Windsor Castle. There have been calls to return his remains to the motherland, while Theodoros' other children – who lived out their lives in Ethiopia – have long been forgotten, place of burial unknown.

HERBERT VIVIAN

FROM *Abyssinia: Through the Lion-land
to the Court of the Lion of Judah*, 1901

Menelik and His Capital

My last march towards the capital seemed as though it would never
end. I had been led to expect that I should arrive in less than three
hours, but nearly four had rolled by before I happened to turn round
and ask one of my men, 'When on earth are we ever going to reach
Addis Ababa?'

'But, sah'b, here it is.'

'Where?'

'Here, we have already arrived.'

I looked around incredulously, and saw nothing but a few summer-
house huts and an occasional white tent, all very far from each other,
scattered about over a rough, hilly basin at the foot of steep hills. I
would scarcely admit that I was approaching a village. That this could
be the capital of a great empire, the residence of the King of Kings,
seemed monstrous and out of the question. 'Then, pray, where is
Menelik's palace?' I asked, with a sneer. The men pointed to the
horizon, and I could just make out what seemed to be a fairly large
farmstead with a number of trees and huts crouching on the top of
a hill.

As we advanced, the buildings drew slightly more closely together,
but I still refused to recognise a town in the wide stretches of turf,
broken by deep ravines and studded with rare summer-houses and
booth-like tents.

After a long peregrination we arrived at the British Agency compound, where Captain Harrington was kind enough to invite me to
pitch my camp. The Agency consists of some eight acres of ground
surrounded by a mud wall three or four feet high, and comprising a

number of tents and tukuls. Properly plastered and decorated inside, furnished with civilised carpets, chairs, writing-tables, and wardrobes, it is amazing how comfortable these rude cabins can become. Two huge tents serve as dining-room and drawing-room, and arouse the admiration of everybody by their magnificence. Before I left, Captain Harrington had begun to build himself a regular house, which was to consist of some eight huts, connected by mud passages so as to form a parallelogram enclosing a courtyard. The general effect would be that of a feudal castle, and I should not wonder if by this time it is already complete. Once you can induce workmen to adhere to a job in Abyssinia, they call buildings into being almost with the rapidity of magic. The chief difficulty lies in the fact that every Abyssinian hates work. He thinks that the Gallas or some other slave should do all his work for him. It is only his inordinate greed for money that ever induces him to stoop to manual labour. When builders are needy, they will flock to your call in large numbers and toil away for a week unless you are foolish enough to accede to their demand for payment in advance. In any case at the end of a week they will insist upon being paid for what they have done, and then they will go away for a fortnight or so to spend the money they have earned. Neither threats nor promises are of the least avail to lure them back until they have completed their orgy.

They are, moreover, extremely lazy while at work, and it is only by employing great numbers of them that you shall build fast, though the process is excessively easy. A circle is drawn on the turf and a number of fairly deep holes are made in it. Into these are planted stout sticks some eight or ten feet long. Great buckets of mud are brought to smear against them and in a day or two they have caked quite dry in the sun and wind. The roof is made of similar sticks laid so as to taper to a point, and finally covered with thick thatch. The thatching is really very artistic, and constitutes perhaps the only successful Abyssinian industry. A few days after the thatch has been completed your tukul is ready to be occupied.

Regular houses are very rare, and consist for the most part of glorified tukuls two or three or four times the usual diameter, which is rarely more than nine feet. The Emperor and a few of the foreign representatives have succeeded in causing stone buildings to be erected, but only by the use of forced labour and with very indifferent results.

Some nine years ago Menelik's capital was at Entotto, a couple of hours' ride up the hill behind Addis Ababa. Now only two churches and a few brown ruins remain of a town which must have comprised fifty thousand souls. The reason of its abandonment was that all the wood had been exhausted for building and fuel. The Abyssinians are most improvident in the matter of wood, cutting down forests in a haphazard way and never troubling to replant. The consequences of this are already being felt at Addis Ababa; wood is now brought thither from a distance of sixteen miles, and it is certain that within a very short space of time Menelik will be obliged to shift his capital once more to the neighbourhood of fresh woods. This is not by any means the hardship which it would be in a civilised country. The capital is rather a camp than a town, and there is no particular trouble in rooting up a tukul and planting it elsewhere.

The only other form of architecture which remains to be described consists of the hovels were the soldiers go. These barracks can only be compared to a number of hollow haystacks or mows, which cover enormous stretches of ground, figuring in a bird's-eye view like a flock of sheep. Their furniture consists of little more than a gun and a pan or two, and they are scarcely more elaborate than the lair of a wild animal, merely serving to keep out the wind and wet.

To appreciate Addis Ababa it is necessary to realise that this strange capital covers some fifty square miles, and contains a very large population, which has never been numbered. Streets there are none, and to go from one part of the town to the other you must simply bestride your mule and prepare to ride across country. Three-quarters of an hour at least are necessary for a pilgrimage from the British Agency to the Palace, and as much again to the market. On either of these journeys you must cross three or four deep ravines with stony, precipitous banks and a torrent-bed full of slippery boulders. Generally in the course of any expedition I chanced to cross a single rail, which seemed to lead nowhere. I had some difficulty in meeting with anyone who knew the use or meaning of this. At last I learned that it had been laid for the purpose of conveying goods and building material to and fro, but the Abyssinians are so conservative that nothing would induce them to spare themselves labour by making use of it. Similarly, when the Emperor introduced wheelbarrows, labourers only made use of them when they were under their master's eye. Directly they were left to their own devices, they hastened to return to their old accustomed method of carrying things on their backs.

Herbert Vivian (1865–1940), journalist, author and Jacobite royalist. Vivian founded *The Whirlwind: a lively and eccentric newspaper* and worked for a number of newspapers as a correspondent – the *Morning Post, Daily Express, Royalist International Herald*. He is remembered for his book on Abyssinia, but also works on Serbia, Tunisia and Italy.

ARTHUR RIMBAUD

FROM Letter to his Mother, 30 April 1891

A Sunken Boat

Aden, the 30th of April 1891

MY DEAR MOTHER – I have received the two stockings you sent as well as your letter, which reached me in trying circumstances. Seeing my right knee continuing to swell and the pain in the articulation, without finding any remedy or counsel, as in Harar we are surrounded by Negroes without there being any Europeans, I took the decision to go down. Leaving unfinished business, which was not an easy thing to do, as I had money scattered all over the place, but finally I managed to completely liquidate just about everything. I was laid up in Harar for twenty days, completely incapable of making a single movement, suffering atrocious pains, and never sleeping. I hired twenty Negro porters, paying each 15 thalaris, from Harar to Zeila, I had a stretcher put together covered with a tarp, and it is by that means that I have just covered, in 12 days, the 300 kilometres of desert that lie between the hills of Harar and the port of Zeila. I don't need to tell you what horrible pain I suffered en route, I could never take a single step from my stretcher, my knee was visibly swelling and the pain increased constantly.

Upon my arrival I went to the European hospital, where there is but one room for paying patients, and I occupy it. As soon as I showed my knee to the English doctor he cried out that it was a synovitis, that it had reached a very dangerous stage because of the lack of care and fatigue, and he immediately spoke of cutting off the leg. Then he decided to wait a few days to see if the swelling would go down after the medical treatment. That was six days ago, but no improvement, except that, as I am resting, the pain has greatly diminished. You know that synovitis is an illness of the liquids of the knee joint, and its cause can be hereditary, or accidental, or due to many other reasons. For me it is obvious that it has most certainly been caused by the fatigue of marching on foot and by horse in Harar. Finally in the state in which I have reached, it is not to be hoped that I be cured before at least three months, under the most favourable circumstances. And I am lying down, my leg in bandages, trussed, tied up, enchained, in order that it not be moved. I have become a skeleton, a frightful sight. My back is all flayed from the bed, I do not sleep for a minute. And the heat here is now very extreme. The hospital's food, that I pay quite a high sum for, is very bad. I do not know what to do. On the other hand I have not yet closed my accounts with my associate Mr Tian. It will not be finished for another week. I shall exit that business with about 35000 Francs. I would have had more, but, because of my inauspicious departure, I am losing a few thousand francs. I want to have myself removed to a steamer, and to come to be treated in France, the voyage at least would distract me. And in France medical care and remedies are cheap, and the air is good. It is therefore very probable that I shall come. The steamers bound for France are presently sadly always packed, as everyone comes back from the colonies at this time of year. And I am a poor invalid who has to be transported very gently, well, I shall see what happens in a week's time.

Do not be frightened by all this, nevertheless. Better days shall come. But it is a sad reward for so much work, so many privations and troubles! Alas how miserable our life is.

With fond greetings

RIMBAUD

P.S. As for the stockings they are useless, I shall sell them some-where.

Translated by YVES-MARIE STRANGER

Arthur Rimbaud (1854–1891). It is impossible to exaggerate the importance of Arthur Rimbaud in the pantheon of French symbolist poetry, a place that he ironically cemented for eternity by running off to various exotic locales to evade his budding fame and a literary coterie that had become burdensome to him. His twelve years seeking fortune in Ethiopia, by running guns and selling and buying different commodities, have long been misunderstood by French litterateurs and his silence on his poetry and refusal to write another line – besides company accounts and geographical treatises – have bemused them and goaded one after another to explore the poet's silence and find the 'true' meaning of his life in Ethiopia.

FROM *A Sporting Trip Through Abyssinia*, 1902

Sore Backs and Olfactory Tricks
on the Hunting Trail

Next morning the mules were so fresh that quite half the number
took four to five men each to hold and load them; but when once the
packs were secured only one animal succeeded in getting free from his
burden. For two hours we were crossing a grassy, undulating plain,
and while we were doing so a mounted man overtook us with the
news that Nasser and Adarar, who had stayed behind in Addis Ababa,
would catch us up that evening. The horseman, having delivered his
message, tried to sell me his mount. He exhibited its paces, and Hyde
gave it a turn; but when I had the saddle taken off we found the poor
beast's back in a shocking state, and so declined the deal. Soon after,
we reached a highly cultivated plateau and passed a large square
enclosure, divided and subdivided, the outer walls 6 feet high and 8
feet thick, built of stone without mud or mortar. In form it was like an
immensely strong cattle-pen, but as to what it was, or by whom built,
I could get no information, except that it was very old and probably
was erected by the Gallas. We camped by a stream at the foot of this
plateau, Nasser and Adarar coming in later. Next day our route lay
over a great undulating grass-plain with very little cultivation. With
the glasses I spotted two reedbuck, and after a long crawl bagged
them both. My shots brought a crowd of Gallas together, who seemed
very much interested in me and my rifle. Meanwhile, my mule had
bolted, and led us in a long chase before it was recaptured. I told Ali
to cut the throat of one of the reedbuck, to make it lawful food for the
Somalis, and Nasser, that of the other, thinking that this would make
its meat acceptable to the Abyssinians. I soon heard that many of the
men would not touch it, as they said Nasser was not a real Christian,

because he ate meat which Ali had hallaled. This food-question
proved a continual source of trouble. If a beast fell dead at once, or if
I hallaled it, only two or three of the Gallas would eat of it; if one of
the Gallas cut its throat, none but Gallas would touch it. Only when
a Somali hallaled one beast, and another received its *coup de grâce* from
one of some half a dozen Abyssinians, whose orthodox Christianity
was above suspicion, did everyone get fresh meat. Now nothing causes
so much discontent among one's followers as a long deprivation of
meat, or for one half to see the others feasting while they have none,
and so I often had to shoot game for meat alone.

We were approaching by a series of easy slopes the tongue of land
between the river Wenza, Kowart or Moguer, as different natives
called it, and its tributary the Gora Goba, which drains the Entotto
range. Both of these run in deep, rocky valleys, with sheer cliffs on
either side. That day camp was pitched close to the edge of a deep
precipice above the Moguer, just below the point where its five head-
waters meet. It was a grand bit of scenery – the rolling grass-plain,
dotted about with trees, abruptly bounded by the bare rugged cliffs;
while, far down in the valley, the glistening threads of water, with
great trees and clumps of bamboo along their banks, showed indistinctly through the haze, till one wondered if it was reality or
mirage.

On the fourth of March, while the mules were being loaded, I went
to the edge of the cliffs, watching the light of the rising sun as it
caught ridge after ridge of the spurs below me. Suddenly I saw a head
bob up close to me, and, moving a little, I beheld a troop of monkeys
working along a ledge of rock. The king of the troop was a splendid
old fellow, with a mane and coat of hair which swept the ground.
Although I wanted a specimen, it was useless to shoot, as to secure the
body would have taken hours. The mules were now ready, and we
began the descent of a series of rough zigzags, to negotiate which took
three-quarters of an hour, the going being very bad in some places,
though fortunately the path was dry. A long, easy slope and another
zigzag brought us in an hour and a half to the shade of a great tree
close to the Gora Goba. The difference of temperature between the
breezy plain above and this shut-in rocky valley had to be felt to be

believed; the heat was so great that I decided to put off the climb up
the opposite side till the cool of the next morning. A caravan of
merchants from Gojam, on their way to Addis Ababa, halted under
our tree in the afternoon for a rest and a chat with my men. I showed
them my rifles and some illustrated papers. Portraits of the Queen, as
a girl and at the present day, and of our generals in South Africa
excited the most interest. Later on, I weighed myself and most of the
men. In breeches and short-sleeves, without boots, I pulled down 158
lbs. Warsama, at 121 lbs., was the lightest, and Hussein, at 140 lbs.,
the heaviest of four Somalis; while Adarar, 102 lbs., was the light-
weight among the Abyssinians, and Destar, 151 lbs., a Galla, the
heavy-weight. After this the men did various tricks, of which, I think,
standing with the feet close together and picking up a stick from the
ground in the teeth, was the most agile. Then Hussein Hadji gave us
an exhibition of his sense of smell; first telling which of three stones
had been touched, and then, which of four of us had touched a
particular stone. He and other Somalis said this was nothing, and that
some could tell which man in their own tribe had handled a spear
belonging to another, and went on to recount instances, which, if
true, proved these men to have a keener sense of smell than a dog.

Early next morning I crossed the stream of clear water – only
some 30 feet wide and knee-deep – before the caravan, and worked
along some scrub, but saw no game. Half way up the cliff, from a
little cultivated plateau, I took some photos of the valley before
commencing the long climb to the top. Running along the steepest
part was an ancient wall, 4 feet high and 7 feet wide, built by the
Salali Gallas to defend their country against the inhabitants of Metta.
It still marks the boundary between the two provinces. At the top of
the cliff was a farmstead with a fine stretch of green grass, watered by
a little stream running through it. It was very hot, the place tempting,
and as I was told that the next water was a long way off, I gave the
word to pitch camp. After tiffin a man came in to say he had seen two
klipspringers close to the top of the cliff, and I seized a rifle and ran
in the direction indicated. Just as I reached the edge, and looked over
on some broken jungly ground, I saw two klipspringers dash up a
little rise and stand 40 yards off, but for a second only. A snap-shot

and they disappeared. Running after them, I heard one call, and saw it standing almost hidden in long grass below me; I fired, and, as it fell to the shot, I saw a leopard, which had evidently been hunting them, sneak off through the underwood, but could not get a shot at him. While I sat still, hoping he would show himself again, first one and then another hyrax, or dassie, as they are called in South Africa, came out from a crack in a rock close to me, and, as I kept perfectly still, gradually the whole family assembled and watched me intently with their beady black eyes, till, getting tired, I moved, when all vanished instantly. My men afterwards found both the klipspringers. The first I fired at had rolled into a bush, and the second lay where it had fallen. It shows how much luck enters into sport, that, during the whole of this trip, great part of which was in leopard country, this was the only occasion on which I saw one; while, in my previous shooting expedition in Somaliland, and I bagged three and saw nearly a dozen, though, I think, I only had a shot at one other. Next morning my men came to tell me that a dog had carried off both my klipspringer skulls, and as I had warned Hussein to be careful (one being the largest head shot so far), I was very angry. While camp was being struck, I went along the top of the cliff and found a big troop of the long-haired monkeys. I clean missed one big male that was dodging about looking at us, but knocked another off a ledge stone-dead. His companions seemed fairly astonished, and ran about to different points of vantage, craning their necks to gaze down at the place where he had fallen. At first they did not see us, but when they did they showed their teeth and seemed to fairly shake with rage, while their language, if we could only have understood it, was, I am sure, more forcible than polite. Some six or seven dassies came out and solemnly gazed at the monkey's body. They seemed on the best of terms with the monkeys, sitting side by side with them. I picked out one other very large male and rolled him down close to his companion. It took a long time for Hyde and another man to go round and down, in order to bring the skins back. We passed a good deal of cultivated land and saw numerous herds of cattle, besides horses, mules, donkeys, sheep, and goats. Near one village, a long line of men were beating out with green boughs a grass fire that threatened to envelop their huts. The head man ran after us and, shaking me by the hand, insisted on my waiting while a great bowl of fresh milk was brought me to drink. I reached camp at five, in a heavy downpour of rain. After tea Abyssinians came to me in a body and asked for salt, chillies, and clothes, and requested that they should not have to carry skins. I told them that the wages and conditions of their service had been settled before we started; that if they did good work they would be well rewarded, but that, if they were dissatisfied, they could leave at once, as I could not agree to make any further concessions, or say that they should not do this or that. I then had an inspection of the mules, and found six sore backs – a bad beginning.

Major Percy Horace Gordon Powell-Cotton (1866–1940), hunter – some say his trophy collection made him the largest killer of game ever – but also conservationist, maker of ethnographic films and museum creator. A number of animal species are named after him. Attacked and mauled by a lion that he had shot in Kenya, he was only saved by a rolled-up copy of *Punch*, which one can still see in the museum he founded. An avid and trigger-happy shooter, in keeping with his times, he was granted the right to hunt throughout Abyssinia by Emperor Menelik himself – a right he used well. His book, besides recounting his shooting exploits, is full of details about customs and mores that no longer exist. A point of interest for the contemporary conservationist is his bagging of an Ethiopian Wolf in Gojam – a location in which the animal is now all but forgotten.

JULES BORELLI

FROM *L'Ethiopie Méridionale*, 1890

A Rainy Season Diary

Entoto. Saturday, 3rd of July
It rained during the whole night. This morning, I was to visit with Machacha-Seyffou, the king's cousin, and Saleh-Selassie's grandson; but this prince is in mourning for his mother, and is not receiving.

The weather is dreadful; after the rain, a thick fog; you can't see at twenty metres and the paths are slippery. I remain at home. One of my barometers is faulty. It is difficult to have a fire; wood is scarce and so wet that it barely smoulders. It does not alight and produces a suffocating smoke that finds no issue. My house does not have any more windows than the others and my fire is placed in the middle of the sole chamber that composes it.

Entoto. Sunday, 4th of July
I leave my abode; I have found another larger one, a quarter of an hour away.

Entoto. Monday, 5th of July
I have finished my move. My new abode offers little more conveniences than the one I left: a palisade of woven branches, that encloses three round huts, in very bad shape. I have set up as well I can in the largest of these huts.

Entoto. Tuesday, 6th of July
The king had me called. After two hours of waiting, I am introduced into the *adérache*. It is a rotunda of twenty-two metres in diameter and a dozen in height. The roof, similar to that of all Amhara houses, is covered in dry grasses, thin and long. Two doors, of four metres of height and two and a half of large, open in vis-à-vis to each other.

Three superposed algha make up the throne from which the Negus presides over meals and ceremonies; above it, a crude painting represents Menelik between two lions; it is the work of an artist from Godjam or Tigré.

My crates and my guns are there. The king invites me to open them in front of him. His attention is particularly attracted by the embroidered silks, the mechanical toys, the tin soldiers . . . etc. etc. He is enchanted by my parasols. I offer him the one I had chosen for him; it is in red silk, decorated with the arms of Showa, embroidered with golden thread; he takes from me all the others. Cloths, red sheets, black and white, coloured silks, everything was appraised; a quarter of my effects remained in the royal hands.

Menelik insisted a lot to have a watch. I answered him that to my great regret I was not able to satisfy him and, to avoid his pressing demands, I had to declare that I only had one left, and that it was indispensable to me in order to always have the solar time.

He grabbed my excellent telescope, telling me that he had a most mediocre one and that he would give it to me in exchange. He was good to his word. He also wanted to take a certain number of my guns 'to frighten the Oromo'; I answered I wished to keep them with the same goal in mind. His Majesty did not declare himself beaten; he assured me I would need nothing of the sort, as he would not allow me to go to any place I would risk incurring any danger. Truly it is too much solicitude.

My perfumes pleased the king; he took a lot of them, all the while assuring me I had too many. Finally, he seemed enraptured by the silk stockings and the embroidered slippers that I entreated him to offer, in my name, to her Majesty the queen. Sadly, the feet of Taitu, without being long, are very large. This intimate detail, that leaves me indifferent, evokes regrets in Menelik.

That the Negus is fond of gifts, it is natural; curiosity alone would excuse him and nobody expects of him an even relative discretion; but should he not, at least, grant to the donors help and good protection? It is said that he forgets promptly. What shall he do with me?

I left the guebi quite late and I returned to my lodgings, in heavy rains, by awful roads.

Entoto. Wednesday, 7th of July
Water is seeping through the roof and dripping into my inhabitation.
To find a refuge, I ten times moved my bed – without success.

The king insists; he had one of my servants called and told him to
bring my chronometer. I refused to give it. I went to the guebi. I
waited for Menelik in his carpentry workshop. He examined my
watch; its appearance is modest; but the king is a connoisseur. The
workings interested him. He offered me jewellery in exchange; but I
have no use of useless things and my chronometer is indispensable to
me. I persisted in my refusal.

Storm upon storm, lightning, thunder and intense fog. If it weren't
for its roof, my hut would be just about liveable: eight metres in
diameter inside; a circular corridor of one metre twenty-five; four
metres of height; but one has to get used to the humidity and to the
draughts; all of the walls are cracked.

I have a view onto the guebi; it is in front of my entrance door.

My hearth is made up of a simple protuberance of earth, that
retains logs and ash. No chimney and humid wood. Which means I
have at all times little fire and much smoke.

My door is made of badly joined planks; open or shut, it allows for
the passage of the same quantity of air.

Entoto. Thursday, the 8th of July
Still the same weather. Entoto's precipitations have a deserved
reputation. Lightning also often falls there and makes many victims.
One can attribute these accidents to two principal causes: the
ferruginous nature of the soil and the altitude. Thunder peels with a
lugubrious effect and prolongs itself sometimes, without interruption,
for an hour or two.

Entoto. Saturday and Sunday, 10 and 11th of July
The rain, despite the mending of the roof, continues to seep through.
The lodgings of my servants and animals are inundated.

Entoto. Monday, the 12 of July
The weather continues to be atrocious. The inhabitants of Showa
have a very original procedure for facilitating the course of justice

when it comes to thievery. Children are trained, mysteriously, in certain practices; they are called *liebacha* – I think that the etymology of the word is *lieba* thief, and *bacha* chief, commander – when the culprit escapes investigations, the victim appeals to the *liebacha*, whose mission is to discover undetected thieves; his decision cannot be appealed. During two or three days, the ordinary length of the search, the robbed party feeds the *liebacha* and his entourage, beasts and people. The young sorcerer is given a beverage to absorb that seems to inebriate him. Suddenly, he roams the house, upsetting what falls to hand; if he doesn't find the thief in the crowd, he enters the neighbouring inhabitations and turns them upside down. All of a sudden, he stops and lies down on an *algha*: it's the thief's bed! Thus designated to the public and private opprobrium, the guilty party is apprehended and delivered to the judges.

The *liebacha* is not always successful in his investigations; he often renounces his search; and this is very honest on his part; for his denunciations are never contested.

Translated by YVES-MARIE STRANGER

Jules Borelli (1852–1941) was an able explorer, scientist and would-be arms dealer, who left us some important if fragmentary descriptions of a certain Arthur Rimbaud (whom he describes as able, hardy and versed in languages), with whom he travelled from 'Antoto' to Harar. His descriptions are often funny in their seriousness and pettiness, and his complaints about being robbed by Emperor Menelik, and of the dreadful weather and lodging conditions he finds at the Emperor's court in Entoto, are a lugubrious delight. Nevertheless, Mr Borelli did show his mettle in his groundbreaking explorations and map-making in the south of the country. Jules' brother Octave was the editor of the *Bosphore Egyptien*, in which Rimbaud published his *Voyage en Abyssinie et au Harar*. Jules himself settled down in France – until deciding to sail to Rome from Marseille in a small skiff in his old age.

J. GASTON VANDERHEYM

FROM *Une Expédition avec le Négous Ménélik*, 1896

Court Etiquette in Addis Ababa

A few French traders, as well as some Greeks, Armenians, Arabs and Indians come and go at the palace. The day after my arrival in Addis Ababa I was introduced to the Negus Menelik by M. Savouré, the director of the Franco-African Company. First thing in the morning, we were on our way to the palace. After having crossed a few court-yards separated by branch palisades and milled about in one of them for a good two hours sitting on a beam, I was introduced into His Majesty's presence. The sovereign not liking one to come empty handed, I had brought a few pieces of silk cloth, and thus His Majesty received me in a charming manner. Squatting on an old soft folding armchair in the middle of a lawn, the emperor was surrounded by a crowd of lords. One of them projected upon him the shadow of a vast red parasol embroidered with gold. The intelligent physiognomy of Menelik is at first pleasing. His slightly greying beard surrounds a very black face marked by smallpox. A coloured silk shirt, white cottonade trousers, a shawl of very fine white cotton and a black satin burnous make up his attire; a large black felt hat with a wide rim and a bandana of white muslin cover his baldness. His hands are enormous, as are his feet, which he places in Molière-style shoes without laces or silk socks. Sometimes, but rarely, he puts on socks and shoes together. The lords that surround him spy on his every move and follow each of his gazes to pre-empt his orders. The audience only lasted a few minutes. The emperor bade me welcome and asked me if I had made a good trip. Upon my affirmative answer he told me that he hoped that I would be comfortable in his country. The Grazmatch Joseph was serving us as interpreter. We took our leave from the Negus bowing in the Abyssinian fashion while embracing our left hand, but we were obliged to remain to lunch at the palace. From that day I had to go nearly every Sunday morning to the palace: it is good to show oneself to the Negus, both when it comes to doing 'business' as from the point of view of 'relations'. When one goes to the palace, one is in a manner forced to lunch, as the doors are closed during the imperial repast and the service chiefs well know how to find the Europeans, which the emperor is enchanted to see at his side. He never fails to chat with them. At the arrival of the couriers from the coast, he always interrogated me on the news arriving from France, in which he was particularly interested. When I learnt of President Carnot's death, I had translated for him the newspapers that gave the details of the assassination, and showed him the illustrations representing the funeral. As he was in correspondence with the President, who had sent him a few years previously the insignia of the Légion d'Honneur, Menelik had written to Mme Carnot a letter of condolence and charged a few months later M. Lagarde with deposing a wreath at the Pantheon. This death irritated him a lot: he knew the nationality of Gaserio, and, as this was the time when his relations with Italy were beginning to fray, he fulminated against the assassin and only seemed appeased when I told him of his execution. Later I announced to the Negus the death of the Count of Paris. He sent immediately, by express courier, his condolences to the Countess, and reminded me of the following treaty made by his grandfather Sahle Selasse, King of Ghoa, with the King Louis-Philippe by the intermediary of Rochet d'Héricourt, in June 1843.

In the light of the good will that prevails between S.M. Louis-Philippe, King of France, and Sahle Selasse, King of Ghoa, in the light of the gifts that have been exchanged between these sovereigns by the intermediary of M. Rochet d'Héricourt, decorated with the insignia of the great of the realm, the king of Ghoa desires an alliance and trade with France.

ART. 1 In the light of the conformity of religion that exists between the two nations, the King of Ghoa dares to hope that in the case of a war with the Muslims and other foreigners, France shall look upon her enemies like her own ones.

ART. II S.M. Louis-Philippe, King of France, protector of Jerusalem, commits himself to have respected as they would be French subjects all of the inhabitants of Ghoa that shall go on pilgrimage and to defend them with the help of his representatives along all the roads against the bad deeds of infidels.

ART. III All Frenchmen residing in Ghoa will be considered as being the most favoured subjects, and, in that respect, on top of their rights, they will enjoy all the privileges that could be granted to other foreigners.

ART. IV All French goods introduced into Ghoa will be subjected to a customs fee of three per cent, once paid, and this fee will be paid for in kind, in order to avoid any discussion or arbitrage on the value of the said goods.

ART. V All Frenchmen will have the right to trade in the kingdom of Ghoa.

ART. VI All the Frenchmen residing in Ghoa will have the right to buy houses and land, the acquisition of which will be guaranteed by the King of Ghoa; the French will be able to resell and dispose of these same properties.

Made in two copies.
Angolala, the 7th of June 1843

This treaty was never applied: the Negus has only begun talking of it since the rupture of the treaty of Outchali and the beginning of this hostility against the Italians. The Emperor Menelik is making his best effort to prevent the castration of wounded in war; but when I accompanied His Majesty against the Oualamo I saw that this custom is rooted in the mores of the Abyssinians, of the Galla and the peoples of Oriental Africa. Despite all his edicts and ordinances, and despite all the respect that his subjects have for him, the Negus can do nothing to abolish this ignoble custom. Abyssinians explain it by saying that they hence put an end to their enemy's progeny. Menelik understands that if he wants to remain independent he must not resemble the

negro kinglets that the Europeans conjure away regularly in Africa
in order to annex their territory. Of an above par intelligence and
possessing to the highest degree the faculty of assimilation, he is aware
of the great leap that his country would have to accomplish in order
that its independence be recognised. His entourage, his generals, and
his subjects, comparing themselves to the neighbouring nations which
fight with spears while they have guns, believe themselves to be very
civilised. But the Abyssinian or Galla who have been to the coast, to
Berbera, Zeila, Djibouti or Obock see how much they have fallen
behind us and the Arabs. As to those who have been taken to France
as servants and from whom one cannot expect anything such is their
laziness, they lose as soon as they set foot back in their native land the
notion of what they saw. I often conversed with the young servant
of M. Trouillet, from Tigray: a real urchin of the desert, he only
remembers of his visit to Paris some parrots on a trapeze glimpsed on
the floor of some fairground. Menelik had to be hard and cruel in
order to roll out his empire as he has done; but the time is distant,
when, having caught sight of the wife of one of his generals, the
Cagnasmatch Zekargatcho, and finding her to his liking, he had her
kidnapped, then ordered her husband put in irons, and shortly after,
assassinated. He wed her and made her the current empress Taitu,
repudiating his first wife Bafana. But Bafana liked the Europeans
whereas the empress Taitu cannot stand them. The empress Taitu
had as first official husband the general Oueld-Gabriel, in the service
of the emperor Theodore, who immediately after this marriage put
his officer in irons in order to keep him out of the way. On the death
of Theodore, she wed the general Taclé-Gorguis, but soon divorced
him to marry the governor of a province, that King John then had
imprisoned. She entered a convent, which she abandoned to marry
the general Zekargatcho. Menelik married her in April 1883, when
she was thirty years old. One must recognise that Menelik does not
lack certain ability. A plot set up in 1892 in the hope of a change of
sovereign having been discovered, there was only a small number of
people at court who were punished immediately. The pretender, a
distant cousin of Menelik, a man of little valour and only chosen as a
rallying point, was locked up. The plotters, kept close by in the palace,

did not remain at a distance for long showing themselves to be the most attentive around the emperor, who in turn bestowed upon them many favours, granting them lands and dignities as if he ignored their having been part of the plot. Then, suddenly he disgraced them, and confiscated their possessions. In this fashion their downfall was all the more terrible; what is more, the nation had no inkling that so many high dignitaries had the idea of overthrowing their sovereign. The emperor is, or rather would want to appear, democratic, and, in spite of the antique usages, the slavery and the serfdom, he listens to the complaints of his subjects who come to the doors of the palace to shout: 'Justice! Justice!' sometimes for hours on end, until His Majesty decides himself to receive a deputation. Often, traversing the crowd, a peasant throws himself at the feet of the Emperor to ask for bread: the order is then given to serve him the *kaleb*, a grain ration distributed on a monthly basis to the imperial workmen or . . . to chase him away with a bastinado! Every day Menelik goes to the Chapel of the Guebi; on Sundays and feast days, he listens to mass with the Empress in the Church of the Trinity, located not far from the palace. It is in front of this palace that, on feast days, the priests dance and vociferate religious songs while shaking copper rattles, and shaking towards the sky the crutch that serves them as support during the offices. Menelik doesn't spare his efforts to combat the actions of the clergy, which shows itself very hostile to all novelties. One day, the priests of his court having reproached him for having had his photograph taken by a European, because the devil was in the apparatus: 'Idiots,' he told them, 'to the contrary it is God that created the materials that permit the execution of such a work! Do not tell me such fairy tales or I will have you whipped!' When the Emperor ventures out, he is escorted by a few thousand soldiers armed with rifles or lances and shields. From afar it is a heaving coloured mass, white, black and russet. The dress of Abyssinians is quite simple. It consists of a light white pantaloon coming to mid leg, a great white peplum bisected in the middle by a red band and that they drape in the antique fashion. Some of them wear a burnous of wool or black silk, and soft wide-rimmed felt hats. A long sword shaped like a glaive on their right side and a bullet belt are the finishing touch to their attire. The rifle and the shield are entrusted to a servant of their retinue. As to the Negus, he makes his way underneath a great red parasol with a golden fringe, carried by a favourite. He is mounted on a strong mule richly harnessed in brilliant clothes and all got up in leather embroidered in gold and silver threads bearing a badge with his arms, that represent a lion holding in his right paw a beribboned sceptre ending in a cross. Soldiers carry his shield, his rifle and often a chair covered in Adrianople fabric. The Empress rarely comes out; her entourage is equally very numerous. She goes riding a mule, sitting astride it, similar to the women of her suite. Her head is veiled by a muslin which hides her face, that very few have been able to see, as, by order, empty spaces are created as by enchantment everywhere she is to go. I was so privileged, Her Majesty having had me asked if I would come and take her photograph, I spent a very interesting morning having the empress Taitu pose, with the princesses and the ladies of the court, who had dressed in their most beautiful costumes, but I little appreciated the lunch that His Majesty had served for his photographer. I think that in order to thank me one had doubled that day the dose of pepper and beriberi! The Empress' complexion is clear and seems all the less dark as the ladies of honour are chosen amongst the darkest in the empire. The Empress has her own people, her service officers, her women and her own privy purse; the price of the foods served up in the palace is paid alternately every other week by the Emperor and by the Empress. I also made on that day the photograph of the princess Zaoudietou, daughter of Menelik. Around the imperial palace, and quite far from each other, are found the Abyssinian dwellings, circular, in stone and mud, or in wood, surmounted by conical-shaped roofs of thatch; the most modest amongst the subjects of Menelik live in *godjos* of straw little more than a metre in height, that shelter them more or less during the night. Here and there, there are encampments, tents that appear and disappear from one day to the next. Addis Ababa is not in reality a town, but an agglomeration of huts, quite similar to a collection of hay mounds, whose conical roofs are silhouetted against the sky. The importance of a chief can be told from the number of partisans that he trails around in his suite when he comes out and by the number of huts constructed around his house. The feudal system exists in Ethiopia.

The lords that govern the territories entrusted to them by the Emperor have above them other chiefs; these command to others, and henceforth downwards to the peasant, who is in reality little more than a slave, on whom falls the full weight of this organisation. On an expedition the generals lead their men in the wake of the Negus; each soldier is himself followed by servitors that take part in combat and become soldiers as soon as they have killed an enemy and brought back to their chief some prisoners. Addis Ababa is divided by several rivers fordable during the sunny season, but impassable during the rains. These torrents separate monticules less elevated than the one on which is found the Guebi. On one of them is the abode of Ras Makonnen [Menelik's cousin and governor of Harar Province]. On others, the church, the house of the Abouna Matheos (the Coptic catholic bishop), etc. Nearly all of the important houses are in view of the Guebi. It is not rare, while about, to step on a skull or upon human or animal bones. The corpses of indigents are not buried, as the hyenas and jackals that lurk at night around the houses take care of cleaning them of their flesh. Two years ago, at the time of the famine, the spectacle was terrible!

Everywhere one could see human remains partly chewed up, that the satiated hyenas abandoned, chased away by the light of day. The Abyssinians have no registry office – they are born, marry and die without official acts. On a little plain, at the foot of Ras Makonnen's house, is held the daily market, and further along, in a less cramped space, the *tebj* weekly market. On Saturdays, at noon, the animation is great. Transactions are carried out under the gaze of the nagadi-ras, the chief of the merchants. Set atop an eminence, a sort of tribune of stone and wood, under a reed parasol, he judges disputes submitted to him incessantly.

Translated by Yves-Marie Stranger

J. Gaston Vanderheym arrived in Addis Ababa in January 1894 on business – he had already visited his company's posts in Obock, Djibouti and Harar. Taken under the wing of Savouré, a long-time Ethiopian resident with whom Rimbaud had also undertaken business,

Vanderheym was introduced to Menelik, and put his photographic capabilities to good effect as this piece shows. He also accompanied a war expedition in southern Ethiopia, but had to beat a rapid exit from the country after his article relating how Menelik had kidnapped Taitu from her first husband, before having the man poisoned, was read by the Negus.

AFEWORQ GEBRE EYESUS

FROM *Guide du Voyageur en Abyssinie*, 1908

TRAVELLER: I have heard it said that the current Emperor of Ethiopia is good and just and that he is of benefit to his country; is all this true?

GUIDE: Oh, sir! I beseech you. Only question me on past kings, do not ask about those that still live, upon whom I do not have the right to speak favourably or unfavourably. Of these our descendants will speak freely and tell the truth. But if I tell you that out of prudence, do not believe that there is a suggestion; in this respect the current Emperor Menelik, when compared to all of the Ethiopian sovereigns who preceded him, and, even if one could not say as much if one compared him to European sovereigns, is a liberal monarch, to whom Abyssinia owes a glimpse of the light of European civilisation, and the Christian population now lives with a modicum of liberty.

T: Yes, when we compare him to European sovereigns, the Emperor Menelik still falls short in his understanding of many things, which could be very useful to both his empire and to his subjects.

G: That is certain; however, the pattern of all this is that, while European sovereigns govern themselves, at least they govern an intelligent country, of which the peoples have been civilised for centuries and who are conversant with the needs of humanity and the prerequisites of life.

T: Indeed, in Europe it is the people that can be useful to their sovereign and to their country by striving to abandon their ancient customs if the latter disagree with the needs of the day, to adopt better ones; or simply renew or modify them, if they are not quite adoptable.

G: To the contrary, if the Emperor Menelik governs; Abyssinia is a country whose people are still primitive, and they cannot share the burden with him either with their intelligence, or instruction, nor

with their industry or counsel. Despite this the Emperor Menelik
has consented great efforts to accelerate his country's journey on
the road to progress; he has introduced many customs that were
not in usage in the times of the sovereigns that preceded him.
In this respect I can say that faced with Menelik's situation a
European sovereign would have been ill equipped, and could not
have done any better on his own without the support of his people.

T: I can only agree; but the Europeans who come to Abyssinia, did
they not try to introduce their civilisation into the country?

G: Oh, sir, it is not useful to ask me that; it would be better if I did not
speak about it.

T: And why, would it not be useful?

G: Because it is better to remain silent on the subject.

T: What is it that frightens you so?

G: Oh! Sir, no fear to tell the truth, but if I were to speak, I would only
say a single word, do you know?

T: So be it! And tell me that word.

G: Well, sir, then: to the exception of a few individuals, all of the
Europeans who come to Abyssinia not only do they not teach us
the civilisation of their country, but what is more they have no use
of it themselves, and as soon as they set foot in Abyssinia, before
leaving for the interior, they leave at the coast all that they had
learnt from their country, Europe.

T: Really! And why is that?

G: Who knows, sir? It could be, perhaps, in order to not be en-
cumbered by the weight of the load during the journey!

T: You are right, maybe that is the reason. And all of the other
Europeans who have lately come to Abyssinia do they act similarly
to those who came before?

G: Oh! Sir, it is very different and things have completely changed.

T: In which manner have they changed?

G: Nowadays, amongst the Europeans who are in Abyssinia, there
are great characters worthy of all possible respect, sent by their
governments or by their sovereigns. These do not only bring to
Abyssinia the improvements of their countries, but what is more
they teach them anew to the other Europeans who had forgotten

civilisation in the course of their long years of sojourn in Abyssinia. I was speaking to you of those that came to pass long ago in order to seek fortune and who established themselves multiplying like goats or better said, rabbits.

T: And they did this with Negresses or white women?

G: Oh! Sir, those who will have children from all species, do not choose between black and white; for them both are just as good.

T: Now I understand: in truth those people are teaching you everything that they learnt from you better than anybody.

G: Sir, it is not today that the student will better the master in his studies.

Entire Regions Seem Depopulated

T: Countries which seem to be earthly paradises are so depopulated and empty; why is there not a soul to be found? Where is the prosperity of the country?

G: On the one hand war, on the other misery decimate the population, how could the country prosper and the population increase, sir?

T: What is this war which diminishes the number of the inhabitants of Abyssinia?

G: You ask me what war in Abyssinia? Oh, sir! In Abyssinia no one wishes to submit to anyone, in a positive manner, but at each change of sovereign and until one emerges as the victor and seizes the throne, they fight with rage one against another.

T: But how? When one sovereign disappears, is it not his son who follows him?

G: And so it should be in accordance with the law, but since about 450 years, nobody has been a legitimate sovereign, with the exception of our current Emperor Menelik.

T: I had heard said that the Emperor John from Tigre, who died in Metemma, was the descendant of an ancient imperial dynasty; how is that possible? And is it not true?

G: Oh! Sir, dynastic titles can be found without any difficulty; that is to say that every time a miserable head of some obscure family who, after having led a life of skulduggery as a rebel, sees fortune favouring him and placing him on the throne, in that same day of his coronation, he finds amongst his courtiers an historiographer to attest that his dynasty is without question imperial.

T: This is really surprising what you are telling me! How is it that some obscure chief can become king?

G: First of all, it is usual that he become a highwayman, then he becomes a rebel, he lays waste to the country by pillaging the property of its inhabitants and with that he finds, as much as he wants, disgruntled and hungry soldiers who desert and flock to him from all sides. So it is that the ruin of Abyssinia is solely due to the ignorance of its rampaging soldiers who, abandoning the legitimate princes of the throne, who would have thought of the future of the nation, they [the soldiers] give their support to usurpers who afflict the population and lay waste to the country, only thinking of themselves and of their supporters. Foreigners, who see our country so depopulated and so deserted, then call the women of our nation barren, whereas, in reality, the decrease of the population is due to the barbarity of the soldiers and to the cravenness of the feudal lords of the country itself, who take from the population, and to the tyranny of the usurpers.

T: And so?

G: And so! Well . . . You have heard what the Emperor Theodor and the Emperor John of Tigre did.

T: So that is how it was! The newspapers in Europe, however, spoke rather in favour of the Emperor John as if he was the legitimate heir of the throne of Ethiopia rather than the Emperor Menelik.

G: Oh, sir, let us leave aside newspapers which, if things are as I have heard them to be, always seek to talk over the truth. What is more these newspapers would have learnt this false story from the people of Tigre, I believe. Anyhow, now it is the Emperor Menelik who is the sole and true legitimate sovereign of Abyssinia, which hence finds itself governed by the legitimate prince that he is.

T: To resume, Abyssinia is now happily governed by its legitimate prince Menelik; is this accurate?

G: Certainly, sir.

T: What difference exists between the government of the defunct

Emperor John and the government of the current Emperor Menelik?

G: What sort of comparison are you asking me for, sir? Your question is equivalent to this one: 'What is more unctuous, honey or aloe?'

T: Which of the two can be compared to honey, and which to aloe?

G: He who is honey is Emperor Menelik, and aloe the Emperor John. The latter had sat on the throne of Ethiopia solely in order to destroy Abyssinia and afflict her poor inhabitants.

T: Myself, I had only heard of the tyranny of the Emperor Theodor who annihilated the population and destroyed the whole country, but I had heard nothing said of the Emperor John.

G: Let us leave aside the Emperor Theodor who with his mental hallucinations, led a devilish life; for myself I only speak of the Emperor John who made efforts to unite hell to paradise and sought to make a home in each.

T: In what manner?

G: On the one hand he would go to church, during the nights, to pray and give to believe that he was chaste and saintly, while on the other hand he oppressed the poor people.

T: In what manner did he afflict the people?

G: In all manners and especially by obliging the population to billet in each family and during four or five months of the year soldiers and to entertain them giving them all that they desired. When the poor people no longer had enough bread and wheat to give food to the soldiers billeted on them, and after all their resources had been exhausted by these same soldiers, these poor people were then tied up with their hands behind their backs and whipped and often chased from their home so that they would suffer the terrible cold of night and the terrible heat of day.

T: And what did the Emperor John say of all that?

G: The Emperor was in agreement with his army and he knew every-thing that his soldiers inflicted on the population. You know what that sovereign did.

T: No; what is it that he did?

G: Listen to me then: in the winter of 1880–81 while a terrible hunger crushed the population of the regions of central Abyssinia, the

Emperor John came back from his native land of Tigre to spend the winter as was his custom in Debre Tabor. During this winter, the population of Begemder, reduced to the greatest of misery could no longer as in the past support and feed the armies which it was obliged to give lodgings and feed. For this reason they were then forced to empty their granaries and sacrifice all their fortune to reap the wheat while it was flowering and to crush it to make a porridge which was then served up to the famished soldiers. Moreover, all of the families that could no longer continue to take care of the soldiers billeted in their abodes, were condemned by the magnanimous sovereign, the Emperor John, to give to the soldiers that they were called upon to house and feed, the feed for their cattle, and if they had no cattle, to give up one of their sons as a slave. Now you can judge yourself if this monarch was not a truly saintly monarch!!

T: One verily sees that he was a truly saintly monarch.

G: Having done all that, and as death is inevitable, this monarch laid himself down dead between hell and paradise stretching out his arms towards both as the proverb has it the mother of twins dies lying down on her back (to say: a mother lies down on her back between her children that she can thus embrace both at once without making any distinction, to not make a difference between one or the other).

T: Astounding! I for myself admire greatly the people of Abyssinia who show such patience when faced with the tyranny of all of these daemons cloaked in the dignity of Christian monarchs.

G: You are right, sir, the people of Abyssinia really deserve to be admired.

The Peasants of Abyssinia

T: Are the peasants of Abyssinia not lazy?

G: No, sir, the peasants of our country are truly hard working and indefatigable while ploughing the land; it is the soldiers who are lazy and only know how to mock the poor people, to oppress and to rob them.

T: If the peasants show dedication in working the land, why then are all of the lands so depopulated?

G: Oh, sir! When we see that the fruits, produced by their sweat is destined to the nourishment of soldiers; that the best of the animals that they have reared with such difficulty only serve to fatten feudal lords; that the mules and horses they have kept in order to barter them against cows of good breed and that the oxen in the field are chosen and seized upon by local authorities; from the moment that they cannot seek repose when they come back from the land tired of their fieldwork and that they find their home occupied by these oppressive soldiers who command as master, what is the sense of putting your heart into your work?

T: What is to be done then?

G: In this case many of the landowners shut up their house, abandon their lands, buy a shield and a spear and leave for good to become soldiers: that is all, sir, it is for this reason that regions become deserted and arid.

T: And what is the advantage in being a soldier?

G: The best and sole means to live in Abyssinia is only to take on the occupation of soldier, not really to live happily; but it is better to live from pillaging than to be pillaged oneself.

T: Why do the sovereigns of Ethiopia not defend the pillaged against this domination? Would it not be better to allow farmers to peacefully work their lands; to encourage traders to trade, so that the nation would be rich and bloom and the population could instruct itself and become civilised? Do they not know that the development of the nation and the wealth of its inhabitants is the prosperity of the army and the well-being of their kingdom? Is it not true that man likes milk and butter and that for that he should seek to fatten his cow and not to let it starve, or kill it; for in this case he will be left with just dry leather.

G: This is true, but in order to have such a noble idea one has first of all to be a legitimate king elevated to the throne of one's ancestors; but as soon as any usurper can come and elevate themselves to the throne of others they never take into account the well-being or the future of the nation but rather seek out only what is their personal advantage.

T: Why do they not look to the future of the country?

G: Because they understand that a usurped throne leaves just as it came and that it will never be handed down to their descendants.

T: That is certain. But now that the Emperor Menelik is the legitimate sovereign of Ethiopia, will all of these barbaric customs be abrogated?

G: Already in the kingdom of Showa the custom of billeting and feeding soldiers on the population did not exist; I think that henceforward it shall not exist such a bad custom in any parts of the empire of Ethiopia; otherwise it would be a great shame for a legitimate and honourable sovereign such as Emperor Menelik.

T: I believe myself as well, that the Emperor Menelik who loves European civilisation, shall abrogate all of these inhuman customs. Otherwise what shall be the reputation that he will enjoy with the Europeans if he does not prove his fairness towards his people by establishing freedom and equality between peasants and soldier?

G: Myself I do not doubt that the Emperor wishes to carry out all these things, but you know that as long as we will have a feudal regime in the empire of Ethiopia equality and freedom will never reign.

T: And the feudal regime, does it also exists in Showa?

G: Oh, sir, the feudal lords of Showa are just as terrible!

T: How so?

G: Because the vassals of Showa are terribly persecuted by their chiefs and their feudal lords who, under whatever pretext, confiscate all their properties without even leaving them a single needle.

T: Is this possible? Are there no judges, no laws which determine if these people can be confiscated or not?

G: Each feudal lord has the right to judge his vassals and when he wants to seize their properties even if they are innocent, they become all of a sudden, under any pretext, guilty and are henceforth arbitrarily condemned to prison and to the confiscation of all of their property.

T: And what about the capital punishment? Can these feudal lords pronounce an execution sentence?

G: No, sir, this is the responsibility of the supreme magistrates of the capital that is presided over by the sovereign; otherwise these devilish feudal lords would have decimated the poor vassals condemning them to hanging too then seizing their property.

T: What an infelicitous population! If any of this reaches the ears of the sovereign what will become of these oppressive chiefs?

G: Oh, sir! Despite the goodwill of the sovereign, the poor vassals will never be right and always condemnable.

T: These knaves do they digest everything that they so arbitrarily dispossess their vassals of?

G: Oh, sir! If you only knew the indignities which these unhappy vassals are submitted to as they grind wheat, bring the flour, the grains, the honey . . . etc. up to the residences of their chiefs, for whom they cut the wood for the construction of their houses or for their hearths or for the fences of their inhabitations; they plough all the lands of their lord and finally during expeditions they follow their chiefs loading tents, food provisions and anything else that their feudal lord commands them to do. They even carry the kitchen utensils and the wheels of pottery which serve to cook bread.

T: To sum it up, Abyssinian subjects are truly slaves.

G: Worse still, sir, for if slaves work for their masters, they are at least fed, whereas the subjects feed their feudal lords for whom they work without remission.

T: All of the provinces of the Galla how are they governed by Abyssinian Christians?

G: When Christians are so terribly oppressed by Christians when they are brothers, just think of the poor pagans, they are treated as church dogs.

T: We can see that in Abyssinia one still lives as one lived before our father Adam begun to sport his little moustaches.

Translated by Yves-Marie Stranger

Afeworq Gebre Eyesus (1868–1947). Author, grammarian, satirist, and *de facto* collaborator in the eyes of many, Afeworq was a leading intellectual and a remarkable Amharic writer. Besides grammars, essays and language primers he penned what is considered to be the first Ethiopian novel (*A Story from the Heart*, Rome, 1908).

Afeworq was born on the shores of Lake Tana and first received a traditional church education, before arriving in Addis Ababa in the 1880s where a blood connection with Empress Taitou ensured him privileges and standing at court. After impressing the Italian ambassador with his artistic skills, he was sent to Italy to train formally in the arts. Afeworq came back, only to leave again on the eve of the Italian invasion of Ethiopia, an invasion he wholeheartedly sided with, just as he would support the fascist invasion of 1936. Made Afe Kesar (Mouth of the Cesar) by the Italians, Afeworq was nonetheless exiled to Italy for a while after the attack on General Graziani's life in 1937, and was exiled once again, this time by Haile Selassie, to Jimma, where he died.

BENITO MUSSOLINI

FROM *Introduction to the Italian Campaign of Pietro Badoglio*, 1937

What the Romans Did for Ethiopia

This book of the Marshal of Italy Pietro Badoglio is the book that narrates and consecrates the African victory. Its style is simple, nearly dry, because the events are in no need of literary amplification. It is a military style, in close correspondence with the Marshal's psychology. The categorical imperative of the African war was that of all wars: it was necessary to vanquish. But to this imperative, the circumstances added another, not less categorical: it was necessary to win quickly.

No war, and certainly no colonial war, was ever carried out in more singular circumstances. Italy not only had to fight against and beat an enemy that had been prepared by European instructors, and equipped with modern weapons on the high plateaux of Ethiopia; she had to fight on two other fronts: the political front and the economic front, as a consequence of the sanctions adopted and carried out, for the first time, by the Society of Nations, which, if the vicissitudes of war had not been propitious to the Italian armies, would have probably come to more drastic measures, that many parties favourable to the Society were indeed demanding openly or in a roundabout manner. The *time* factor was therefore an element of the solution. If the war had become chronic in the manner of so many other colonial wars, time would have worked against us. In order to avoid this terrible eventuality, it was necessary to give to a war that all foresaw to be colonial in character, the character of a great continental war, and, in consequence, have sent from the motherland elements of a size and quality such that we would obtain a sure victory, crushing, with the shortest delays possible.

Initial provisions were therefore multiplied by five; when it comes to numbers there were not 100,000 but 400,000 men plus 100,000

workers, material sufficient, and beyond the foreseen and the unexpected. All this required a logistical effort of nearly unimaginable
proportions; but this method also revealed itself to be the most
economic one. A war that the most optimistic calculations foresaw to
not last less than six years was wrapped up in seven months, and, as I
write these lines, three months after the end of the hostilities, a good
third of the troops have been repatriated or are on the way back.

When Marshal Badoglio arrived on the front, at the beginning of
December, the Italian flag had already been flying on Makale for a
month. The occupation of Makale had certainly stretched the supply
lines, but if we had not undertaken this first audacious act
of occupying Makale, it is very probable that we would not have
undertaken the others either. The deployment presented the bulge
of Makale, but what took place in this advanced position in January
and in February shows that the dispositions taken by De Bono, then
by Badoglio, to shatter any offensive efforts were perfectly efficient.
The penetrative force of the enemy only showed itself in the episode
of a very small proportion of Mai Timchet-Dembeguina. The first
battle of Tembien concluded itself in a very important defeat for the
Abyssinians. We can say that, already from this time, the offensive
possibilities of the Ethiopians were definitively broken. Already from
these days they had to passively suffer our initiative, and it is only in
the Vth act of the tragedy that the Negus, on Lake Ashangi, tried to
thwart this in an effort that was both useless and desperate.

The preparation of Marshal Badoglio who asked, between December
and January, a few weeks of cessation, was therefore an indispensable
condition. Marshal Badoglio could only jump onto his target once
ascertained of his launching pad. The battles were all manoeuvred,
conceived along the most classical lines of both the most prudent and
the most audacious strategy. That of Enderta remains a model. That is
why the five battles were resolved by decisive victories with important
losses for the enemy, light for us. After the battle of Lake Ashangi, the
regular forces of the Abyssinian army were in disarray. Badoglio could
have stopped and waited. But the *time* factor was bearing down on us.
When the enemy is in crisis, he must in no manner be allowed to collect
himself: you have to hunt him down and destroy him to the last man.

Only a commander of the stature of Badoglio could conceive and undertake the march Dessie–Addis Abeba. And it is only with the occupation of Addis Abeba that the war could come to its triumphal conclusion.

One has to be grateful to Badoglio to have dared to the point of temerity. In war one must be bold, for he that dares courts the probability that, nearly always, fate will come to his aid. One must be bold, especially when the human element is made up of the steel of the African legionaries, raised in the atmosphere of the Revolution of the Black Shirts. And that is why the war extending from the 3rd of October to the 5th of May can rightly be called 'fascist' as it was carried out and won in the spirit of fascism: promptness, decisiveness, spirit of sacrifice, courage and resilience beyond human strength.

The considerations that Marshal Badoglio exposes at the end of his book shall be meditated upon as they should. This 'people's' war as it was called in the Pontinia speech, was won by the people. Badoglio recognises this and reserves his admiration for the Italian people: combatants and civilians. All were worthy of this victory that, for the first time, not only did not receive any help from abroad, but had to puncture the front of the world coalition. The Italian people salutes in Marshal Badoglio the craftsman of the military victory and the conqueror of the enemy capital. The tricolour of Italy was raised on the 5th of May on the Ghebi of the lion of Judah. Four days later the new era of the empire of Rome had begun.

Mussolini
Rome, 6th of October, year XIV, F.E. [1936]

Benito Mussolini's (1883–1945) war on Abyssinia and the drama it caused in the middle of the 1930s at the League of Nations, and among peace groups and African and black liberation movements the world over has been much forgotten – not least because of the Allies' decision, at the end of World War II, that they simply could not afford to prosecute the Italians over their misdeeds against Abyssinia. The Italian army's ready use of attack gases, and its ruthless killings of civilians (the Addis Ababa and Debre Libanos massacres being only

two prime examples) throughout the occupation, went mostly un-
opposed by Western governments, and were seen by many as an
omen of things to come.

IAN CAMPBELL

FROM *The Plot to Kill Graziani*, 2010

The Massacre of Debre Libanos

The credibility of Franceschino's report was of no concern to Graziani [Marshal Rodolfo Graziani was the viceroy of Ethiopia during the Italian occupation. An attempt on his life on the 19th of February 1937 led to massacres in Addis Ababa, carried out by the Black Shirts over three days, then to the Debre Libanos killings related here. Graziani came to be known as The Butcher of Ethiopia], so long as it provided a suitable document for the file. It is, of course, inconceivable that the Viceroy really believed that a thousand monks and clergy had all been party to a 'secret' plot, but that was irrelevant. Simion's Plymouth had dropped Moges and Abraha in the general vicinity of the monastery [of Debre Libanos] before their trek into the rugged Shewan countryside, and that was good enough for the Viceroy. The rest of the case was a charade.

In fact despite Graziani's injuries, which traumatised and embittered him for the rest of his life, the Fascist administration must in some ways have viewed Moges and Abraha as heaven-sent. The *Governo Generale* had survived almost unscathed, and now they had the perfect opportunity to solve their problems by eliminating all of their perceived enemies. Nobody could have been more delighted than the Viceroy when he realised where the putative assassins had gone. The question of the monastery of Debre Libanos – 'a den of murderers, brigands and monks absolutely opposed to us' – would be resolved once and for all.

Of all of the premeditated atrocities conducted in Ethiopia by the Fascist invaders, the massacre of Debre Libanos was the most terrible and hideous. The massacre consists of two separate but related incidents: a mass execution at Laga Welde, and another mass execution at Ingecha.

Slaughter at Laga Welde

After insinuating themselves with the monks under the guise of providing assistance to the community, General Pietro Maletti, acting on the Viceroy's personal orders, enticed almost the entire community into the church of St Tekle Haymanot, and detained them there overnight, on the 18th of May, 1937. The following day, he had them transported to a temporary detention camp where resident members were separated from visitors. The residents, consisting largely of clergy, monks and other monastery and church officials, innocent of any crime, were trucked in groups on Friday, the 21st of May, to the edge of a ravine at a site known as Laga Welde, and systematically machine-gunned to death. Meanwhile the aged and disabled at the monastery who were unwilling or unable to climb onto the lorries were shot down where they stood.

Secret Killings at Ingecha

The other captives, consisting of several hundred equally innocent visitors and young deacons, who really had no idea what was going on, were taken through the night to a remote site named Ingecha outside Debre Birhan, some 120 km north-east of Addis Ababa. There they were shot and buried in specially prepared mass graves on the 26th of May, in a manner remarkably similar to the Italian Fascist massacres that were to be carried out in the Balkans (south-eastern Europe). Shortly afterwards, possibly fearing they would reveal what had happened at Ingecha if they were released, thirty young boys captured at Debre Libanos were sent to perish in the horrors of the notorious Danane concentration camp in Somaliland.

In all, between 1,700 and 2,100 civilians were slaughtered in the massacre of Debre Libanos, and over the following weeks, more than a thousand people from the Debre Libanos area and from other monasteries and churches were sent to Denane, many of whom never returned.

Telling the Story

Once the massacre at Laga Welde was underway – and only then – Graziani decided to let Rome know what was going on. On the 21st of May, he sent a personal telegram to Alessandro Lessona, in which he transmitted Franceschino's report blaming the monastery – a report which was, by then, several weeks old.

Having copied out Franceschino's report into his telegram verbatim, Graziani went on to state that he had informed Maletti of the purportedly watertight case, telling him that the Royal Military Advocate had 'gathered absolute proof of the complicity of the monks of Debre Libanos with the authors of the attempt', although no such proof was ever provided, so far as can be ascertained.

Based on that report, the Viceroy informed Lessona, he had on the 19th of May instructed the General to 'execute summarily all monks without distinction'. He then went on to admit that it was actually a *fait accompli*, for at 1 pm on that day, the 21st of May, Maletti had begun to carry out his instructions.

A few days later, Graziani followed up with another telegram to Lessona, in which he assured the Minister that the monastery had finally been eliminated: 'No more trace remains of Debre Libanos monastery'.

By then, however, the Viceroy had become very cautious in his approach to Rome. He was anxious that Lessona, who was pushing Mussolini to remove Graziani on the grounds of mental instability following the attempted assassination, should not be furnished with any ammunition to support his anti-Graziani lobby. The Viceroy was conservative in his account of the executions. The reports were brief, the number of victims had shrunk to a few hundred, and the thirty schoolboys – actually transported to die in Denane – had purportedly been 'sent to their native homes in the various districts of Shewa'.

'The question of Debre Libanos', as Graziani put it, had at last been resolved. Moges and Abraha had, unwittingly, served the Viceroy well.

A resident of Addis Ababa, **Ian Campbell** is an international development consultant, author and speaker, with a specialisation in Ethiopian history and cultural heritage. He is a regular contributor to the field of Ethiopian studies, and has written numerous academic papers on Ethiopian cultural history and on the iconography and architecture of the Ethiopian Orthodox Church. Since 1997 he has been an active member of the Society of Friends of the Institute of Ethiopian Studies and acquisitions adviser to Addis Ababa University Ethnological Museum. His extensive research into twentieth-century Ethiopian history over the last twenty-five years has led to a trilogy on the Italian occupation of Ethiopia: *The Plot to Kill Graziani* (2010), *The Massacre of Debre Libanos* (2014) and *The Massacre of Addis Ababa* (forthcoming).

A Day-trip to Debre Libanos

(Guida dell'Africa Orientale Italiana, Milano, 1938)

A Picnic in Debre Libanos

Excursion to Debre Libanos in *c.* 2.30 hours. – After continuing along the main mule track for about 10 km. on the Addis Ababa motor road, then taking a path on the E, flanked by two churches, one arrives at Debre Libanos, one of the most famous Abyssinian monasteries, which has maintained great importance and large numbers of monks (they superseded for a time 5000). Founded by the Abuna Tekle Haymanot (died *c.* 1312), to whom legend attributes the restoration of the Solomonic dynasty, it maintained a preponderant political influence for many centuries; it is from among its monks that by tradition the *Echege*, the head of the regular clergy in all Abyssinia, has been chosen . . . It forms a whole village, situated on a valley terrace, and in the shade of pretty trees, olive, juniper and eucalyptus. The main church is the octagonal one of Tekle Haymanot, with external and interior galleries decorated with paintings in the usual fashion. The monastery does not possess a library; the church does however preserve precious antique manuscripts. Close to a thermal spring, which used to be attended by the pagan Galla.

Translated by YVES-MARIE STRANGER

MARCUS GARVEY

FROM *Ras Nasibu*, 1937

Ras Nasibu

A king has fallen on the field –
The field of war, but not by shot,
Nor even through a broken shield:
He died in exile – awful lot!
Ras Nasibu of Ogaden
Is he – the greatest of his tribe –
The man who led his valiant men
With Wehib Pasha at his side.

He died in Switzerland – afar,
Of broken heart in his exile:
He saw the end of that sad war
In which he fought without a smile.
The Brute of Italy had sent
His liquid flames of steady death
And tanks that ploughed and also rent
The land and stole the hero's breath.

This Mussolini, vile of heart,
Who plagues the world with devil tricks,
Has caused a king to lose his part
In building glory with his bricks.
The dream of Abyssinia, great,
Was dear to Nasibu's own heart;
But he has met an awful fate,
And failed in this to do his part.

The Negroes of the world shall wait
To take their stand against the foe,
And when they fight to win their State
They'll make Italians drink their woe.
A Fascist king shall never rule
The Blacks of all the lands we know:
The Negro shall be no footstool,
But give to all the seeds they sow.

Let's honour Nasibu's fair name,
And damn the Mussolini tribe:
This Abyssinian's splendid fame
Shall live through pen of Negro scribe.
Look out for time, that's coming soon,
To strike Italian Fascists down:
To us 'twill be a glorious boon
To have them sprawling on the ground.

Marcus Mosiah Garvey, Jr. (1887–1940): Jamaican political fire-brand, orator, entrepreneur, writer – and later a prophet for certain of the Rastafarian churches – was never one to shy away from a political fight with natural allies or avoid a problematic alliance (he famously met with the Ku Klux Klan imperial giant Edward Young Clarke, while the NAACP's Du Bois called Garvey 'either a lunatic or a traitor'). Nor would he make do with simple but workable plans when a grand vision could be painted. Garvey advocated both for the involvement of African diasporas in African affairs (to 'redeem' the continent) and a mass exodus back to Africa for all people of African descent. His frequent references to 'a king crowned in Africa' in his writings, and his activism for the cause of Ethiopian independence during the Italian invasion of the country, endeared him to many at the time and has earned Garvey permanent status as a founding father of panafricanism and as a prophet of Rastafarianism.

THOMAS PAKENHAM

FROM *The Mountains of Rasselas*, 1959

Climbing Rasselas' Happy Amba

There is a note in the 1860 edition of Murray's *Guide to Egypt* which reads: 'If the traveller inquires whether the oriental dress be necessary, I answer it is by no means so; and a person wearing it, who is ignorant of the language, becomes ridiculous. One remark, however, I must be allowed to make on dress in the East – that a person is never respected who is badly dressed, of whatever kind the custom may be, and nowhere is exterior appearance so much thought of as in the East.'

These severe words, which I took to apply to rural Ethiopia today as well as they had to the Egypt of the Khedivate, were indeed food for thought. I realised that my gold jacket, khaki trousers and third-rate topee were not impressive as a costume. At this crisis in my affairs I needed every assistance I could get. But my smart clothes were aggressively Ethiopian. I had bought an outfit of Ethiopian dress – baggy white trousers called Tafari-cut after the Emperor, and long Arab-style smock here called jitterbub – in an American tailor's in Addis Ababa, more for their merits as fancy dress when I returned, than for their practical use on the expedition. I wondered if I should appear ridiculous if I wore them now, speaking hardly a word of the language as I did. I glanced at Teshome and the Governor. In their eyes I was clearly a figure of fun already; nothing then could be lost by wearing it before them. But to the unsophisticated majority – the villagers, and the priests – they would appear most impressive. At any rate I enjoyed the absurdity of wearing them. I struggled into the white robes, tied camera, compass and Coptic cross around my neck (there were naturally no pockets) and followed the Governor and Teshome down the pebbly hill towards the church, who were led by a young man from a village with the frizzy and goat-like appearance of a satyr.

Where the path forked, one path going up to the church and the other continuing down the valley, the two priests sat awaiting us. A cool wind blew through the silver leaves of olives shading the path. The priests greeted us gravely; as before, the Governor went forward and kissed the proffered silver cross, and the rest followed suit. In my white robes I felt bold enough to hazard a kiss too. The elder priest held the cross up to my lips and I touched the four corners as ritual demanded. The priest replaced the cross in its red calico handkerchief, and began to address the Governor. From time to time the Governor nodded in assent.

The priests, it appeared, were warning us of the dangers of trying to climb the *amba*. Their mood of quietism had changed. As the chief representatives of the village they felt it their duty to warn us. 'What did you say?' I asked the Governor rather peevishly. 'Did you agree with them?' The Governor did not reply. We left the two Cassandras under the olive trees.

As the path became steeper, the flowers and shrubs became more luxuriant. The auburn gotom trees of the evening before were thicker here than ever, and at their feet grew white woolly flowers with yellow petals called *injuartz*; there was also a new species, a gina tree, whose thin silver leaves reminded me of an olive, though its trunk was smoother and darker. We had to cut our way past these exotic obstacles, and our hands and legs became flecked with tiny burrs. I was glad of the generous protection of my jitterbub.

After ten minutes, where the defile ran between two craggy rocks, I was excited to see a long wall with grass-choked arrow-slits piercing its side in several places. The lichen yellow stones were fixed together with lime cement. These were clearly the ruins of a fort built by the king of Gondar – even such elementary architecture as this was unknown beyond their sphere of influence – and still more evidence of the importance of the Mountain. Here a check point had been constructed to guard the last mile of the road. Perhaps it was here that one of the few prisoners to ever escape, the future King Hannes, had been recaptured by the palace guards.

Beyond the fort the path became more precipitous still as it approached the foot of the *amba*. We could hardly keep pace with our goat-like guide. He leapt from boulder to boulder with the assurance of long practice, but we were less adroit: twice I slipped and was forced to grasp the spiky leaves of acacia for support. Eventually, perhaps after ten minutes of this slithering descent, we came to a circular wall cemented to the foot of the *amba*. Its stones closely resembled the fort's in shape and colour. Owing to the thick mat of undergrowth it was difficult to see at first that both ends of the wall were attached to the actual rock of the *amba*. But this was in fact the case. The great wall must have been used to enclose the open space where the King and his Court camped when they paid a visit to the Governor of the Mountain. I thought of the scene which must have been enacted here – Bruce describes it at length – when King Yasous set up his camp here and ordered all the prisoners to be bought down from the Mountain. Nowadays the courtyard is choked with tall grass and young saplings. We waded through the grass and stood surveying the *amba*.

The rock path began in a series of steps cut from the volcanic rock like the steps at Petra that lead to the temple called Ed Deir. We could follow the rust-coloured scar for some thirty feet above our heads, until it reached a place where the rock was overhanging; at this point a second fort had been built, cemented on to the rock face like a house-martin's nest. Whether the steps continued beyond was impossible to see.

The moment had arrived for the ascent. The party quickly divided itself into those who felt honour demanded some attempt at climbing, and those who were content to stand below and encourage (or deride) our efforts; the first category comprised only the Governor, Teshome and two of the soldiers who had been most importunate in their demands to be photographed, the brashest of our escort in fact; all the rest, including the local governor with an identical marque of topee as my own, withdrew to a safe distance.

First Teshome, a gallant figure in his wide-awake, started up the staircase. The Governor removed his Sam Browne and topee and followed. I clambered after them. It was easy going up to the fort, as a thick succulent called *andahula* which grew in the crevices between the stairs, provided an excellent handhold. The three of us, installed in the dark interior of the roofless fort, peered upwards at the rock face. Thirty feet of overhanging rock towered above. There were no traces of any steps, but over to the right where it seemed the staircase must have been run, the rock was flaked and pitted by a recent landslide.

For several minutes we sat there without speaking. Asafa and Teshome were, I suppose, relieved that our ascent was cut short with such finality. I was wrapped in a numbing mist of disappointment. 'It is no good,' said the Governor at length. 'Perhaps later we can bring ropes and a long ladder to climb the rock. But let us go down now.' My companions left me.

Suddenly I had a wild idea that I could crawl round beyond the area of the landslide. I crawled along a narrowing ledge till I was firmly and ignominiously wedged. Looking down I could see the men of the escort grinning; this was their chance. I wondered humbly what would happen to me. With remarkable agility, the goat-like man who had led us came flying up the rock face towards me. When he was five feet away he took a sickle-shaped knife, that rested in his frizzy hair like a pencil over an errand-boy's ear, and stretched its handle to me. I seized it gratefully. Soon I was restored to the ground.

The two priests, who had prophesied disaster, had apparently followed us, as they were talking complacently to the Governor when I came up. They had good reason to be smug, I reflected. But how much did they know, I wondered, about the landslide? I asked Teshome to see if anyone they knew had climbed the *amba* before the path disappeared. They replied that years ago, perhaps it was thirty years ago, a priest called Skinder Mariam had climbed up the staircase to the summit. I asked what he had found. 'Oh,' they replied, 'he had found a curiously shaped vase.' 'Where is it now?' 'Oh, it broke – and naturally we threw away the pieces.'

This assertion started a furious controversy among a number of villagers who had followed the priests down to a courtyard. There was said to be an old man in the village still alive who had actually climbed the Mountain. It was he, not Skinder Mariam, who had climbed to the top. 'Wait,' said the goat-like man, 'he is my father. I will call him. He is nearby.' He gave a loud cry which floated across the valley, echoing off the walls of the *amba* to the alarm of the kites above. Soon an old man, very tall for an Amhara, in a particularly dirty grey shamma, stumbled down the path towards us. Both sides waited eagerly to see what story he would tell. Teshome put the question to him. 'Yes,' he replied gravely, 'it was I who climbed with five others from the village. We thought there might be treasure on top. There were wooden steps at that time. When we reached the tower a little distance from the summit, we were afraid to go on.' 'What were you afraid of?' I interrupted. 'They say that devils have lived there ever since the King's sons left in the reign of King Tekla Georgis. But one of our number was braver than we. He left us and climbed to the summit.' 'Did he find any treasure?' 'No, but there were remains of many stone houses – enough for the King's sons who were more than two hundred in number. And in the middle there was a great house.' I tried to discover more about the 'great house', but the old man would only repeat what he had said. 'The wooden steps fell in ruins many years ago. You cannot climb now.' He turned away. 'He will not let his son try,' said the soldiers grinning. 'No one can climb the *amba* now.'

5

GOODBYE ABYSSINIA,

HELLO ETHIOPIA (1930–2015)

Introduction

It's Christmas time, and there's no need to be afraid
At Christmas time, we let in light and banish shade
'Do They Know It's Christmas'
Midge Ure & Bob Geldof

Is it still possible to call Ethiopia *biblical* – as is done on a regular basis?
Today, not only does this approach airbrush the yellow jerricans tied
to the donkey's back out of the picture, it also divests the nativity
scene's actors of their sneakers, t-shirts and of the battered Nokia
mobile phone stuck in the folds of the *gabi* (often described as antique
and toga-like). Similarly, Ethiopia's Omo Valley is routinely described
as 'stone age' (although the inhabitants also use donkeys, they do not
qualify, it seems, as biblical). For all their lip plates and Kalashnikov
bravado, the Omo tribesmen also relish mobile phones, and speak
enough English to negotiate the price per picture when they take off
their t-shirts and sneakers to pose as noble savages in the African
Eden.

Famines are routinely described as 'biblical' too – as if dying of
hunger can best be described in the verses of the King James Bible.
But why this choice of language? Could the same language be used to
describe the famine which occurred during the Great Leap Forward
in 1960s China? In the 1970s, Ethiopia became famous for its own

famine, but it was the Chinese who died in biblical numbers, and by a factor, when compared to Ethiopia, of perhaps 30 to 1. And yet the reputation lingers on, and it is only nowadays starting to be shaken off, with the last few years throwing up a steady slew of stories on Ethiopia's fast development, soaring school enrolment figures and decreases in maternal death rates. Whether or not Ethiopia will truly shake off the shackles of poverty and develop into 'a middle-income country by 2025' as the government intends, is anyone's guess – the jury is still out, although the outlook is generally positive.

It seems, in a way, that Ethiopians have written themselves into a corner by insisting on the biblical connection for so long themselves, and on the descent of their monarchs from Solomon; claiming a legitimacy derived from sacred texts, first for their Christian state, and then for their culture.

The Ethiopian Church, isolated for so long, conserved many early Christian traditions, and byzantine controversies – such as whether to respect two Sabbaths or just the one – raged throughout the land. A Biblical land indeed. When Ethiopia opened up again in the nineteenth century, and travellers started to visit, they found a bizarre land in which peculiar practices struck them as throwbacks to things they had last read of in medieval or antique accounts. Visitors, taking their cue from the Ethiopians themselves, compared these mores to the Bible, or to ancient Rome and Byzantium. Twentieth-century Ethiopia did begin to modernise in fits and starts, but first the Emperor, then the Derg, controlled things with a heavy hand and top-down bureaucracy. Poverty – which, it seems, makes people think of the Bible – and the relative scarcity of modern baubles combined with an abundance of donkeys did the rest.

Donald Levine's excellent book *Wax and Gold* is an in-depth study of Ethiopian efforts to modernise in the mid-to-late twentieth century. The title refers to the lost-wax casting process used by goldsmiths: the jewellery or sculpture to be cast is first modelled in wax, then the wax model is encased in clay and placed in a hot oven, where the wax is melted out – lost – leaving behind a hollow clay mould ready to be filled with molten gold – dull wax is replaced by brilliant gold. This wax and gold process is also the origin of the name given to the widespread use in the Amharic language, with its many near homophones, of a sophisticated punning technique where one phrase has two distinct meanings. According to Donald Levine, this taste for ambiguity, in which wax is the obvious inter-pretation, and gold the concealed meaning, is one of the keys to understanding of Ethiopian society. He finds wax and gold's Midas touch running like filigree throughout Ethiopian culture. He sees this love of obfuscation – of saying one thing while meaning another – as symbolic of a serious clash between deep-seated Ethiopian cultural mores, and their desire to modernise and rejoin the concert of nations – in a word, to become more global. As the writer Senedu Abebe once rhetorically asked me, playing on the similar sounding English word 'global', and the Amharic *mgedel* (to kill): 'How do you say globalisation in Amharic?' before answering herself in a peel of laughter '*Gedelisation* . . . ' ('A killing').

Today's Ethiopian state – the Federal Democratic Republic of Ethiopia – is pluri-ethnic and secular. The use of local languages is encouraged in print, education and media, and the country's ethos is boldly developmental and modern in outlook. This may seem strange in a country that is resolutely devout – be it Muslim or Christian – but Ethiopia, behind its seemingly strange and byzantine traditions is also, in a quirky fashion, quite capable of adaptation and change. And yet it remains an extremely poor country. Leave the capital's shiny new buildings and new urban railway, walk off any of the asphalted roads for a couple of kilometres and you are going to see what most will still describe as a biblical scene. As Paul Henze's book *Layers of Time: A History of Ethiopia* makes explicit, the effort to understand the significance of the accumulated layers of time and culture takes dedication and uncountable strata of one's own time. Sometimes, a donkey is just a donkey, and to think otherwise is just asinine.

However, even as Ethiopia modernises and its diaspora – in Israel, in the US and in Europe – goes from strength to strength, this biblical imagery will lose none of its potency. In some diaspora communities, you can see it becoming sturdier as communitarianism takes root and these immigrants begin to strongly identify themselves as

American- or Swedish-Ethiopians (what Tefera Degefe liked to call *hyphenated Ethiopians*), and they reclaim ownership of the old stories – and old stories are often the best.

Philip Marsden's *The Chains of Heaven*, the account of his pilgrimage from Lalibela to Axum, begins with the sound of a horn blown at dawn in the streets of Lalibela by the public herald, announcing the death of a local notable. This is the kind of detail that visitors to Ethiopia relish, as it seems an obvious throwback to something both medieval and biblical. Likewise, fifty years ago, Dervla Murphy's *In Ethiopia with a Mule* emphasised traditional customs and foibles, and she makes her distaste for modern Ethiopia and Addis Ababa quite apparent. I remember reading somewhere that Murphy says she would hate to visit Ethiopia again today – for surely, the country she knew no longer exists.

Tefera Degefe's memoir, *Minutes from an Ethiopian Century*, is one of the best examples from a recent wealth of autobiographies of Ethiopian men (women seem less intent on making their mark in print), born in the first half of the twentieth century, seeking to make sense of their lives, and of Ethiopia's progress. Books with titles such as *I Saw a Lot*, *What I Saw and Heard* or *My Life Story* try to bridge the gap between 'Auld Ethiopia' (tradition, empire), the blood-soaked hiatus of the revolution, and today's relentless march towards a brave new world of hydro-powered industrial development. Diaspora writers have also begun to try to forge the hyphen into a link, rather than a sign of division. Novels such as *The Children of the Revolution* by Maaza Mengiste, *Cutting for Stone* by Abraham Verghese (born in Ethiopia into a family of Indian descent), or accounts such as *Notes from the Hyena's Belly* by Nega Mezlekia, try to make sense of the turmoil of revolutionary bloodshed and exile. And in so doing they are re-creating the old stories all over again – for a modern audience and their own contemporary sensibility.

But there are also diaspora Ethiopians out there who seek to discard the label altogether, and with it the country's overarching blueprint. They are first and foremost Oromo, Tigre or Amhara, rather than Ethiopian. Tefera Degefe had not foreseen the emergence of these sub-Ethiopian groupings, which clamour their differences in tones that range from jolly creative folklorism to aggressive ethno-nationalism, and shrilly proclaim the wrongs inflicted by the dominant narrative (which they call imperialism or colonialism).

But in truth, Ethiopia's written manifest destiny has already prevailed, and these latter-day narratives will never be contenders. They arrived too late in the game. They have not taken root, and remain on the margins, blotted out by a centuries-old tale which has inked page and consciences alike. These new ethno-nationalisms have also conveniently forgotten their own complex origins, and feats of bloody conquest, as they creatively write down their simplistic founding myths – sometimes, to not have a written record is no bad thing, when it allows for amnesia over the bloodiest pages of your own history. Nobody would have placed a bet on Ethiopia's survival as a unitary state at the 1991 fall of the military Derg regime. But it has not only survived, but flourished in its new guise as a federal state (which has sought to answer some of the grievances of the past). But in reality, Ethiopia, similar to France, is a democracy with a strong underlying monarchical ethos.

Early photographs of Ethiopian monarchs show them confidently posing astride their best mule – for a man of means in Ethiopia never travelled on horseback. Too dangerous, too uncomfortable. Then, in the early twentieth century, the mule vanishes, and Haile Selassie is only ever photographed again atop of broad-chested horses. Someone had plucked up the courage to inform the king that mules didn't travel too well abroad.

There is a danger that Ethiopia's sturdy hybrids will be replaced by more simplistic steeds. A country made up of rival regional power-bases for most – nay, all – of its history, now lays claim to being near immutable in time; an economy based for millennia on plunder and the slave trade is held up as a champion of African anti-colonialism. Not only were millions of slaves exported to Arabia and the Ottoman Empire over two millennia, but millions more tilled the land in the country itself, and this well into the twentieth century. And the southern 'independent' kingdoms, who would recast themselves today as colonised and subjugated, were some of the worst offenders on both counts. The currency value of slaves was so devalued in their main areas of 'production', that the ruler of independent Jimma, Abba Jiffar, offered the explorer Jules Borelli five women and six eunuchs in the late nineteenth century – for one Winchester rifle. And in 1910, the population of Addis Ababa was two-thirds made up of slaves.

It is also a nation that prides itself on a tortuous relationship to skin colour, and yet it became a shining light for the Senegalese writer Léopold Sedar Senghor's Négritude movement (he even titled a major poem collection, *Les Ethiopiques*) – and for Pan Africans all over the continent. Yet you'd be hard pressed to find an Ethiopian calling himself African who is not either a politician, an intellectual making a point, or a member of the diaspora living cheek-to-cheek with *other* Africans abroad. What is more, a kingdom whose peasantry often endured a fate worse than serfdom has been transformed into a utopian model ruled by a just king by the dispossessed descendants of slaves in the West Indies . . .

This is of course part of a necessary transmogrification in the globalised world in which Ethiopia must find its place. National branding has always been a simplistic affair. Adapt to global trends or perish – go global or ride your mule off the *gedel* (*gedel*, besides to kill, can also be rendered as 'a cliff' in Amharic). All countries do it, but nevertheless – a horse is not a mule, and the latter are far superior to the former on Ethiopia's rocky terrain. What made Ethiopia special – often infuriatingly so – is boxed up for easy commodification and the global sensibility. Think of the Greece first encountered by Patrick Leigh Fermor in the 1930s, with its goat-herding pastoralists sleeping under coarse tents full of the pungent aroma of smoke and curdled cheese – and today's country.

But whereas it took more than half a century of mass tourism to bury Greece's traditions, in Ethiopia it is being done in less than a generation. This is no lament for a country in which forty-year life expectancy, illiteracy or death in childbirth were the norm. But a pervading essence, a quintessential 'Ethiopianness' that cannot be defined, but whose absence can only be felt once lost, evaporates for ever in the process – for lack of a better definition, call it the short difference between the length of the ears of a mule and those of a horse.

If you do want something that stings the eye, that is unsentimental and still reeks of Ethiopianness, read Jacques Mercier's *Asrès, le Magicien Ethiopien*, which plunges the reader into the mindset of an Ethiopian sage, an excerpt from which follows. Or you can read the factual accounts of the travellers of old. They're prejudiced, but they do tell it straight. Maybe those mule-riding emperors, who would have had all foreigners attempting to scale their table mountain beheaded, were on to something. And perhaps Senedu Abebe, for all her easy manner and laughing, was on to something too – you can read a warm description of Senedu in the extract from Sébastien de Courtois' *Eloge du voyage*, in this very chapter.

But I must confess here, that for all my contrary musings on biblical figures and donkeys, I am quite partial to them myself – *asinus asinum fricat*, donkeys like to praise each other, as the saying goes. The good thing about donkey photo-opportunities in Ethiopia is simply that you can always find one – the country has the second highest head-count of them in the world – only China, typically, has more. I am also rather fond of the overlapping cultures we see today in Ethiopia – a barefooted nun, all decked out in a saffron robe with a skull cap to match, eagerly chattering away on her mobile phone, for example. Meanwhile, near my home in the booming heights of Addis Ababa, where cement mixers can be heard all day long, dawn still often arrives with the announcement of a death in the neighbourhood, blown on a horn by the public herald, just as I tune into the BBC World Service. Finally, it should be noted that both Philip Marsden and Dervla Murphy travelled not by donkey, but by mule.

JACQUES MERCIER

FROM *Asrès, le Magicien Ethiopien*, 1988

The Emperor Haile Selassie Breaks Wind

Upon their return to Talia in July 1922, Asrès and Berhanu hear of Duke Hailu's departure for Addis Ababa. In October 1923 the Duke is at the coronation of Tafari, who takes the regal name Haile Selassie I. Upon this occasion, Hailu himself becomes a prince, and is assigned residence in the capital. Complaints against his misrule accrue. Court cases abound.

Duke Hailu was condemned to pay back the monies of the goods he had seized, as well as the sums levied as taxes on the hot springs, and those of the fines levied against those who fired their gun without good reason, the taxes imposed on Zegue, everything he had squeezed out of his province.

When I learned of the Duke's worries, I shared my concerns with the cleric Berhanu.

'Listen,' said the cleric, 'let us think hard about this business. Now that he is being forced to cough up everything he was able to confiscate, he is going to be hard pressed for cash. How can we remain complacent, we who have gobbled up his money without restraint during all these years? Let's give him back what is rightly his!'

'You have nothing to worry about. Don't fret so much! In truth you are satiated. What restlessness! Me myself, I am sick. I won't leave. Take what you will and return it to the Duke. But stop mouthing off!'

I departed with a she-mule and a mule from Sennar, both of towering height, that the Duke had tasked us with putting through their paces and teaching to amble; more than five hundred thalers; three Tripoli carpets confiscated from an octroi; and four revolvers each equipped with fifty cartridges. My servant Abebe Mercha had a relative in Addis Ababa. He accompanied me for a salary of three thalers. On the third day, as we entered Dedjen, the she-mule fell ill. I placed her with someone:

'If she dies, hack the tail and the mane off in front of witnesses and keep them safe for me. If she survives, take care of her until my return,' I said, handing over to him four thalers.

With the mule I made for the capital where I presented myself at the Duke's residence. A factotum ushered me in. The carpets were unrolled. I spread out the revolvers, the cartridges, the thalers.

The Duke arrived.

'Your health is good. Your brother is well too?'

'He was taken ill. He was unable to come.'

'Aïï! . . . ' he exclaimed upon seeing the money. 'Why go to such extremes? Why worry so much? While so many are hoarding my money in their granaries! Aïï! May God give it back to you!'

We counted the money. The Duke had Amsalu and Meche Haregwein beckoned!

'Look,' he said, 'you hold against me that I cherish foreigners and accomplish nothing for you. But the people of my country, who are hoarding my money, when did they come to pay me a visit? These two fellows of little means have come to show me their concern for me. But look! Who has done this much for me, in these trying times? His brother is sick and had to stay put. This one, he came alone. And what if highwaymen had fallen upon him, what if they had done something to him . . . It is God who has protected him! Aïï! Look well! And you condemn me by accusing me of giving my preference to foreigners. Behold what they do, when they are loved! Take it away! Give your brother a revolver with fifty cartridges. The other is yours. And there are forty thalers for each of you.'

We were near the entrance.

'Pull the curtains aside!' he orders a servant.

He observed the coming and goings of the dromedary-sized mule.

'Marvellous! Marvellous! It will carry my provisions. The other is the same as this one?'

'Yes,' I said.

'Bring a saddle! Ride it!'

The mule was saddled, someone mounted it. Whee! . . . It ambled off at a good pace. In truth, the cleric Berhanu had no rival when it came to putting mules through their paces!

'O Duke!' someone exclaimed, 'it shouldn't be used as a pack animal. It should be ridden.'

'That is well. So it should be. If the she-mule recovers, she is yours,' he told me. 'And if not, you can come and take this one. Now that prison beckons, of what use can he be? What have I done for you? Did I entrust other animals to you?'

'Upon my daughter Yideneku's birth, you gave me a milk cow. She is still with us. Upon the birth of Taddesse you gave another one. They remain, with their progeny.'

They had calved eight times. As I was afraid lest the Duke would take them back, I reduced their number by half. Unforgivable!

'You were to return them to me after having used their milk?'

'Yes.'

'Well, let me give them to you. When was Yideneku born?'

'In fourteen.'

'And Taddesse?'

'In fifteen.'

'Alemu, write what I dictate to you: "In the year of grace fourteen, I give this cow to Yideneku, the cleric Asres' daughter." And write again "To Taddesse I give that cow . . . " '

And he affixed his seal.

'Let them be yours! It is a gift! Keep these letters in order that they not be confiscated from you.'

Didn't he know that his province was slipping out of his control?

Thereupon, he contrived to have the Infant Iyassu escape and was himself thrown into prison.

Duke Imru, who was then appointed to Gojjam, proclaimed that all those who had cattle or goods belonging to the Duke Hailu were to return them. I went to see him with the letters.

'And you, what do you have?'

'Two cows. When I announced to the Duke the birth of my first child, he gave me a cow. And then another upon the birth of my second.'

'And they are with you?'

'Those that died died; those that lived are alive.'

'You have proof?'

'Yes,' I said.

And I showed my letters.

'It has been quite some time that the Duke Hailu gave them to you, and yet the paper is like new . . . '

'When I received these letters I put them away in a chest. I just took them out to bring them to you. What more can I say?'

'There was present there the Chamberlain Desta, that Duke Hailu had brought up and who had become close to Duke Imru. He knew me.'

'For what reason did he give him these animals?' Duke Imru asked him.

'When an epidemic would strike, he and his brother would sprinkle and cleanse the kitchens, the prison. When the household people were sick, they took care of them. Right now his brother is not around. But there are two of them in this line of work.'

'Well, as long as we have a paper . . . We will not have their animals brought in order to slit their throats. These people can be useful to us too. All is well, you can return to your house.'

And my animals were not confiscated.

After giving him the two letters, Duke Hailu detained Asrès until evening. During the conversation the latter shared a dream he had recently.

'It was all as if I had never seen the Emperor before. I only knew him by name. I hadn't ever caught even a glimpse of him. He had taken himself to the Kebena neighbourhood to pray in the church. Saying to myself: "How is it possible that I remain without seeing his face? Will I die without knowing it? I must see him! Which way did he go?" I had taken myself there with my servant Abebe. The Emperor, surrounded by his entourage, was taking part in the mass under a large tent that served as a church. As I milled around, trying all the while to catch a glimpse of him, a man busy reading his Psalter asked me, "What is it with you, my friend? Is something amiss? Everyone is praying in silence. Why are you so agitated?"

' "I have never seen the Emperor. I wish to see him."

' "Are you Christian? Say, 'In the name of the Father', and when he comes out, I shall show him to you."

'I said, "In the name of the Father . . . " Upon which the mass ended and the Emperor emerged.

' "Look at him! That is the Emperor Haile Selassie. The others are his retinue."

'I tried to catch a glimpse of him in the midst of the crowd: his cape and his hat were in a black cloth called *letaken* (moiré). All of the clothes he wore were black. There was nothing white, besides his body itself. His mule was harnessed with gold and covered in a large drape that came down to the ground. Its ears pointed through the brocade. The Emperor climbed into the saddle without assistance and took off. The mule surged forward without touching the ground with its hooves. Only the drape covering its back swept up the dust. The mule glided off with the Emperor in the direction of the palace.

'Duke Hailu stood at his side. The crowd was thick. I followed the Emperor with my gaze. His hat covered even his shoulders. I could not see the nape of his neck, nor his face. Only his black clothes and hat, all was black. It was even impossible to make out the colour of his mule's coat.

' "Aïï," I lamented to myself, "am I to remain like this without having seen his face? Let me run to the flank of his escort!" But I remained unable to see him. So I went to the front and mixed with his people. When I made to turn towards him, they nearly would have trampled me underfoot.

' "Aïï! . . . I have not seen him!"

'We had arrived at the place where the Jubilee Palace is now located, close to the buildings of Emperor Menelik. The path was hemmed in by bramble bushes, hawthorn, by *agam* and *gumero* that closed in on us until they prevented any passage. All of the servants had vanished. Not one could be found. The Duke Hailu alighted from his mule while the Emperor remained on his.

' "O Majesty!" said the Duke.

'The Emperor nodded his head in acknowledgement.

' "How many days will it take us to find a way round these brambles? Why not cut them down and open ourselves a path, O Lord?"

'Another head nod.

'The Duke took him in his arms and took him down from this mule that towered as high as the heavens. He took off the blanket and laid it down on the brambles and hawthorn.

'There was a lot of *kentafa* especially, a creeper with hooked and very sharp thorns. In the old days, when an Emperor inaugurated his reign with a war campaign a proclamation was read out: "Cut down the *kentafa*!" That is to say, remove the brambles from his path. The word *kentafa* also means "one lost day". And he set down the Emperor who settled himself in, facing towards the west, his head inclined, hidden underneath his hat.

'The Duke measured with a stick a distance sufficient for the Emperor to not be bothered by our presence nor by our breathing: "You, sit yourself down here! And you, there!" he told us. He placed us, myself facing the Emperor, and Abebe a little further back.

' "I am going to measure the distance from this path to the palace and I shall return," said the Duke.

'And he left bearing his stick.

'Upon which I felt very happy, as I could now observe the Emperor at leisure. All these tribulations that I had undergone, were they not for his face? He resembled a peasant who would have remained too long on the threshing ground, covered in straw and dust. Shrivelled up, all askew, with crooked legs. And the edge of his eyes were stained by watery humours, similar to runny butter.

' "Aïi! . . . And you are the one who governs this world!" I lamented to myself in my bosom.

'The Emperor thrust aside the panels of his cape and began to search his pockets. On his right he didn't discover anything, then, on the left, he found four lemons. Without adding a word he silently nodded. It must be for me, I told myself, as there is no one else around. I moved closer and stretched out my open hands, in order to touch the Emperor's. He placed the lemons there. Three remained while one fell. I kissed the ground, picked it up and returned to my sitting place.

' "Aïi . . . If I give two to Abebe, he will say that I gave him too many, and if I give him just one, he will say it is not enough. Aïi . . . Too bad!"

I thought, and gave him the one that had fallen on the ground. He was a lucky lad. Abebe made a cut in the skin and began to suck the lemon. I did as much. As we squeezed and sucked on our lemons, a fart erupted. A formidable noise. The sky and the earth shook. It was the Emperor who was farting.

' "Aïï! Poor me! This lad will go and tell somebody about this, and he will have me hanged. Poor me! Did he hear it?" I did not venture to ask him. But I furtively cast a look in his direction: he did not seem to have noticed anything and was still sucking on his lemon. "Praise be to God! He heard nothing." The Emperor didn't turn a hair.

'At that moment Duke Hailu returned carrying a modern pickaxe, an Italian double-edged pickaxe.

' "Be standed, Majesty!" he said. "Here! Dig from here!"

'The Emperor began to dig and, by turning inside what was out and bringing out what was inside, he buried all of these brambles, all of this hawthorn, all the *kentafa*. Everything disappeared. The Emperor dug all the way to the palace and, just as he entered it, I woke up.

A few days later, the Duke, back from visiting the Emperor, was chatting with the cleric Asrès. So I recounted to the Emperor that dream in which you saw him farting. I told him: 'A man from my country saw a dream! He even took you for a monk!' 'Bring this holy man,' he said to me. You are in luck to still be around.

Dumbstruck, I could only look at him.

'What is upon you? Of what are you frightened?'

'Am I to tell the King of Kings that he farted?'

'Of course not! Don't worry, Alemu will redact it for you. Alemu! Come over here! Copy down his dream putting "I saw you commit an indiscretion," in accordance with court etiquette. If he questions you, do not be afraid to talk to him clearly. There is no harm in having seen it, as it is in a dream. It comes down from the Holy Spirit. He will rather congratulate you upon it. He will not hold it against you. Do not be afraid! Take courage!'

The following day, at the end of the afternoon, one of the Duke's servants took me to the palace with the paper. He handed it over to a certain Amanuel who was waiting for us at the top of the stairs and who ushered me in. It was at dusk. The lamps were being lit. The

Emperor was sat at a desk. The major-domo unfolded the paper and placed it upon a sort of lectern made of leather.

The Emperor read it and read it again, then said, 'And how did I break this wind, my friend, when you saw me commit an indiscretion?'

His voice was soft. He raised his head as he said that and looked at me. I bowed my head and, my eyes staring at the floor, terrorised, I said to him, 'It was when you farted.'

'When you told this dream to Prince Hailu, what did he say to you?'

'Something important is going to happen to the kingdom.'

'You did not tell it to anybody else?'

'At Saint George of Zegue lives the Abbot Tekle-Giorghis. I went to see him and I told him: "I saw an important man in a dream farting. What do you make of it?" He answered me: "The fart, is fear, but death is not upon him. Something momentous is to happen to his possessions, to his wealth. But he has nothing to fear for his life." '

'Is this Abbot part of the plot against Duke Hailu?' (The inhabitants of Zegue were embroiled at the time in a court case against the Duke in Addis Ababa.)

'No, he is not a person who would conduct himself in such a manner. He keeps to himself. He is an elderly man.'

'You didn't tell him that it was I that was concerned?'

'No.'

'There is no threat to his life, he told you . . . Be it what it may, have you ever had a taste of the food of this house?'

'Yes, a long time ago, at the time when the Emperor Menelik was ill, we would come in with the children to eat out the leftovers in the bottom of the baskets at the end of banquets. Then, in the era of the Infant Iyassu, people would take me in and put me in charge of proffering the meats to the guests.'

'Maybe you are poor and penniless, but, look, those leftovers that you ate brought you this vision for the government, for the whole world. It did not come to just you, but for the world as well. And it did not only come to you solely for the world, but also for yourself. It will be good for you. Amongst all the saints in seclusion in the deserts, not one has seen something similar. If, without having tasted a morsel from my hands, you have seen such a thing, then, how many more will you see once they shall have fed you. Take him away, Amanuel. Have him fed and escorted back home. As to you, do not forget me! For myself, I shall remember you. Come and see me again.'

Amanuel took me to have dinner and, after giving me ten thalers, had me taken back home in a cart to the Duke's abode in Gulele, who also rewarded me. The following day Amanuel invited me to his home. I spent the day drawing up talismans for his pregnant wife. He too rewarded me.

'The fart means fear. Something ominous is going to happen to his possessions, but death is not upon him,' the Abbot Tekle-Giorghis had said. Soon the Italians invaded the country and the Emperor left for the Maichew campaign. He took fright and came back. The brambles he cleaned up are the Italians: he expelled them from Eritrea that they had governed for sixty years. Thus was this dream interpreted.

As to this Abebe to whom I had given a lemon, what did he gain? When the Emperor left for Europe after the Maichew defeat, his palace was plundered, as you know. Abebe was in Addis Ababa at the time, staying with his uncle. He went to the palace and found there a bag full of thalers. That bag is the lemon! As to myself, I received much money from the hands of the Emperor upon his return.

Translated by YVES-MARIE STRANGER

Jacques Mercier was a researcher at the CNRS (Centre National de la Recherche Scientifique) and a member of the Laboratory of Ethnology and Comparative Sociology at Paris-10 University, when he published *Asrès, le Magicien Ethiopien*, in 1988. The book, the fruit of an enchanted ten-year relationship with an Ethiopian 'sage', sought to plunge a Western reader into the stream of this wise man's words, unlike most so-called ethnological autobiographies, which are shaped, or even fabricated, through anthropological questioning. From 1973 to 1997 Jacques Mercier studied Ethiopian esoteric and medicinal practices. Since then, he has been working on Ethiopian art and architecture.

WILFRED THESIGER

FROM *The Life of My Choice*, 1980

Barbaric Splendour

James Bruce had no doubt witnessed similar scenes in the 1760s when victorious armies returned in triumph to Gondar. Few other Europeans have seen the like; certainly never before had two small English boys watched such a spectacle in Abyssinia. Even now, nearly seventy years later, I can recall almost every detail: the embroidered caps of the drummers decorated with cowries; a man falling off his horse as he charged by; a small boy carried past in triumph – he had killed two men though he seemed little older than myself; the face of Ras Lul Seged's young son, and the sheepskin over his shoulder. I had been reading *Tales from the Iliad*. Now, in boyish fancy, I watched the likes of Achilles, Ajax, and Ulysses pass in triumph with aged Priam, proud even in defeat. I believe that day implanted in me a lifelong craving for barbaric splendour, a lasting veneration for long-established custom and ritual, from which would derive later a deep-seated resentment of Western innovations in other lands, and a distaste for the drab uniformity of the modern world.

Major Sir Wilfred Thesiger CBE aka Mubarak bin London, is best known for *Arabian Sands* and *The Marsh Arabs*, books which hark back to the seemingly happier times of the Anglo–Arab infatuation, and Thesiger is often seen as some sort of latter-day Lawrence. But in truth not only was he born in Ethiopia (in one of the Addis Ababa's British Legation's tukuls, where his father was the ambassador), but he also chose to live out his last years in the barren wilds of Kenya's north-east frontier, not far from the Ethiopian border. Thesiger recounts how an early victorious war procession, marching back from the battle they had won against King Mikael of Wollo, and witnessed from the relative safety of the British Legation entrance gate, was to instal a lifelong love of adventure in him – and it was also in Ethiopia, when personally invited to the coronation of Ras Tafari in 1930, that he launched his dual career in adventuring and travel writing, with his exploration of the Awash River in 1933 (*The Danakil Diaries*). Thesiger remained a lifelong supporter of the Ethiopian monarchy, played a role in its liberation from the Italians with Wingate and also served as an adviser to the crown prince.

EVELYN WAUGH

FROM *Remote People*, 1931

Waugh on Rimbaud

I went to the cathedral and there met the Bishop of Harar, the famous Monsignor Jerome, of whom I had heard many reports in Addis Ababa. He had been in the country for forty-eight years, suffering, at first, every kind of discouragement and persecution, and attaining, towards the middle of his career, a position of great influence at Court. He acted as Tafari's tutor, and many people attributed to him, often in harsh terms, the emperor's outstanding skill as a political tactician. Lately, as his pupil's ambitions have become realised, the bishop's advice has been less devotedly canvassed. Indeed, it is doubtful whether it would still be of great value, for he is a very old man now and his mind is losing something of its former grasp of public affairs.

It is his practice to greet all visitors to his church, but I did not know this at the time and was greatly startled when he suddenly swooped in upon me. He was tall and emaciated, like an El Greco saint, with very long white hair and beard, great roving eyes, and a nervous, almost ecstatic smile; he advanced at a kind of shuffling jog-trot, fluttering his hands and uttering little moans. After we had been round the church, which was shabby and unremarkable enough, he invited me into his divan to talk. I steered the conversation as delicately as I could from church expenses to Arthur Rimbaud. At first we were at cross purposes, because the bishop, being a little deaf, mistook my *poète* for *prêtre*, and inflexibly maintained that no Father Rimbaud had ever, to his knowledge, ministered in Abyssinia. Later this difficulty was cleared up, and the bishop, turning the name over in his mind, remembered that he had, in fact, known Rimbaud quite well; a young man with a beard, who was in some trouble with his leg;

a very serious man who did not go out much; he was always worried about business; not a good Catholic, though he had died at peace with the Church, the bishop understood, at Marseille. He used to live with a native woman in a little house, now demolished, in the square; he had no children; probably the woman was still alive; she was not a native of Harar, and after Rimbaud's death she had gone back to her own people in Tigre . . . a very, very serious young man, the bishop repeated. He seemed to find this epithet the most satisfactory – very serious and sad.

It was rather a disappointing interview. All the way to Harar I had nurtured the hope of finding something new about Rimbaud, perhaps even to encounter a half-caste son keeping a shop in some back street. The only significant thing I learned from the bishop was that, living in Harar, surrounded by so many radiant women, he should have chosen a mate from the stolid people of Tigre – a gross and perverse preference.

Arthur Evelyn St John Waugh (1903–1966) was a cornerstone of English letters throughout the twentieth century with his bestselling novels, biographies, travel books and journalism. Waugh's interest in Abyssinia was kindled while covering the 1930 coronation of Tafari Makonnen (Haile Selassie) – his descriptions of the 'thread-bare robes', and the obtuseness of Ethiopian protocol are a pleasure to read, and even more so when read together with some of the more dithyrambic descriptions of the same events – for example Wilfred Thesiger's. He is much reviled to this day in Ethiopia for his sympathetic portrayal of the fascist invasion of Ethiopia and his apparent dislike of Ethiopian foibles. While his novel *Black Mischief* does seem to take fun-poking a step too far, his memoirs *Remote People* and *Waugh in Abyssinia*, and the novel *Scoop*, remain indispensable reading on Ethiopia.

DONALD LEVINE

FROM *Wax and Gold*, 1965

The Road to Modernity

The legacy of Manz and Gondar

Thus far the significance of Manz and Gondar has been discussed from the point of view of an outsider. We have attempted to assess, on the basis of the best available evidence, the respective historical and cultural roles of these two noted Amhara regions. We turn now to a different though related question, namely, the significance of these two places in the minds and feelings of Ethiopians themselves.

Two kinds of reaction are conspicuous. To the Ethiopian modernist, Manz and Gondar are seen primarily as outlying pockets of conservatism. Their commitments to the past move them to resist certain changes promoted by the national government, with Manz protesting modern education, and Gondar defending itself against nationalist centralisation. They are regarded as backward areas, representative of the many forces that are 'holding Ethiopia back', and to a certain extent are disdained.

To their inhabitants, on the other hand, these places are objects of intense loyalty. For differences of identity among the Amhara are defined chiefly in terms of their *agar*, or 'home country'. The size of one's *agar* is relative; it depends on the context in which the symbol is used, and may be as small as a district or as large as a province. Whatever the referent, one's *agar* signifies more than a place of residence or provenance. It means 'home', and all those whose families live there are regarded with special affection, while those outside are regarded with reserve and suspicion, if not hostility. For this reason the word of native local authorities has always carried more weight than that of imported or distant authorities. For this reason the names of bars and cafés around Addis Ababa today are to a large extent place names. For this reason the type of voluntary association which has aroused the most enthusiastic interest in Addis Ababa in recent years is the association based on a membership drawn from the same *agar*. Regionalist sentiments are so intense in connection with these groups that some members of the Manz association, for example, have asserted that they would not admit to membership a person whose family originated in a district only a few kilometres outside the boundaries of Manz.

This type of orientation to Manz, Gondar, and the many other regions in Amhara country may be regarded as an instance of the more general phenomenon referred to above as 'primordial sentiments'. These are sentiments which are based on the awareness of certain given qualities shared by the members of a group, qualities such as race, language, religious affiliation, tribal affiliation, as well as region of origin. The primordial sentiments account for much of the cohesion and much of the vitality among the members of any traditional society. How these allegiances are affected in the course of modernisation has considerable bearing on the future shape of the rapidly developing nations.

A number of factors inherent in modernisation work to erode the primordial sentiments. Increased physical and social mobility tend to uproot the individual from the setting of family and home community in which these sentiments are produced and reinforced. Occupational position comes to replace membership in primordial groups as a primary determinant of status and identity. Secondary education, military training, and the development of national institutions and symbols promote the sentiment of nationalism to which these narrower allegiances are subordinated.

Other aspects of modernisation, however, work in the opposite direction to intensify primordial sentiments. The education of members of minority groups gives them both a heightened sense of grievance and a voice with which to protest. The creation of new forms of wealth and power provides new bases for competition and conflict, processes which tend to be structured along lines already laid out by cleavages based on primordial differences. The insecurity aroused by the threat to tradition inherent in modernisation also produces defensive reactions which often take the forms of heightened allegiance to such groups.

This intensification of primordial loyalties during modernisation presents a problem which, for all their differences, nearly all the nations of Africa and Asia have in common. Whether the critical differences revolve about language, as in India; religion, as in Lebanon; geography, as in Indonesia; or tribal affiliation, as in sub-Saharan Africa – the passions spent in the conflict of primordial groups have impeded the development of a civil society at the national level. The problem is of such moment that Clifford Geertz has defined the nature of the effort required to cope with it as of a revolutionary order.

Because of the disintegrative implication of primordial loyalties, so conspicuous in transitional societies, the ideas usually set forth for dealing with them have a tendency to reflect what we have called the 'conciliatory' perspective. On the one hand are those who conceive of tribalism or its counterparts as a major obstacle to the development of a national community, and see the chief hope for transitional societies in the effort to promote symbols and situations which excite the sentiment of nationalism as a substitute for logical advantages of retaining primordial identifications, and look rather for political and social mechanisms which will keep under control the explosive aspects of primordial loyalties.

Without denying the practical importance of such ideas, we would like to suggest an alternate emphasis, an emphasis on the positive aspects of traditional patterns – on their potentialities for reformation rather than for elimination or control. There is advantage in defining the durable aspects of tradition. The vitality of a people springs from feeling at home in its culture and from a sense of kinship with its past. The negation of all those sentiments acquired in childhood leaves man adrift, a prey to random images and destructive impulses. The only plausible alternative for a society which has been so uprooted is an order based on a rigid ideology and secured by a high degree of coercion. The most productive and liberating sort of social change is that built on continuity with the past.

This assumption may be elucidated by considering the nature of personality development. The human ego grows by incorporating new elements, discarding some old ones, and constantly recognising what it retains. The strongest egos, however, are those which have retained some solid identifications from childhood. The man with a strong ego may have substituted new religious, political, and occupational values for those of his father, but he has kept some general sense of oneness with his father, or original father-figures, all his life.

It is with respect to such general, archaic identifications that traditional primordial sentiments can be of positive use in times of rapid change. The specific content of early identifications can be replaced without sacrificing the deeply rooted, vitalising sense of oneness with the original objects. In the Amhara case, Manz, Gondar, and other regions constitute such objects of identification: widely diffused symbols whose content must be modified with the times but which can endure as source of inspiration in a changing society.

In what ways may the content of a primordial symbol be revised to benefit the developing nation society? One way is through enlarging the scope of the referent. This is particularly feasible in the case of regionalist sentiments among the Amhara, for their concept of *agar* is, as we have seen, highly flexible. A native of Agantcha, for example, may think of his *agar* now as Agantcha, now as the sub-district of Gera Meder, now as the district of Manz, now as Shoa Province, or even as Ethiopia as a whole. In each case, a feeling of inclusiveness would attach to anyone within the boundaries of the region in question, and he would be defined accordingly as *yagare saw* ('my countryman'). Thus a focus on the more inclusive reference of *agar* in the mass media and in educational institutions may serve to diffuse the libido invested in regional symbols and so extend, rather than destroy, the psychologically integrative functions of regional identifications.

A different process of reorientation is that which, instead of broadening the object of the particularistic attachment, focuses on aspects of the culture of the primordial group which are valuable in terms of universalistic criteria. One remains attached to the symbols of one's primordial group, not because it is uniquely 'chosen' in some way, not only because of the accident of birth and upbringing, but also because it embodies certain qualities which are intrinsically valuable according to the beliefs of the larger culture and/or which related to some special function performed in behalf of the larger community. It involves a process of redefinition that might be termed a 'rationalisation' of primordial sentiment.

This process was exemplified, with an understandably high degree of self-awareness, in the personal experience of Sigmund Freud. Cosmopolitan though he was, Freud had a very intense primordial attachment to the Jewish people as well as its traditions, both the religious mythology of Judaism and the chauvinistic concept of a Jewish nation. Yet throughout his life he maintained, and drew strength from, a lively sense of his identity as a Jew. In his own words, he was attracted to a symbolism of Jewish identity by 'many obscure emotional forces, the more powerful as they are ineffable' and by 'the clear consciousness of an inner identity, the secret of sharing the same type of soul'. In addition, he thanked his Jewishness for two qualities which he found of essential importance in his career: freedom from prejudices which hamper the full use of the intellect, and the readiness to accept a position of solitary opposition.

In Freud's assessment of what it meant for him to be a Jew, we find an articulation of the three elements which constitute this process of rationalisation of primordial sentiment: (1) rejection of exclusivist, particularistic beliefs and values, (2) retention of the basic emotional tie and identification with the group in question, and (3) elaboration of the virtues of the group in terms of universalistic criteria.

This is a type of orientation to the primordial sentiments which has the effect of maximising both traditional and modern values, for it retains the source of security and identity provided by tradition yet defines them in ways that promote national solidarity and the creative resources of the national culture. It is an approach which may be illustrated, in concluding this chapter, by the case of two modern, educated Amhara who identify themselves, in part, as a Manze and Gondare.

'Balatchew' is an American-educated official of the Ethiopian government. Born and raised in Addis Ababa, his family originated in Manz, and he still has relatives who reside there. He is an ardent moderniser, anxious to see progressive leadership and expansion of educational facilities provided in the provinces; yet he is also very sentimental about Amhara traditions and, in particular, his *agar* Manz.

To Balatchew, Manz symbolised hard-core loyalty to blood and to land. It also symbolises the will to fight stubbornly for one's rights and for what one thinks right. He sees the government's keen concern for its territorial boundaries as a direct reflection of the Manze's determination to retain and acquire land. Balatchew gets much pleasure out of telling stories about the Manze's almost foolhardy bravery in combating the Italian invader. He reveals a 'clear consciousness of an inner identity' with the Manze in this regard, and says of himself: 'You know, even as a child, and ever since, I have not been afraid of anybody.'

'Makonnen' is a government official who was trained in Western Europe. His family lives in Gondar, though he spent little time there after leaving for secondary school in Addis Ababa. In the course of his studies abroad, he had become estranged from the traditional ties and symbols of his Gondar-Amhara background. And yet now he speaks with great respect of the virtues of Gondares, their cultivated manner in personal relations, and their pride and wit in the use of language. The meaning of Gondar came to him almost in the manner of a revelation:

> In the midst of my studies in Western Europe I had the chance one summer to visit a number of West African countries and then to return home and spend some time in Gondar. I had not thought very highly of my people before that trip, and what I experienced was a great surprise. What I found – what we have, that I did not find in the African countries I visited – is a special sort of dignity of manner. When I talked with the elders at Gondar I was moved to tears. That is something priceless; something that is a great and irreplaceable national resource.

It is a scant vision to regard the Ethiopian past only as a source of obstacles to modernisation, or as a matrix of primordial loyalties whose only issue can be discord and disruption. It is likewise constricting for

Ethiopians to regard their past as useful only as a façade for exacting admiration from outsiders. The Ethiopian past can be, as the cases of Balatchaw and Makonnen demonstrate, a source of identifications which are associated with specific virtues of national significance, and which Ethiopian cultural leaders can draw upon to help define for their country its unique composite character in the company of transitional societies.

Donald N. Levine (1931–2015) was a Professor Emeritus of Sociology at the University of Chicago.

RICHARD PANKHURST

FROM 'Caves Around Addis Ababa' in
the *Ethiopian Observer*, 1973

Caves Around Addis Ababa

Caves appear to have been extensively used in Ethiopia in the past, and a search, which for logistical reasons has been limited to the environs of Addis Ababa, suggests that they were perhaps more interesting as well as more numerous than is sometimes assumed.

The general area of the present-day Ethiopian capital, it should be emphasised, was, in the past, as is well known, of considerable political and economic importance, particularly in the sixteenth century, but the historical geography of the region has still been little studied, for several of the most important places mentioned in the literature of former times have thus far not been located.

These include:

1 Barara, which an Ethiopian monk, Brother Nicholas, described to the Venetian scholar, Allesandro Zorzi early in the sixteenth century, as the 'chief city of Presta Jani', i.e. Prester John, 'with the castle of the patriarch', while another of the Venetian's informants, Brother Zorzi, referred to it as the 'metropolis, where the said Presta Jani makes his residence for the greater part of the time, and on the mountain is a castle where abides the patriarch'; a third monk, Brother Thomas, called this place a 'great city . . . where is the Patriarch with a great church, and Patriarch on the mountain'. According to one of Zorzi's informants the city lay by the Awash river.

2 Ufat, described by Thomas as half a day's journey from Barara, and situated on 'a mountain on which above the city (is) a great church of monks in numbers about 3,000'.

3   Wis, a place mentioned in the chronicle of Emperor Zara Yaqob
    (1434–1468). Zorzi's informants state that it lay on the River Awash
    six days' journey from Barara, while the chronicler of the Muslim
    conqueror Ahmed Gragn refers to it as a market town.

4   Ugie, thought by the modern British historical geographer,
    O. G. S. Crawford, to be another name for Wis, and said by
    Brother Thomas to be six days' distance from Barara.

5   Satai, or Sadai, apparently also known as Saba, said by Brother
    Nicholas to have been 'a great city', which, according to Brother
    Thomas, was a day's journey to the east of Wis, and was situated,
    another of Zorzi's informants says, on a mountain 'above which on
    the south rises the River Auoz', i.e. Awash.

Firm identification of these and other such sites mentioned in the
sixteenth century would do much to unravel the historical geography
of the area under discussion.

The project of the present article is, however, somewhat different,
namely to introduce the reader to some of the numerous but still
little-known cave antiquities within a day's journey of Addis Ababa,
and which deserve to be taken into consideration in any attempt to
reconstruct the past of this area. The account is admittedly most
tentative, for the author, and the friends and family mentioned in the
text who carried out these investigations on Sunday, and occasionally
also Saturday walks, had neither the time to embark on an exhaustive
study on the ground nor the physical strength, ability or equipment
with which to reach all the caverns here mentioned, many of which
are indeed entirely inaccessible without the aid of ropes and other
climber's tackle. Lack of time, skill and resources have likewise
rendered it impossible to make accurate measurements, let alone to
attempt the drawing of plans; all this is left to others in the future.

The study of these caves, which incidentally reveals the existence
of a long-established troglodytic tradition in Ethiopia, is important,
we would argue, in that it shows the antiquity of settlement in
the Addis Ababa area which has too often been overshadowed by the
better-known antiquities of northern Ethiopia. The innumerable

caves here discussed are, moreover, evidence that the Ethiopian tradition of working in the living rock, as exemplified by the famous monolithic churches of Lalibala, was geographically far more widely established, and also much more profoundly engrained in the Ethiopian culture than has been often assumed. These cave antiquities which make use of columns, windows, wall niches and the like, must thus be seen as the products of a deeply rooted national building skill which made possible the beauty and elegance of the better-known rock churches, the creation of which, if looked at in this light, requires far less supposition of 'foreign influence' than has too often been supposed.

The Awash Area

One of the most interesting clusters of caves, which has apparently never been described since the time of Alvares, lies by the Awash River south of Addis Ababa, a little downstream from the prehistoric site of Melka Kontoure on the Alem Gena–Butagira road, and can best be reached from that road.

This location was visited in 1523 by Alvares, who remarks:

We happened to keep one Lent at the Court of the Prester John, which we kept in the furthest part of the country of pagans called Gorages, a people (as they say) who are very bad, and none of them are slaves, because they say that they let themselves die, or kill themselves, sooner than serve Christians. This country in which the Court was encamped had belonged to Gorages. As it appears, and as the Abyssinians say, these Gorages dwell underground (that is, they make caves in which they live). All the Court and we were encamped above a great river, which made great chasms, and on each side was a (verdant) plain, but a foot below it was all like that of Carnache dos Alhos, in Portugal; and in all parts of the river there were innumerable houses placed in the cliffs, one above the other, and some of them very high, which had no more door than the mouth of a large vat, through which a man could easily pass, and above these doors, an iron in the stone to which they fastened cords so as by them to know the house; and they had them now because in these little houses many of the lower people of the Court were lodging, and they said that they were so large inside that twenty or thirty persons could find room inside with their baggage.

The area described by Alvares, if our identifications are correct, was on the stretch of the Awash River here under consideration where there are, as we shall see, a truly remarkable number of man-made caves.

Describing a fortified town in this locality, Alvares continues:

And there was on this river a very strong town, which, on the side towards the river, was a very high scraped rock, and on the side towards the land a very deep hollow, which was fifteen fathoms deep, and six wide, and on both sides is indeed the river, and inside this hollow on both sides there were everywhere houses like the aforesaid; and inside the enclosure (which is like a field) were small walled and thatched houses in which Christians now live, and they have a very good church inside. The entrance to this town is (underground) of (tufa) stone, and low, with many turns so that it seems that neither mules nor cows could go in; yet they do go a good way in, for the space of a third of a league.

The site of this 'very strong town' appears to have been on the northern bank of the Awash at a place now known in Gallinya as Dubatu, where the river, which flows at the bottom of a deep gorge, makes a large bend, thus encompassing the area in question on three sides, north, east and west. At either end of the fourth, and southern, side, there are two fairly deep gulleys leading down to the river, as Alvares suggests. Easy access to the camp could therefore be effected only through a relatively narrow stretch of land to the south, and here the presence of numerous stones, apparently in a line, suggests that there may once have been a wall or other fortification. The most notable feature is, however, at first sight, invisible. As inspected by Rita and Alula Pankhurst, Tsegay Tafesse, and myself, this is a large and obviously man-made cave in the centre of the promontory where the land, which rises steeply from the river's edge, becomes almost completely flat, and in a few areas around it there is a series of *warqa* trees (*Ficus dahro*).

This cave has two entrances. The one to the south, that is to say on the land side of the fort, is small and narrow and slopes down steeply so that people or cattle entering could do so only by clambering in single file, and with some difficulty, as Alvares seems to indicate, while the entrance to the north, i.e. towards the interior of where the town may have stood, is broader, permitting of relatively easy access. This large, obviously man-made cave, which is well fashioned and still bears the signs of the tool with which it was excavated from the surrounding limestone, is composed of two windowless and hence dark chambers with a narrow passage between them. Each chamber could easily have held 'twenty or thirty persons . . . with their baggage', as Alvares reports. The southerly, or external, cave is supported by two pillars, and has a possible third entrance through a man-hole in the roof which was closed with a large stone, a feature which, as we shall see, is characteristic of many of the other caves examined in the environs of Addis Ababa. Each chamber has shelf-likes niches in the walls.

Within the area presumed to be that of the town described by Alvares, about half a dozen smaller caves, all of them apparently man-made, are to be seen. One of them has a single column with a cut-out niche in it, while another, because of the subsidence of the land is now almost closed.

A further feature of the area of the assumed town is the existence, particularly to the north above the edge of the river, of a dozen or so small holes in the earth, each apparently only large enough to hold a single individual in a prone position. These holes, assumed by the local boys to be the abode of wild animals, could conceivably have been the sleeping places for the courtiers mentioned by Alvares.

The Portuguese priest continues his narrative by describing a nearby cave monastery which, he states, also lay by the river:

Upstream, there was a great rock scraped from top to bottom, and at the top all level ground. Nearly in the middle of this rock there is a monastery of Our Lady, and they say that there was the palace of the king of that country and kingdom of Gorage. This crag faces the rising sun, and they climb to this monastery by a movable ladder of wood: and they say that they raise it every night for fear of the Gorages, when the Court is not here. After that one climbs by stone steps to the left hand, and a gallery runs past fifteen cells of monks, all of which have windows over the water, and very high, and further on are their pantries and refectory, and little rooms for keeping their provisions. Going round to the right by a dark path one comes to broad daylight, and the principal door of the monastery, which is not made of the same rock, only it seems that in former times it was a great hall, and the form is of a church with little walls: it is very light and spacious, because it has many windows over the river, and there are few monks. Many of the people of the Court used to come here to take communion, as they venerate this house and its monks, because they say that they live good lives, and suffer much injury from the bad neighbours they have.

The monastery here mentioned by Alvares seems to have been a little upstream from the promontory assumed to have been the site of the royal camp, i.e. it is more or less in the location suggested in his account, for to the west of the said promontory we find several distinct complexes of remarkably finely worked caves which have been cut in the often precipitous banks of the river, and are indeed in many cases almost inaccessible. A couple of caves, with doors and windows which can be clearly discerned from part of the promontory, are to be seen beneath us on the southern bank on a small, narrow and relatively low-lying lip of land which juts out eastwards from part of the right bank of the Awash and is separated from the rest of the highland by a small but steep ravine. The land on the far side of the river, we are told, is locally known as Wagide. A second, larger and more impressive group of caves comprising over a dozen grottos, which may be very roughly said to consist of three horizontal rows each more or less above one another, has been cut in the side of a bulge of rock forming the right bank of the Awash. This complex of caves is visible from the aforementioned lip of land, but partially out of view to the observer on the promontory of the royal camp. A third and smaller group of caves is at the end of the lip of land, more or less on its northern side, and faces the right bank of the river from which they are separated by the already mentioned ravine. This third group of caves appears to be virtually inaccessible.

The second of the above group of caves, the only group up to now to be examined, by Adrian Mansfield, Jeremy Wyld, Alula Pankhurst and myself, consists of an interesting network of man-made grottos, large and small, most of which are interconnected either by manholes in roofs or floors, through which one clambers with some effort, or by open doorways in the walls. The majority of the chambers have large doors or windows overlooking the river and the opposite bank, and are therefore far from dark. Several rooms are supported by pillars, and the majority have shelf-like holes or niches in the walls, as well as perfectly circular holes in the floors, usually about half a metre in diameter and perhaps twice as deep, obviously intended for the storage of grain or other supplies.

Perhaps the most interesting of these caves has in its floor a large rectangular hole, the purpose of which is not clear. In shape and size it exactly resembles a modern bath. Immediately behind the far end of this bath-like cavity is a solid rectangular block of stone which stands waist-high and may conceivably have served as an altar.

Richard Keir Pethick Pankhurst (b. London, 1927) moved to Ethiopia in 1956 to teach Economic History at the University College of Addis Ababa. Founding the Institute of Ethiopian Studies, Addis Ababa University, in 1965, he became its first Director, launching the *Journal of Ethiopian Studies*, and organising the first conference in Ethiopia of the International Conferences of Ethiopian Studies in 1966. Richard Pankhurst has published scores of books, as well as hundreds of articles on Ethiopia and single-handedly laid the corner-stone of modern Ethiopian studies. He was awarded an honorary doctorate by Addis Ababa University in 2004 and an OBE, for Ethiopian Studies, in 2005.

DERVLA MURPHY

FROM *In Ethiopia with a Mule*, 1968

En Route to Yonder

This morning Jock seemed quite recovered. Good grazing had been available all night and his performance today has proved that he took full advantage of it. At 6.15 we left the shepherds, who had been singularly unhelpful when questioned about our route. Whichever direction I pointed in, saying 'Semien?', they nodded vaguely and replied *'Mado'* (Yonder). So I decided simply to follow the Ataba. But when we came to the head of the valley following the Ataba was no longer simple; at the junction of the three massifs lay a confusion of rocky, rushing rivers, sheer precipices and ancient forests of giant, creeper-hung trees. However, somewhere amidst this wilderness there had to be an upward path, and after struggling around in circles for some twenty minutes I noticed a narrow tunnel through the forest, on the far bank of one river. And that was it. From there a track climbed south up a cleft in that mountain-wall which for two days had been unbroken.

At first we were amidst the chill gloom of the forest, where many rotten trees have been caught as they fell by networks of tough creepers which now support the dead giants at strange angles. Then the path was overhung by green and gold shrubs, between which the emerald flashings of the river could be glimpsed far below. An unexpected descent took us down to river level, and having crossed to the eastern wall of the ravine we were again climbing steeply on an open, grassy slope where the path was of slithery earth. (On the west wall it had been rocky, and therefore easy to climb.)

By nine o'clock the sun was reaching in to the ravine, yet the air was getting colder every moment – though this didn't prevent Jock and me from lathering sweat. Half-an-hour later we at last reached level ground, and fifty yards ahead three men were threshing barley. They seemed mesmerised by our appearance, but when I had unloaded Jock and collapsed on a pile of straw they quickly recovered and shared their *talla* with me.

An uneven shoulder of the mountain formed this ledge (some three miles by two), where a few settlements – perched on hillsides amidst stubble fields – were overhung by rough grey crags rising from green forest. Now I really was in the Semiens, at 10,300 feet, and for the next hour I rested here, being revived by timid but generous locals who filled me with *talla* while I gazed joyfully at the heights and the depth all around me.

When Jock was being reloaded I had the ropes tied extra-tight, a regrettable but necessary precaution. Earlier the load had been slipping slightly and on the isolated heights ahead I dared not risk it falling off.

From this ledge the path climbed steeply for half-an-hour before levelling out in a cool green world of tall, aromatic shrubs. Then it curved around the mountain, overhanging an apparently bottomless abyss, and soon was climbing again to the 11,500-foot crest of a ridge of black soil. Here only a few clumps of heather grew between smooth boulders and it was so cold that I stopped sweating.

A short stretch of flat, bleak moorland brought us abruptly into a new world, where on every side the immense slopes, sweeping above and below the path for thousands of feet, were so thickly covered with golden grass that the very air seemed golden too. From here we climbed gradually, rounding one grassy spur after another, while to the east, south and west jagged rock summits rose far above us, severe against an intense blue sky. As we penetrated deeper and deeper into the mountains I realised that our track would have to go *over* one of those summits, improbable as that might seem, for there could be no other exit from this colossal amphitheatre.

I was scanning the various peaks, wondering which escarpment we were fated to tackle, when my eye was caught by a violent disturbance in the long grass on the next spur. At first I thought it must be a herd of alarmed goats – though this seemed unlikely – but an instant later shrieks and screams of an uncanny stridency, shockingly ravaged the stillness. We were then rounding the spur – and I stopped, accusing myself of having a hallucination, for the slope ahead was apparently swarming with misshapen lions. It took me half minute to realise my privilege. This was a herd of some two hundred Gelada (Bleeding Heart) baboons – one of the rarest of animals, which is found only in Ethiopia, and in Ethiopia only on the highest mountains. So my hallucination was understandable, for the magnificent male Gelada has a thick lionesque mane – a waist-length cape of dark fur – and to strengthen the illusion his tail is handsomely tufted.

Our presence was provoking hysterically raucous protests. The Geladas swarmed across the whole slope – above, below and on the path – and the nearest were hardly ten yards away, giving me a clear view of the heart-sized patch of crimson skin on each chest and of their long, powerful fangs gleaming in the sun at every shriek. In the circumstances, I could have done with a less clear view of these fangs. All baboons are reputed to be cowards but apparently Jock and I look unusually innocuous, for this troop was showing not the slightest inclination to move off the path. Then my memory perversely produced what is doubtless an old wives' tale about human bones having been found among others in the Geladas' boneyards. At which point I decided to take action – and a few stones immediately cleared the path, though none of the males moved far away and their hideous peals of rage almost deafened me as we slowly passed through the herd. Luckily Jock had maintained his customary stoicism during this encounter, merely looking relieved at having a chance to stand still.

On the next spur I paused to watch the Geladas' antics. Their many human gestures have the chastening fascination of all monkey-behaviour and in their social life they seem to be aggressive and irritable and to expend a great deal of energy on squabbling, male with male and female with female. But this does nothing to distinguish them from their more advanced cousins – and anyway our intrusion may have upset everyone's nervous system.

Soon after, we were on the western mountain, where our struggle began. Green forest covered the shadowed precipice, icy streams formed miniature waterfalls and whenever I stopped, to quieten my pounding heart, I began to shiver. From here it was impossible to see the summit – or indeed to see any distance ahead, through this dark tangle of trees – and poor Jock had to be urged on with vehement shouts, for which I had little breath to spare, and with occasional whacks across the hindquarters that almost reduced me to tears of remorse. Again the track had become elusive and sometimes we didn't know which way to turn – though at least I realised that our general principle must be to move *upwards*, whereas Jock felt that whenever possible it would be much more rational to move *across*.

As the air thinned each step became a pain. Now Jock's jumps from ledge to ledge would have taxed a steeple-chaser, and often he had to clamber up long slabs of table-smooth rock that lay at dreadful angles, or to leap across deep, narrow gullies, or to keep his balance on inclines where every boulder shifted beneath his hoofs. But, oddly enough, he went ahead willingly at this stage, as though aware that I had become too exhausted either to shout or to whack, and that our climb was now a crisis in which he must not fail me. He was magnificent, yet here I found suspense on his account a far worse agony than aching muscles or lungs. To my inexperienced eye it seemed that at any moment he might break a leg, which would have been much more serious than my doing so; at an extremity he could carry me, but with the best will in the world I could not carry him. I was beginning to wonder which of us would collapse first when suddenly we were out of the trees, on a narrow ledge of yellowed turf – and looking up I saw the summit two hundred feet above. Inspired by this sight, I was about to take the lead – but apparently Jock had been inspired too, for he made an heroic final effort and got there first, to stand with head hanging and sides heaving. Poor fellow! As I pulled myself on to the top I longed to be able to unload him.

However, on seeing what we had conquered I forgot everything else. We were now at 13,800 feet, and directly beneath the northern verge of this plateau lay a fierce, sombre scene of geological anarchy. One fancied that at the time of creation some basic law had here been forgotten – and nothing grew or moved amidst the grotesque desolation of these riven mountains. Then, looking north-east, I saw beneath me the countless strangely-eroded peaks and ridges that from the Ataba valley had looked so high; and beyond them I could recognise the mountains of Adua and Aksum, amongst scores of other ranges. In three directions I was gazing over hundreds of miles through crystal air – away and away to far, far horizons, where deserts and the sea are 'as a moat defensive . . . ' No wonder I felt like a mini-Hilary, with all Northern Ethiopia lying at my feet.

Dervla Murphy (1931–) is an Irish travel writer with some twenty-six books to her name. Her first and most famous, *Full Tilt* (1965), tells of her bicycle ride from Ireland to India. Now in her mid-eighties, she is still travelling and writing.

ABERRA JEMBERE

FROM *Agony in the Grand Palace*, 2002

Luck at Last

An epoch is remembered as good or bad depending on the nature of the events that take place in it. History will decide on how the Derg period will be characterised based on the weight of events perpetrated under its rule.

One thing is clear though. During the period of the Derg, people in great numbers were imprisoned and killed in a manner that history will not forget. Not only the emperor, the nobility, the patriarch and the priests, but also ordinary people were victims of mass imprisonment and cruel deaths. Thus, from those crammed into the prison in the Great Palace, the fate of some was death while that of others was languishing in prison indefinitely. When those still living saw what they built come crumbling down because they had been deprived of their freedom; when they saw the economy of the country heading for disaster, human rights being violated, human dignity being degraded, Ethiopia losing her place of honour in the international fora and the friends obtained over a long time turning their faces away from her, they were embittered. Often they wished they were dead because their imprisonment seemed to have no end and their being burdens to their families was something they could not bear. It was one such time when they were in this state of mind that a miracle happened.

Usually, the Derg released prisoners on the eve of the New Year. In 1982, no one was called at that time, and everyone became desperate and overcome by a sense of hopelessness. Nevertheless, the prisoners brought themselves together and prepared to celebrate the New Year with greeting 'cards' from materials available in the prison cells and sent them to their families. The significance of the cards was not in their material quality but in their symbolism of the deep feelings they had for their families.

On the Ethiopian New Year, September 11, 1982, just after the celebration of the Mass had been conducted in the two cells, prison guards came and summoned the representatives of the two prison cells, Ato Ketema Abebe and Ato Abitew Gebre Yesus. Everybody waited with great anticipation, wondering what they could hear or who would be called this time. Soon after, the representatives came dashing back, 'Prepare to go! All of you! Freedom is near!' they shouted. They were heralds that healed broken hearts and restored impaired minds. Many could not believe their ears for they had given up the idea of being released, even more so the idea of everybody being released at the same time; it was unthinkable.

People were excited and confused. Those who had not changed their clothes for the holidays were seen trying to put on their better outfits in a hurry; their hands shook. Words came out of their mouths incoherently; they were not aware of what they were saying.

The prisoners recalled the last two words of the sermon that day by Abba Habte Mariam Workneh. Everyone believed that God had put the words into his mouth and they gave heartfelt thanks to the Omnipotent. The sermon he had given that morning was based on Isaiah Chapter 61, verse 1–2. The verses read:

The spirit of the lord God is upon me, because the Lord has anointed me to preach good tidings unto the meek; he has sent me to bind up the broken-hearted, to proclaim liberty to the captives, and the opening of the prison to them that are bound.

Those who, even in that prison life, labelled each other as progressive and reactionary lined up all together to get out of the prison cells. Many remembered their fellow prisoners who were not lucky enough to have lived to this lucky day and that sad memory mixed with their happiness.

There was no roll call; there was no order to pack up belongings. 'Get dressed, come out and climb on to the buses lined up out there!' was the only order. No one hesitated. We bundled up our belongings, put them aside, rushed out and climbed onto the buses before someone in authority changed his mind and altered the direction of things.

The buses, carrying fifty-five prisoners, headed for the former Imperial Bodyguard's headquarters at Jan Meda.

The families that had come to the Palace, bringing with them whatever food their means had allowed them for the New Year holiday, were lined up at the checkpoint when they saw the buses coming out one after the other. They were then told that prisoners were being taken to Jan Meda, a huge open field in the north of Addis, to be released. All the families that had come to the Grand Palace and had heard the good news rushed to Jan Meda, carrying their food. They surrounded the hall at Jan Meda in which, according to the language of the day, prisoners about to be released were given a 'conscientising orientation'. In September, the families made Jan Meda look like Timket, the Epiphany ceremony celebrated there with much colour and pomp in January. Children and adults who had come there in their holiday best made the place rich with colours.

That sweet Saturday of September 11, 1982, was, for prisoners, not only a holiday marking the New Year but also a second birthday, a day of resurrection, marking a new life. The families also considered that day as the day of their re-creation, a regeneration of freedom. It was a day of the fulfilment of prayers and of the grand miracle of family reunion.

The total number of prisoners freed that day, including the political prisoners brought from the Grand Palace, was 716. That mass release was a great miracle, a work of God, which neither the families nor the society as a whole had expected.

Lieutenant Colonel Wolde Meskel Gonite, speaking in the name of the Provisional Military Government [the DERG] and addressing those prisoners from the Grand Palace and the Fourth Army Division, announced their release with the following words:

When conditions were difficult, our Revolution was forced to keep some people under detention in order to protect the interest of the masses and also to defend itself. Because the aim of a socialist revolution is not vengeance but to orientate people to follow the right direction and helping them to become active participants in the nation building process, and because our revolution has come to stage where its security is guaranteed, you are hereby freed.

When the prisoners came out of the hall, the families that were anxiously waiting outside burst out in ululations. There was a frantic commotion of hugging and kissing. It was at this time that Nurlin, my second son, shouted: 'There, I see his pointed shoes!' He had earlier noticed the pair of shoes when they were being sent to his father. As he could not see my face over the crowd, he looked down at the feet of the prisoners and recognised me by my shoes.

All the families went their separate ways. I went, with my family, to Saint Gabriel's Church and offered my thanks to my Creator.

Thus, by the will of God, the last political prisoners in the Grand Palace were freed and were able to rejoin their families. May God be honoured and glorified!

When the fifty-five prisoners that were in the Grand Palace were freed, they were given a certificate. On that certificate, the reason for their detention was given as: 'Suspected that he would disrupt the Revolution.' The reason for his release was given as: 'Pardoned.' The contradiction in these statements is obvious. After incarcerating people for years and causing them untold suffering, instead of offering apologies and paying damages to families for the injustice and deprivations they had suffered, how could the Derg speak of pardon? Imprisoning on grounds of suspicion is itself illegal and inhuman. But the Derg did not understand the consequences and did not care to understand, for it was not concerned with justice.

The final act of the Derg to humiliate the prisoners was taking them to the Central Bureau of Criminal Investigation and taking their fingerprints, as if they were proven criminals. It is clear that it was not the unfortunate prisoners but the Derg that had dirty hands.

Dr Aberra Jembere (1928–2004) was an Ethiopian legal scholar, writer and public figure. Born in central Ethiopia into a peasant family, Aberra Jembere excelled in his legal studies, which he completed at Addis Ababa University. He began his civil-service career in the Private Secretariat of the Emperor, and was at the time of the 1974 revolution the head of legal and parliamentary affairs in the prime minister's office, with rank of Minister of State. He was imprisoned without charges for eight years in the cellars of the Grand

Palace by the Derg, an experience he relates in his book *Agony in the Grand Palace*. After his release in 1982, he attained a PhD in Law from Erasmus University in Rotterdam, Holland. Aberra Jembere devoted himself to research, teaching and writing, publishing a wealth of works on the legal history of Ethiopia, noted biographies of famous public figures, as well as personal accounts and testimonials on his own life and times.

KEVIN RUSHBY

FROM *Eating the Flowers of Paradise*, 2003

Chewing on Paradise in Addis Ababa

I opened the banana leaf wrapper and took out the khat bundle – about thirty two-foot-long stems tied at the base with some grass. The leaves were very dark green while the stems had a maroon tint that shaded into grey-brown lower down. I undid the grass and threw it on the floor in front of me, then plucked out the last five inches of one stem.

The taste of khat varies but generally it is bitter. Western travellers from times past until the present are fond of describing its taste as being 'like privet' – as though that clarified the matter for most readers. The first reliable account from a European who definitely tried the leaf was by Caresten Niebuhr, leader of a Danish expedition to Yemen in 1761. He was not impressed with the 'disagreeable' and 'insipid' substance, adding, 'We did not relish this drug.'

William Makin, who wrote a melodramatic account of adventures in the Red Sea in the 1930s, gave it, not inaccurately, the flavour of dry lettuce and radishes, adding in distaste, 'I swilled the mess down with some coffee and lit a cigarette.' Presumably, he was initiated by an Ethiopian as the Yemenis neither swallow the khat, nor drink coffee with it. But at least he tried it: Norman Stone Pearn, an American of the same era, did not approve at all. Gamely setting off into Yemen, despite having heard that 'Maxwell Darling, the locust hunter from the Sudan, had been manhandled by beduins in the interior,' he barred his guide from using the leaf, telling him that, 'I had no whisky and he should not have the advantage of me in Carte leaves, Carte blanche or Carte anything.'

Like a two-year-old who knows perfectly well that brussel sprouts are disgusting without trying them, many European travellers were quick to condemn. Those that did experiment were no less critical: 'I have never met one [European] yet who liked it,' wrote Wyman Bury. 'The habit has become a serious social evil, undermining the mental and physical health of the native population; the foe alike of thrift and industry.' Bury dedicated his book *The Land of Uz* in a manner Maxwell Darling might have approved, to 'All who have supported a firm hinterland policy'.

But some khat can be pleasant to open-minded first-timers: the thickened tips of stems yield and snap in your fingers like young carrots or asparagus, then give the same tactile pleasure as crunching through an iceberg lettuce. Others can be pretty astringent, requiring a developed palate or large accompanying doses of sweet drinks, some have the fizz of rocket salad or a lingering nuttiness, many varieties will make water taste sublime and tobacco, too. But the scent never varies: when I first detect that delicate, almost herb-like fragrance, then I am in San'a as surely as the smell of a newly cut lawn takes me to an English summer evening. And what is certain is that to the khat regular, nothing tastes better.

My companion was certainly a regular, tucking in with relish and frequent small grunts of pleasure.

'Are you from Saudi Arabia?' I asked, knowing from his African features that he was probably not.

'Somali,' he said. 'Born near Hargeisa, you know it because it was the capital of what was British Somaliland. I am working in Jeddah.'

He had left Somalia as an eight-year-old and never returned except for short visits, spending his life working on the fringes of the Arabian peninsula: Aden, Abu Dhabi, Bahrain, Kuwait, and now Jeddah. Although in exile for so long, he could still recite the names of his camels which relatives looked after for him in the countryside around Hargeisa. In 1992 his wife had been killed in the Somali war and his son disappeared while living in Mogadishu.

'A year later I was in Jeddah and a man came to my house. He said he had news of my son – that he was alive and in Najran near the Saudi–Yemeni border.'

Abdi had travelled down to see him and given him some money. The youth had escaped by dhow from Mogadishu and survived a gruelling journey across the Arabian Gulf to Yemen. With 180 people aboard and water running low, the armed crew had taken to selling drinks to those who could pay. They landed at night on a deserted beach where most of the passengers, too weak to move fast, were soon picked up by the Yemeni Army and taken to refugee camps. Abdi's son managed to evade them, walking by night through the mountains until he reached San'a. There a distant relative was called on and helped him on his way north, eventually crossing the border into Saudi Arabia.

'Is he still there?'

'Yes, he's got a good job now – plenty money.'

'What does he do?'

'He smuggles khat from Yemen. When he walked across, you see, he found out some special paths that the smugglers use and got to know some of them. They carry about sixty kilos in a sack on their backs and that brings a very good price in Najran. The border is very dangerous though: there are spies everywhere because there is a reward for information on khat smugglers. Sometimes they get shot at but usually that's just the guards trying to get them to drop the khat and run away – then they can take it and sell it, you see.'

'But the penalty if he's caught – it must be tough?'

'Fifteen years and forty lashes.'

It is one of the remarkable features of khat that societies and cultures have reacted so differently to its use, but nowhere is that difference so clearly seen as across the Saudi–Yemeni border. Abdi described khat sessions in Saudi: behind closed curtains with trusted friends, each bringing his own khat hidden down his trousers.

'What about other drugs?'

'Plenty problems. There's nothing to do for young people so they get pills or khat or whisky – anything. Everything is smuggled into Saudi Arabia. And khat is very mild really and it is a sociable thing – it gives people chance to meet and talk. Is that not good? And the Koran does not forbid it. Now they make khat-eaters criminals just like cocaine or heroin addicts. For the young people, they think there is no difference – try khat, then try something else. It is all drugs.'

'Where do all these drugs come from?'

'Khat and guns from Yemen, whisky and pills from Djibouti. The Red Sea is full of smugglers.'

I asked about Somalia, or at least Somaliland, the northern region.

'Yes, they smuggle a lot: they take things to Ethiopia by camel at night through the desert. Then khat goes down to Hargeisa by fast four-wheel-drive trucks. Everything is smuggling.'

He talked about the politics of the area: names coming thick and fast, factions and acronyms. For a man who had not been home since 1984, his grasp of events was impressive. It was from Abdi that I first heard the name Ittihad.

'They are fundamentalists and want Dire Dowa and Harar to be part of a Somali nation. You should not travel down from Harar to the Somali border. They will kill you. For me, no problem; for you, very dangerous.'

I thought of Richard Burton who had passed along that route, disguised as an Arab merchant for the same reasons of religious and racial intolerance.

'But I want to take that route – the old trade road.'

'It is all smuggling now, the only real trade route is the railway to Djibouti and that is no good either. I tell you these people will do bad things to you.'

Abdi's view of the region's politics was pessimistic and tinged with black humour.

'The leaders of America, Russia and Somalia all died and went to heaven and God called them all in separately to tell them what they did wrong in life. The Americans went in and after an hour they came out the room, crying and wailing. The Russians went in and after two hours came out, crying and wailing. Then the Somalis went in and a long time passed – many hours – then God came out crying and wailing.'

Kevin Rushby started travelling as a teenager and has never really stopped, reporting from every corner of the world in a style that is erudite, entertaining and often comical. He is the author of several acclaimed travel and history books, an award-winning documentary film-maker and chief travel correspondent of the *Guardian*. His first book, *Eating the Flowers of Paradise*, was an account of a journey though Ethiopia, Djibouti and Yemen in the late 1990s, a time of great volatility and change for the region.

YVES-MARIE STRANGER

FROM *African Train*, 2012

I Served the King of Ethiopia

'Le Buffet de la Gare, c'est moi.'

Mme Angèle Assimakopoulos – most often known, somewhat irreverently it always seems to me, as Mme Kiki – was born in 1928 in the railway town of Dire Dawa. Her grandfather, a Greek, boarded the steamer from America to work on the rails in the time of Emperor Menelik. Her mother was a Greek too, from Djibouti, and like Mme Kiki's uncles was of French nationality. She will herself learn the indispensable *lingua franca* of the day – French – with the Catholic Sisters in Djibouti. But she also speaks her family's native tongue – as well as Arabic, Amharic and Italian. Mme Assimakopoulos arrived at Awash Station in 1948 – she was nineteen years old.

Fittingly, the neon tube on the empty veranda where we sit has gone out, and Mme Kiki tells me of the past, reclining comfortably in the shadows. Her husband was given the Buffet de la Gare as a retirement posting, back in the late 1950s. I had found Mme Kiki sitting at the end of the veranda, with her back against the wall, her bare feet and legs stretched out on an extra chair. An old-fashioned mobile phone lay on the formica-surfaced table. When I had first caught a glimpse of her in the morning, she had contrived to issue orders from a doorway behind the bar, remaining in the shadows.

This evening, as I walked up slowly, she greeted me searchingly, in French. And when I offered her a drink, she declined, but graciously accepted that I join her table. The light came on by itself, flickeringly, and Mme Kiki said that they normally left them off so as not to attract mosquitoes. I sipped my ouzo and asked about malaria. She said no, not now, but yes, later, in September. Now that the light had come on, I could see she had blond hair and that pale blue eyes looked out of her exposed face. Later, she would say that when she went to Switzerland to have her foot operated on, the nurses had laughed: how could an Ethiopian have blue eyes?! For Mme Kiki was an Ethiopian. She was quite sure of that.

'One hundred per cent Greek and Ethiopian.' And then she added – a touch mischievously:

'I've been to Greece, but as a tourist, you see.'

I take a sip from my Ethiopian-made ouzo. Mme Assimakopoulos again declines to join me, but calls out sharply until my drink is replenished. 'One hundred per cent Greek *and* Ethiopian,' I say, raising my glass, to which she smiles wryly, but remains silent. 'You know,' she says, 'we served the Emperor of Ethiopia! He slept here, yes, right here,' and she gestures to a door further down the veranda, deeper in the shadows. 'And the King of Greece, and General de Gaulle. When the trains came in, we would have 300 for lunch, and for supper again, as trains crossed, from Addis Ababa and Djibouti, and back again.'

Mme Kiki's pale blue eyes survey the pastels of the veranda, the faded posters on the restaurant walls extolling Ethiopia's '13 Months of Sunshine'. *'Il était très gentil, l'Empereur,'* she says, twice. The veranda is empty, save for us and a couple of geckos. The restaurant at noon had seen a party from Save the Children's local office hold a workshop. The Emperor's imperial train carriage had pulled out of the station long ago, and wasn't scheduled to return anytime soon.

As the shadows deepen, Mme Kiki tells me of her son, Dimitri – a professional hunter here in Ethiopia – and of a daughter who runs a garage in Addis Ababa. I mention some old Armenian friends in the capital, and she of course knows them all, and adds names and family connections that I had ignored. I thought it inappropriate to mention a recent visit I had taken to the Gulele Foreigners' Cemetery in Addis Ababa, where close to 5,000 of her compatriots are buried – together with another 5,000 Italians, and the same number again of Armenians. Instead, I told her how, when the Scottish traveller James Bruce visited the springs of the Blue Nile in the late eighteenth century, he was led there by an enterprising Greek established in the country.

The *Compagnie du Chemin de Fer Franco-Éthiopien de Djibouti à Addis-Abeba*, which was to attract so many fortune seekers who would build Addis Ababa, the Eucalyptopolis of the highlands, was the last strong spurt of what had been a steady stream of traders, adventurers and soldiers. They came to Ethiopia to work and do business, then married and settled down in a country they found salubrious and welcoming. The Greeks, the Italians, the Yemenis, and the Armenians formed the majority of this cosmopolitan crew. The construction of the *Chemin de fer* represented the heyday of a certain idea of Ethiopia, one which was called Abyssinia and was ruled by a mysterious Negus. A country full of opportunities. At the upper levels of society, men in pith helmets shot gazelles from carriage windows, and ladies in safari suits and matching silk handkerchiefs made the long journey from the oppressive Red Sea coast to the cool hinterland. But the bulk of the foreigners were middling Greeks, Armenians and Italians. In Gulele Cemetery you can read on their worn tombstones their hardy occupations: cobbler, mechanic, seamstress, engineer, steam-roller driver and saddle maker.

Today, their descendants in Ethiopia would fit in a couple of train carriages. And yet, to take a walk down the aisles of the Gulele Cemetery is to take a roll call of all that was needed to build a capital city and a country: Zahouri Ghourlian, seamstress; Adolphe Gerbal, administrateur de la Compagnie du Chemin de Fer Franco-éthiopien; Apraham Keorhadjian, treasurer of the imperial palace; Ali Bin Abdallah, private, East Afr. Army Serv. Corps; Marcello Mini, money lender; Yervant Hatsakordzian, baker; Count Pierre Tatistcheff, count; Sarkis Hovhanessian, caravan leader; Franz Payr, purveyor of strawberry champagne to the court of Emperor Haile Selassie . . .

And then there are the Agapitos, the Aslanides, the Antipa, the Autis, the Divanakas, the Fili, the Charmanis, the Christodoulou, and the Harmani; the Gliptis, the Ganotokis, the Fokion and, of course, the Assimakopoulos. The list reads like the staccato of an Addis Ababa-bound express. Many were driven out during the Italian occupation. The remainder packed their bags after the 1974 revolution – Mme Kiki's father had had to leave at this point, as he was Greek by nationality. But Mme Assimakopoulos was granted citizenship by the Emperor in 1955 so she remained. She battled on with her Buffet, even as the country, the economy and the railway that had been a lifeline and a national pride, went into terminal decline. The revolution had become a train wreck of historic proportions. Like so many other Ethiopians, Mme Kiki saw her house and assets seized – only to have them returned when she petitioned comrade Mengistu Haile Maryiam, the revolution's leader himself, after a good lunch had mollified him somewhat – a lunch taken at her Buffet, *bien sûr*.

The Buffet de la Gare, like the train itself, seems to have pulled into its terminus a long time ago. This is oddly comforting, in a country where nothing stands still for long – high-rises and roads appear almost nightly in Ethiopia these days, and the country's surging population is itself a runaway train. There is even talk of laying 5,000 kilometres of new railway track, to Jimma in the west, to Gojjam in the north, and beyond. This will of course be done by the Chinese. Will an ageing Mme Li or Mme Ki hold forth in the Buffet de la Gare in a hundred years' time, telling stories about the old glory days of Chinese railway building?

Of course, I did not ask Mme Kiki this whimsical question, but instead bade her goodnight in French, to which she responded with other-worldly politeness. Whether her polished manner was Ethiopian or Greek, as she contemplated me shrewdly but not inimically with her pale blue eyes, it is difficult to say. Mme Angèle Assimakopoulos, who served the Emperor of Ethiopia, is the last woman left standing in the brake van of the Chemin de Fer Franco-Éthiopien.

Désormais le train, c'est elle.

SÉBASTIEN DE COURTOIS

FROM *Eloge du Voyage*, 2013

Dropping in with Rimbaud in Harar

A sizzling dish of goat tebs, harari chips, and a Dashen beer. Ice cold. Saint George defeats the dragon on the label. We offer a toast. A pause in these hurried times. We evoke Rimbaud as if he were a disappeared friend. We're on first-name acquaintance with him now. He has become more accessible to me here, through his African experience. Now indispensable. I like his hesitations, his anger, his bad moods inhabited by the *fievra Francesca*. He was not one to sit and talk idly. This famed poet had been an abstraction before I came here myself. For me this is an unexpected meeting. And I find myself tempted, in turn, to speak of him using only his first name. With Arthur then! But we were not alone, that evening at the Hirut Bar. Senedu came to join us. Jean-Michel Cornu's Ethiopian companion, his alter ego in life and in literature. She is writing a book on the poet, she tells me. 'Rimbaud became fully Ethiopian, he belongs to our history. *The Drunken Boat* has been translated into Amharic by Berhanou Abebe,' she continues, 'a writer of French expression, nearly a friend, the incarnation of an epoch.' Senedu has been several times to Charleville-Mézières, in the north of France, to visit the poet's house, and to pay homage at the tomb where he was buried following the Catholic tradition.

Senedu is originally from Wollo, a region of central Ethiopia where people believe in djinns, in sorcerers and in *Zars* – facetious, or evil, spirits. 'It is not uncommon that people become mystical when they reach the middle of their life, and then they take to the roads,' she tells me. And also, she does not really understand why the poet left his home, when he lived in such a beautiful province, so green, so rich.

'Do you also have evil spirits where you come from?' Senedu asks me.

Which makes me think again of Michel Leiris and his *L'Afrique fantôme*, when he fell in love with Emawayish, the daughter of a possessed sorceress from Gondar . . .

'Does boredom have a meaning in Amharic?' I ask her, thinking of the poet's dark melancholy.

Senedu thinks for a while, without finding the right word. It seems the notion doesn't have an exact equivalent . . .

'What can the poetry of Rimbaud represent for Ethiopia?'

'A lot. I find there the soul of a country, an impulsion carried by the verse, that touches me. That revolt could have been mine,' she says with simplicity.

Senedu grew up during the Derg, Mengistu's regime, that had toppled the picturesque Emperor, the 'sublime fiction' of the descendant of Solomon, to use the expression coined by Victor Segalen to describe the Middle Kingdom. In reality, a palace revolution, far from the people, like so many Ethiopia had known before. Euphoria was short lived. The feudality of aristocrats was replaced by the feudality of political commissars, villagisation, repression and organised famine followed by a war of liberation. 'In the morning, on our way to school, we would count the bodies of those who had been assassinated during the night. The regime had transformed us into criminals!' Senedu is now a publisher, and a reigning figure in the Ethiopian underground scene . . . 'She published a book that made a great scandal,' Jean-Michel explains to me, lifting a veil on one of Ethiopia's great taboos: prostitution. *The Song of Songs of Kazantchis* recounts the voyage of an alienated young man into the nocturnal limbo of Addis, in those changing neighbourhoods where young peasant girls come to sell their bodies for a fistful of Birr, and where alcohol, insults, dejection and illnesses soon wear them out, making them ready for an anonymous death far from home. 'The book sold in the tens of thousands; no publisher had the courage to take on the book before she did,' he continues. It circulated from hand to hand and people enjoyed it in secret hypocritically. A thunderbolt in the 'society of exquisite politeness'! 'Aow, aow,' 'Yes,

yes,' Senedu concurs, her golden locks shaking above her lipsticked mouth. Senedu approves without exactly following our conversation in French. She lights another Nyala, having removed the filter beforehand. She is relieved to find kindred spirits in her fight for justice.

We go home on foot. We go down ill-lit alleys without a soul in sight. The Old City, *Harar Jegol*, looks like a citadel looming in the shadows. Only a drawbridge and guards with golden lances are missing. I think of the castles of Gondar, of the Black Forest, and of the palladian abodes of the aristocracy abutting the Via Appia. Antique princes also haunted these walls. If the ins and outs of the city have not given up all of their secrets, we now know our way around here – all the way to the Abbadir Sanctuary, seen one night under a full moon. The rain has stopped. 'If you see creeping vines, it means there is a mosque, or a saint's tomb,' Jean-Michel suddenly tells me, inspired by his ouzo. The stars are cool. The smells drifting in from the countryside envelop Harar in a heady veil. People don't linger in the streets at this time, except in the vicinity of the watering holes managed by Christian pimps where you can drink *tedj*, a sort of bittersweet honey wine – while gawping at scantily dressed young girls. Senedu has called Amir, one of the masters of this nocturnal life, but not just any life, for this is the nocturnal life of the soul and the sufi brotherhood; a city within the city, where everybody knows the codes, and where to find khat and prayers, two evenings a week. Amir is one of the keys of this parallel world. You have to show *patte blanche* to be accepted. First you have to find some khat, the *salad*, then get some cigarettes – you don't turn up empty handed. Amir has come to meet us, a little before midnight, just at the end of Reconciliation Road.

Amir speaks a little French as he was a pupil at the Lycée Guebré Mariam in Addis. Twenty-seven, two brothers, three sisters, he is the youngest. I guess he has a complicated family story, with dispersed parents, and ancient linkages to Harar. He welcomes us first to his home where his young wife prepares coffee with the help of an Oromo servant with ivory teeth who grinds the coffee attentively. Amir's round-faced wife smokes a hookah while conversing with Senedu. Amir recounts for us with enthusiasm the conquests of Gragn, the emir from Harar, who ravaged Christian Ethiopia in the sixteenth century. I lose the thread of the supposed cosmological explications for this supposed 'mission'. I understand the fury of the Abyssinians, the rage of Menelik in these lands: they had nearly been obliterated! Amir munches his khat with gusto. The thump of the mortar, the smell of the embers. We enter into the night. By the time the session is about to start, the combined effect of coffee and khat has banished sleep. Amir is inviting us to go to a *zikr*, an 'invocation' in Arabic, a night of ecstasy. The Abbadir Brotherhood is meeting this evening – we are in luck. On the road to the sanctuary we stop at the mosque of his great-great grandfather, Kebir Khelil Abogn. The grandfather wanted Amir to come back to Harar to continue the lineage. Amir, like his grandfather, knows the Koran, but for Amir, its real meaning is hidden: 'Sufism enables us to go beyond the text, to read the invisible. It's that simple!' Near the sanctuary, the *zabania*, the guard, lets us in. The question is ritual: 'To which *afocha* do you belong?' The *afocha* is a neighbourhood brotherhood, and the city has several of them. The drum has already begun. Senedu goes to the women's side. Amir explains to us that they have their own evening, their own *zikr*, in another house. They will come in the course of the night to participate in Afar dances, aligned in the yard, wearing below their blouses the traditional pantaloons of Harari ladies.

Amir puts on his white skull cap, before jumping into a packed room. The elders, with thick-lensed eyeglasses, sit against a wall, feverishly engaged in cascading the pearls of their *tespih*, the prayer-bead necklace. They all chant while following the surats with their fingertips. Meanwhile, the sheik, a black colossus, sits in the place of honour with, in his lap, an open Koran. He is setting the rhyme with long intonations and, with a nod in our direction, signifies to us that we are allowed to go and take refuge in a corner. In front of the door are two *kabaro*, drums placed atop tyres. The young sing and dance frenetically clapping their hands. Amir enjoys a certain prestige. He comes and goes several times. Hours slip by, in sweat and rhythm. I remain outside in the cool air, sitting on a mat where I chew khat and smoke. A curious band of reclining figures surrounds us. One of them stands out, with a thin face, and a black and white keffiyeh knotted atop his head, and a thick necklace of prayer beads around his neck.

He takes in long inspirations on his cigarette holder. He says nothing and observes us. The poor regroup under the branches of a giant fig tree, the *chola*, for a distribution of low-grade khat. 'For Ethiopians, these trees are the place where the spirits of the deceased congregate,' Jean-Michel tells me. 'You should not fall asleep under their branches or you risk being visited in your sleep . . . ' Amir comes back to pay us a visit, the dances continue. 'Several cycles are being interpreted this evening,' he tells us, covered in sweat. 'God is great. We hold up to three sessions a night!'

Mirkana, the altered mental state induced by khat, has now made its appearance – not very far from nirvana, I think. Euphoria and an absence of fatigue. A neighbour is chuckling into my ear with insistence. Another is producing rapid movements with his forearms as he counts the stars. Grins are green and fixated. I take a look inside. The men are grouped in circles, hopping and clapping, repeating warrior-like incantations. The text soars. The senses become interiorised, as all seek contact with the forces from the other world. Amir seizes the lead and takes the drum. He is the absolute master now, boum, boum, boum, boum . . . All fall into line. The sheik stares at him and approves. Quicker still, with naked feet, upper bodies staggering, then the breathless incantation of the sufis, la Ilah, illa Lah, la Ilah, illa Lah, la Ilah, illa Lah, la Ilah, illa Lah, la Ilah, illa Lah, la Ilah, illa Lah, la Ilah, illa Lah, la Ilah, illa Lah, la Ilah, illa Lah – repeated dozens of times, quicker and quicker, like a hypnotic mantra. Ali and Hussein are invoked, heads swim, some fall over, while others began swirling with closed eyes and turn on the spot dervish-like with outstretched arms. I am sweating. A sachet of ginger is circulating, perfumed powder. 'It's to accelerate the effects of the khat,' Jean-Michel says. 'You take a pinch and leave it to dissolve under your tongue.' My neighbour swallows a sachet whole, in one go. A pause – coffee is served, the music dies out, a woman reappears. The sheik comes to join us in silence. Tray, plastic glasses, a teapot circulates.

'Rimbaud was completely in his element in Harar; he would have attended such ceremonies; he may even have become Muslim, a way of life that agreed with him. He didn't seek assimilation, the town assimilated him,' Jean-Michel continues. Sufism allows for this sort of connection. Perhaps Rimbaud saw in the *zikr* the 'total poetry' that he refers to in *The Letter of the Seer*. He often writes during his sojourns in Harar: 'Like the Muslims I only know what happens, or, as they say – it is written!' and adds, 'It's life, it is not great fun.' The dance has begun again. 'Speaking Arabic,' Jean-Michel explains with passion, 'Arthur could comment on the Koran and take part in the ceremonies, even sing perhaps . . . ' He shares his doubts with me on the myth of a Harari society closed in on itself, as we are here witnessing the exact opposite. 'The only problem he had, is when he poisoned some dogs who were pissing on his coffee bags. The inhabitants were frightened for the lives of the hyenas!' Jean-Michel says smiling. He received death threats and was menaced with expulsion. 'They say that nowadays they call him Rimbaud or the terror of dogs,' Savouré joked in 1889.

I no longer know what to write down. My notebook is filling too quickly. My sentences are becoming briefer. My vision is growing dim. Already five o'clock in the morning and Jean-Michel is now telling me the history of the city, and its mixed Christian and Muslim neighbourhoods. The gentleness of the people. He evokes the possibility of a woman in Rimbaud's life, a young Argoba who lived in a house organised by Djami. Soothing news. Even if the letters mention nothing of the sort, Jean-Michel has come to this conclusion by putting new random elements together; he found the photograph of another young woman, an Abyssinian draped in a white *gabi* – Mariam maybe, met in Tadjura, a silver cross on her forehead – then traces of her sister established in Aden. The resemblance is eerie. The smiles enigmatic. Descendants then? Rimbaud juniors with the visage of the rebel, maybe in Tadjura itself, where that face glimpsed in the shadows had struck me. 'Everything is possible,' Jean-Michel answers mysteriously. Daybreak is close and a cup full of water is being passed around so we can blow upon it for the curing of the ill. The women are returning and they invite us to supper. Not with them, alas, as I would have liked to wrap myself in their skirts, but in a room reserved for the *misafir*, the guests. Chicken and rice at this time, yes, it is good. I chew slowly. We wash our hands, both before and after. As we return to our abode, drunk and haggard, we lose our way near the

Italian market. But there are no hyenas at this time and anyhow, even if my thoughts are somewhat disjointed, I somehow know I am no longer afraid, and that I shall return. Yes, I shall return.

Translated by YVES-MARIE STRANGER

Sébastien de Courtois is a freelance journalist based in Istanbul since 2009. After a memorable journey in South-Eastern Turkey at the end of the twentieth century, around Lake Van and the holy mountain of Tur Abdin, he decided to give up his career as a lawyer and to go back to his first passion: writing and travelling. Within a few years, after a PhD in History at the Sorbonne, he had become a specialist in Turkey and its various religious minorities. His latest books and articles focus on the question of Eastern Christians, following the paths of these lost communities from Iraq, Syria, Iran, on the Silk Road and in Eastern Africa, Ethiopia and Sudan. He also produces a bi-monthly programme on Spiritualities for French National Radio.

PHILIP MARSDEN

FROM *The Chains of Heaven: An Ethiopian Romance*, 2006

Bladdy Hawzien

Hiluf went off with Kidanu's son to continue the mule-hunt; I walked down to buy supplies in the market.

Onions . . . garlic . . . potatoes . . . *potatoes!* . . . chillies (chilli a day keeps the parasites at bay) . . .

'Farenj! Farenj!' A trail of boys was following me through the rows of women 'Give me pen!'

Tomatoes . . . no oranges . . . no papaya . . .

'Farenj! Money – money!'

Salt . . .

'Farenj – '

'HEY!' It was a voice from behind me. '*Hid!* Scram!'

A man was bending to pick up a rock. He made to throw it and the boys scattered.

'Jeez!' He chop-wiped the dust from his palms. 'They're like bladdy mozzies!' Fikre was Tigrayan but he spoke English with an Australian accent. 'Apologies!'

We crossed the square to a two-table café. A girl was sleeping on her hands at the counter and for a couple of hours Fikre and I talked – or rather he talked and I listened. Behind his odyssey crouched the horrors of recent Ethiopian history, but he delivered it like a vaude-ville entertainment – one part tragic to two parts comic. He kept reminding me of my friend Teklu, whom I'd travelled with all those years ago. Both had come of age during the revolution; both were Tigrayan – Fikre was visiting his parents in his home town of Hawzien; Teklu had been born near Adwa. Fikre fled Mengistu's Ethiopia by walking to Somalia, Teklu by walking to Kenya. Fikre ended up driving a taxi in Sydney, Teklu running a liquor store in Denver.

Fikre had returned with his savings to open a small hotel in Addis, and a few years earlier Teklu had, according to a cousin of his I'd met in Addis, done something similar. But it hadn't worked out. He had returned to Colorado. Fikre's hotel venture was also having problems. Two weeks ago, someone had lobbed a hand grenade into the bar. Ten people ended up in hospital.

'When I left Ethiopia, that sort of violence was only permitted by the government. Now anyone can do it. That's democracy!' Fikre gave a shoulder-shaking giggle. He had the rubbery movement of a born comedian. He did not so much tell his story as act it.

He was born and brought up in the 1960s. At that time Tigray was governed by Ras Mengesha and his court. 'These guys, they were like gods *[Fikre swells his chest]*. They were somewhere up there, in the clouds! And then suddenly *[whispers]*, suddenly we are hearing a song, a song about how these gods suck the blood of the people. We couldn't believe it – a song *against the gods.*'

One of the Derg's first acts when they came to power in 1974 was the *zemecha*. Fifty thousand students from high school and university were sent out to spread the good news of the revolution and set up peasants' associations. Fikre went to a camp in western Tigray.

'We were just getting used to this Derg when we started hearing about something else. Soon in the countryside everything – the wind, the trees, even the dogs – everything was whispering it – the TPLF! Suddenly we all had such a warm feeling for the TPLF, we were such big sympathisers! But secretly all of us were thinking *[drops voice]* – What the hell this new one? What the hell this bladdy *teepee-elef*?'

While Fikre was in the *zemecha* camp, his father died. He was given leave to return to Hawzien for a few days. When he went back to the camp he found it empty. 'Every one of those bladdy students had gone to fight for the rebels!' So he returned home – there he found his mother and all her neighbours celebrating.

'I see them all jumping about and singing and I am thinking *[cocks head]*, is father alive again or what? And my mother has an envelope from Addis Ababa! I have a place at bladdy uni! But when I saw the envelope, I cry and cry. They say, why sad, boy? I tell them, now who will look after mother? So then they fall quiet and all look at each other and start crying too *[loud wailing]*. All bladdy crying like a loada frightened sheep!'

'Did you go to university?'

'My mother say – go Fikre, I look after myself. When you have a top job – top job! *[straightens imaginary tie]* – then you send money to look after yer poor old mum. So I go to Addis, three days on a bus and I walk up and register at the biology faculty. In the faculty toilets, they have graffiti and I look closely at it and suddenly I am feeling at home! It reads: *TPLF are the only Real Marxists!* Didn't know what the hell it meant but I like the way it sounded. So I found the other Tigrayans and we wrote it in every damn place we could.

'At night the soldiers began to visit the dormitories. They wake us Tigrayans, one by one. I am lying in the bed *[drops voice]* hearing the soldiers and thinking it is me now. Is it me now, and if it isn't me now will it be me tomorrow? So I enrol at the Pedagogical College in Bahir Dar and escape up there.'

Fikre leaned forward to drink his coffee.

'So what happens in Bahir Dar? *[feigns bewilderment]* What happens? The bladdy terror comes to Bahir Dar's all!

'Yes, yes. They used to have this damn thing. *Magalata*, they call it – revolutionary council confession. They call all together and everyone has to confess and it is a very good thing they say because after confession everyone feels so damn clean and nice. So they point the guns at us and say – What have you done! They go down the line and I know to say nothing but some of the others said, Well, I did see a pamphlet or I did once listen to this man talking . . . Those ones were taken . . . You know what? One of those guys from Bahir Dar I saw last year. He was on the street in Addis. He was nothing, just a crazy beggar. They beat him so badly he went crazy. Is he alive now or dead, I dunno . . . '

Fikre looked away and for the first time I saw a sadness cross his face.

'I graduate from that institute and apply for a job. When I saw the list, I had been sent to Sidamo, Sidamo! Sidamo is no bladdy good! Sidamo is too far from the border. Beside me is a man from Sidamo and the list says he must go to Alemayu College in Harar but of course he would rather be in Sidamo. So, we just swap round! *[crosses hands]* At the college, I am quiet, I am a good student. No one knows I am from Tigray and I am just waiting, waiting for the chance to escape!

'That is all damn fine but who should come to the college? *[throws up hands in despair]* Only a bladdy singing group from Tigray! And of course because I'm Tigrayan I had to put my arms around them and hug them. They were good Tigrayans now and went round all the places singing songs about workers and what-have-you. When they go up on stage they say there are still people around who are afflicted with "narrow thinking". Even in this room there is someone with narrow thinking. Someone here wants to do *magalata* – he wants to confess . . . I just kept mum but after that I knew I had to be quick.

'I went to see the right people and those people knew the right people who could help me reach the Somali border. And one Monday I slip from the college and go down to Jijiga – and I wait, and I wait . . . and the damn bladdy man doesn't turn up! What can I do? If I return to the college, the cadre will smell me *[sniffs]* – the cadre knows how to sniff well and he knows how escape smells. But I am a stranger in Jijiga and they have their own cadres there spotting strangers. Well I go back to the college and luckily that cadre is away in Addis. Next time I go to Jijiga I make sure it is on the weekend so I can return to college if it doesn't work.

'But there is the man! And he gives me Somali robe and Somali turban and we leave the town. There is a camel behind me and a camel in front and we are walking across the desert, we are walking for days . . . walking . . . walking *[bobs head in slow, camel-like fashion]*. And I am thinking each step, each damn step is taking me further from bladdy Mengistu!'

Philip Marsden is the award-winning author of a number of works of travel, fiction and history, including *The Crossing Place: A Journey Among the Armenians*, *The Bronski House*, *The Spirit-Wrestlers*, *The Chains of Heaven*, *The Barefoot Emperor*, *The Levelling Sea and Rising Ground*. He is a fellow of the Royal Society of Literature and his work has been translated into more than a dozen languages. He lives in Cornwall with his family and a number of boats.

CHARLIE WALKER

FROM Charliewalkerexplore.co.uk, 2013

A Cycle in the Park

At this point some survival instinct kicked in and I found myself fighting my way to standing, swinging around wildly and unleashing a primordial roar; a war cry both enraged and terrified. The people (mostly boys and young men) fell back into a stunned silence.

I gingerly worked my way through the crowds, receiving the odd slap or thump for my troubles, and rushed out the other side of town. Darkness was falling and I was frightened of the atmosphere of rapidly rising hysteria. It was time I got off the road, hidden among the bushes and into my tent. However, the road was busy with people coming and going. There was no chance I could slip away unseen, even in the failing light, as people were continually shouting at me, shattering my cover.

Night arrived and still nowhere to hide. The 'super moon' (14% larger, 30% brighter full moon caused by elliptical orbit) rose in the east, illuminating the land. It immediately seemed forbidding to me. There was madness in the air and my uneasiness grew as I passed through a small village every mile or so with a knot of people engaged in ever more frenzied celebrations. I kept as low a profile as possible while edging through these wildly pulsing crowds and managed to stoically accept the occasional blows that landed on me.

In one of these small villages a particularly large crowd of about 200 people saw me coming, illuminated by a brief flash of motorbike headlights. There was no way around so I put on a polite smile and tried to ease a passage through the tight barrier of pungent-smelling bodies.

From here things happened quickly. The crowd suddenly flared into a mob and closed in on me. I was pulled from my bike and pushed to the ground. I think it must have been only about 15 or 20 seconds that I was cowering in the foetal position while people desperately jostled to land a blow on me. Strangely it seemed that most of the hits were slaps rather than punches or kicks and I think I was saved by the disabling closeness of the crowd preventing any well-aimed or particularly hard knocks.

Standing alone in a small clearing with hot-blooded aggression all around me, I had an instant to make a decision. My bike lay nearby and amazingly unplundered. I picked it up, and trying to retain an air of authority and dangerous unpredictability, I began wheeling it at the wall of uncertain people. A single old man with a stick was trying to clear a path on my behalf. To my relief and surprise the wall gave way and a narrow passage appeared; a gauntlet in which I didn't want to linger.

I mounted and started riding but only got a yard or two before two young boys ran forward and spat at me, one in my face. This seemed to unstop the temporarily corked bottle of mob anger. The hail of rocks and shoes began. I kicked hard on the pedals and made my escape with hard objects bouncing off my back and shoulders.

I suddenly found myself riding along and with the frantic roar fading fast behind me. My hands were shaking and adrenalin was streaming though me. I dashed on a mile or so with ears closed and very suddenly veered down the bank and between two bushes. There, with heartbeats drumming in my ears, I listened for any shouts but heard none. I pushed through some more bushes and came out in a cornfield with a tree in the middle. Under the tree, and in the shockingly stark moonlight, I put up my tent with trembling hands and tumbled in. I broke into pathetic sobs for a while. This catharsis completed, I tried to analyse what had occurred. I could surmise no further than the incident being the result of over-excitement, the liberating mob anonymity of darkness, and plain racism.

From then on I was mentally out of Ethiopia. My patience was truly at an end. For two days on the road I looked dead ahead, listened to music, and largely ignored the world around me. I worried what might happen if I was further provoked. Sure enough, on a dirt road a boy threw a stone that hit my side. Quick as a flash, I'd dropped my bike, scooped up a small pebble and hurled it at the running twelve-year-old. It clipped his heel and he went down hard. I waited until I saw him get up before riding on feeling cold and remorseless. I am now ashamed of what I did: he was only one boy with one stone; but so, in fairness, was I.

To my relief, I caught up with the Scots and two couples in 4x4s that I'd also met in Addis and we camped together on a hilltop in a small town called Konso overlooking the Rift Valley. A night of good company refreshed me and I set out on the road again with slightly restored confidence.

It was a long descent into the valley and the heat rose accordingly. A young girl hurled a rock at me from about two metres away as I raced downhill. It struck my head and my speed worsened the impact but I retained balance on the bike and didn't really register what had happened. My fury was spent. I rode on while a lump rose on my head.

Leaving the tarmac and turning onto a dusty track, I soon found myself in sparsely inhabited land with very traditional tribespeople. Bodies decorated with colourful beads and hair fashioned with butter into thick coils, these people wander mostly naked through the inhospitably hot and dry bush with their herds (and often AK47s). They seemed afraid of me and would scatter into the trees when they saw me coming. Fearful faces would peer through leaves but this suited me down to the ground. At last I had peace and could enjoy the hard toil of the sandy, rocky track. I could feel the exasperation draining from me.

In Turmi I caught up with the little motorised convoy of tourists again and we spent a pleasant day camped in the cool shade of fecund mango trees. We went to market and the seven of us bought a goat to slaughter and cook for dinner.

A ten-puncture ride (due mostly to a knackered tyre) brought me to Omerate where I woke the immigration official and got stamped out of Ethiopia. I spent my last pittance of Ethiopian money on a dugout canoe to carry me across the Omo river and into no-man's-land. Here I had a little glimpse of the indigenous tribes for which Southern Ethiopia is famous but I was soon on a mud track through utter wilderness.

I reflected on my unique experience in Ethiopia: a country with vibrant cities and a rich history. I would go back, I honestly would, and I would advise other people to visit – but not on a bicycle. I saw relatively small pockets of the large country and didn't get to the high Simien mountain range in the north or the baking Danakil Depression in the East. I didn't see the famous monolithic churches at Lalibela. The country genuinely has a lot to offer.

Eventually I arrived at a thin rope slung limply across the path. Beside it, under a sheet of corrugated metal, was Peter; a lonely Kenyan borderguard. I made us tea while we talked. He asked about Ethiopia and seemed unsurprised by the hostility but sympathetic towards me.

'Come and stand over here, opposite me. OK? Now, you see those mountains in the distance over there?'

'Yes.'

'They are in South Sudan. And everything to your right there – that is technically Ethiopia. Now, you see where your right foot is?'

'Yes.'

'Welcome to Kenya!'

In 2010 **Charlie Walker** set off by bicycle and returned four and a half years later with 43,000 miles behind him. He cycled through Europe, Asia and Africa documenting his experiences with photography and an award-winning blog. His journey included walking 1,000 miles solo across the Gobi desert and riding a horse 600 miles through the Mongolian steppe. In 2014 he descended a little-known tributary of the Congo River by dugout canoe, dodging crocodiles, hippos and rapids along the way. His writing and photography have appeared in publications such as *The Times*, the *Daily Express*, *Wanderlust* and *Sidetracked*. The Ethiopian leg of his journey proved quite a challenge, and perhaps cyclists should bear in mind that an early name for a bicycle in the country was *yeshaitan feras* – the Devil's horse . . .

AIDA EDEMARIAM

FROM the *Guardian*, 1 September 2007

A Short Trek in the Wollo Hills

I knew, when I was growing up in Addis Ababa, of the fabled places of the Ethiopian north, but except for Gondar, where I went a couple of times to visit my grandmother and to improve my somewhat wobbly Amharic, I had never seen them. I had heard of camping trips to the high, cold Simien mountains, explorations of monasteries on Lake Tana, but they were by expats: Mengistu Haile Mariam, who came to power in the Red Terror of 1975, was in the ascendant and at war with Eritrea, and the rest of us were subject to petrol rationing so tight there was only enough to go to school and to work on weekdays. In any case, the road to Lalibela, whose rock-hewn churches are called an eighth wonder of the world, was often impassable, and the lands around it, celebrated through the centuries for their beauty, riven with guerrilla warfare.

Last year, I returned to Ethiopia for only the second time in 13 years. I did it in careful stages, spending a day getting re-acquainted with Gondar, its unpaved back roads and crumbling castles, and a couple in Lalibela, where, hiring a guide, I began to encounter a country both foreign to me, and, in a visceral way, completely familiar.

The day I left Lalibela dawned clear and sunny, and by 10am I was being driven in a 4x4 into the towering mountain escarpments that ring the town by Mekedim. We were coming to the end of the small rains, but the stony terraced fields were dry. The centre of the 1984 famine, Sekota, was not far from here, and the area is always balanced on the edge of disaster. If there isn't enough rain, there is no food. At a seemingly random point Mekedim said, 'Stop: let's walk from here.' Minutes later, we saw why: the ground dropped away into a sudden vista of depth and wonder, jagged cliffs soaring down to valleys hundreds of metres below, to mountains upon mountains piling into the distance. The vast sky was punctuated by the grey shrouds of rain showers. They blew past like visitations, soaked everything and were gone. The setting sun shone through the rain; a rainbow began far below our feet and curved up towards us, then was doubled. Everything moved at such speed that just blinking revealed another configuration. Far below was a wide, empty riverbed.

Lightning forked on the horizon, and the temperature dropped precipitously. We may have been only 12 degrees or so above the equator, but Mequat Mariam is also 2,800m above sea level. During the day it's hot, but at night it can be truly, bone-chillingly cold. A fire was lit on the floor of the restaurant *tukul*, and we ate by the light of candles and kerosene lanterns. The cooks murmured and giggled in the corner, chopping onions for the next day. Food is bought in local markets, and the women carry our water on their backs, from springs an hour away. Tired and full, we picked our way carefully through the darkness to our beds.

The next day we set out along the lip of the escarpment. Travellers have for centuries been struck by how proud of being Ethiopian Ethiopians are; our guide Alem Misganew, 45, has little truck with this. 'Don't you hate it?' he asked me, when he discovered I'm half-Ethiopian. 'No, should I?' 'It's so poor, so hard to live in, it has made me bitter.' In a good year, he can harvest five quintals of wheat or barley, worth 210 birr each; in a bad year it can be only one. He chops wood, and walks two hours into town to sell it for five birr a bundle; he cares for other people's sheep. Illiterate himself, he has watched, with increasing frustration, his friends become teachers and policemen, earn more than him; now that he has four children, he's determined they will be educated.

We passed a man setting delicate string pheasant traps; women washing clothes in the suds of an indigenous plant, *indod*; we walked down sweet-smelling avenues of eucalyptus, stopped for a picnic lunch of *injera* (Ethiopian sourdough flatbread) and *shurro* (a sauce made from ground, spiced chickpeas), overlooking the rough valleys. 'That's where the guerrillas hid from Mengistu,' said Elsa matter-of-factly. 'He bombed them from the air.' I looked at the view with sudden, renewed interest. I grew up with reminders of the ongoing civil war, young men missing limbs, soldiers and guns and check-points; later, on the outskirts of Addis and Gondar, burned-out tanks, but I never really imagined the terrain in which the columns of conscripts died. The hills were a misty blue. The sound of dogs barking, roosters crowing, children yelling, carried for miles through the thin air.

A tribe of gelada baboons was silhouetted on the cliff, then scampered out of sight. We passed olive trees, staring longingly at their cool shade, picked our way through rocks and fragrant hillocks of wild thyme, around spiky aloe vera, cowpats. Men called across the valleys – a fox made off with a sheep in the night; beware. We passed a haughty shepherd who muttered to our guide, 'Don't let them get too used to our land.' We're not going to take it, we assured him, don't worry, but he seemed unconvinced.

Ethiopia, and especially rural Ethiopia, is extremely patriarchal; led by a beer-emboldened Mekedim, we discussed the government's new laws forbidding under-age marriage, and requiring Aids tests; quizzed one of the young cooks, singular in having rejected numerous marriage proposals in favour of going to school; talked, surprisingly freely, about domestic violence, which is in many of these places a norm rather than an exception; laughed delightedly at a ribald tale of a woman's revenge.

Driving back to Lalibela the next day, everyone was thoughtful. The fields looked as though they were strewn with the rubble of creation, un-tillable, but there were men out, ploughing them with patient oxen. Crops will grow around the stones.

Aida Edemariam grew up in Addis Ababa. She studied English literature at Oxford University and the University of Toronto and has worked as a journalist at *Harper's* magazine in New York and Toronto. She is a senior feature writer and editor for the *Guardian* and lives in Oxford.

SAMMY ASFAW

FROM *Sangaterra Sefer: The Neighbourhood of the Bull,* 2015

The Village of the Bull

He is still neat and wears the well-cut suits he bought in the Lagar *Ambassador* shop years ago. Looking sharp. But still: I'm getting on, he thinks. I'm no young buck anymore. Right on the spot he is now looking at stood the Tseday Hotel – its food! Its hourly rooms! He cannot recall how many girls he took to the Tseday, and to the neighbouring Quara, Tinsaye and Martha Hotels. Neither can he tell how many nights he spent in the fleshpots of Sengaterra's Arake Bets – back when a shot cost forty-five cents. He shivers a little. It is midday, but yesterday's pleasure dome of tin and mud lies in the shadow of the blue-glass highrise being erected in front of the National Theatre.

Some people called the village *louche* (street argot was full of French in those days. Jazz words too: Jiving. Flipping. Freakiiie!) but he breathed and lived Sangaterra – the Neighbourhood of the Bull – for a good half-century. He was your quintessential Addis Ababa *'y'arada lidj'* (a streetwise kid, the proverbial cool cat in the vernacular of the day). And he excelled in all the tricks of the game. You name it: gambling on *carambola*, the latest trends in burglary and theft, and dating and flirting *legerdemain* too. He spent his money like a millionaire one day, only to then survive with a fistful of coins for weeks on end. He was the neighbourhood's love guru, and a go-to negotiator for people who had lost irreplaceable IDs, along with their wallets and backpacks. He was respected and looked up to in those days. A chief organiser behind the village's largest *ekub*, the saving club.

But now his whole neighbourhood is turning into a pile of rubble. The place he was born in, his entire world – the throbbing heart of Addis. The village where he rubbed shoulders with the nation's worthies. With its judges and doctors; engineers and authors; thieves, chancers, coolies and journalists. They all congregated here, in the Neighbourhood of the Bull; in its bars, its merry, makeshift hotels, nameless whorehouses and mud, tin and plywood *Arake Bets.*

Sangaterra was right in the thick of things, buttressed by venerable institutions such as the Ethiopia, the Ras, the Harambee and Wabi Shebelle hotels. A sea of tin given an air of respectability by the twin buildings of the ministries of health and culture up the hill; kept safe by the ministry of defence on its eastern flank; banked upon by the head offices of the national and commercial banks of Ethiopia, just a stone's throw away. The biggest referral hospital in the country – *Tikur Anbessa* or *Black Lion* – and The Addis Ababa Commercial College, closed the huddled ring around the neighbourhood. Sangaterra's alleyways could provide expertise on any subject, at any time of day or night. From bookworms versed in the complete works of Vladimir Ilyich, to know-how in catering to the specialist needs of military officers of the highest rank, needs they'd picked up in communist, but jolly, Cuba –'Caramba, I blame Cuba!' From lunch-break quickie *khat* sessions to late-night accommodation paid for by the hour, Sengaterra's modest wattle and daub houses could provide anything the human heart may possibly desire – and then some.

Back in those days, he shared his lunch break *khat* chats with journalists from Ethiopian Radio Television and Radio Fana. He spent his chewing sessions in small bookshops, with authors and poets, pickpockets and crazies, sharing expertise and life philosophies (Marcus Aurelius, the pickpocketing expertise of Charles Dickens in *Oliver Twist* . . . etc, etc). Right now, he is looking for a spot to sit and chew on the muddy ruins of Mama Bruce's *Arake Bet*. He had spent countless nights in that house. Counted down the Ethiopian millennium there with his best friend in fact ('Travel to Ethiopia and be seven years younger!') – friend who had gone to the US two years earlier, and come back to celebrate the big day with his family in the homeland. He recalls how they discussed, for old time's sake, how an elderly matron from Gojjam had ended up being called Bruce (it goes like this: one night a drunkard refuses to pay up his handful of cents. But the portly owner kicks the drunk with a stylish move that knocks him for six. There and then after – for all eternity – Bruce Lee became the matron's name and the moniker of her *Arake Bet!*). It has become a drunken ritual to tell this story among Sangaterra revellers. His friend in turn waxed lyrical about the place where he now lives – Phoenix, Arizona. He told him how the city was named after a bird from Chinese mythology that bursts into flames and dies – to be reborn from the ashes, again and again.

Sangaterra witnessed the good and the bad times that shook Addis Ababa and the nation as a whole. From the aborted coup d'état of Mengistu Neway in 1961 to the successful toppling of Haile Selassie in 1974, and the drab but crimson rule of the Derg military regime. The new revolutionary administrative structure for the regions, and the zones and kebeles of the metropolis; the revolution itself, and its tenth anniversary – they were all cooked up and plotted in this very corner, the capital's intellectual *plaque tournante*. Sangaterra applauded the downfall of the mighty Derg when it came; welcomed in the EPRDF's Fuzzy-Wuzzies. It wryly observed its Eritrean residents being evicted to their new country. And it witnessed the great celebrations for the millennium. A new era for Ethiopia, for Addis Ababa, they called it, a *Renaissance*. The village saw a lot. Its residents lived in harmony, sharing their family disputes through thin walls, as well as their communal lavatory blocks and the courtyards where they took turns to dry their peppers and grains. Lending each other support to finance funerals, weddings, birthdays and graduation ceremonies. Sangaterra shed tears of sadness in times of turmoil and tears of joy when the good times seemed to return. Bellowed political slogans when they were enjoined to, and with suitable enthusiasm too: 'Land to the Tiller!' 'Vive la Renaissance!'

The neighbourhood's children – *yesangaterra lidjoch* – are particularly known for their resourcefulness. They are now scattered all over the world. They have travelled on foot, to Libya and Egypt, and sailed on rubber dinghies to Sicily and Greece, and made it through five different countries of Europe to reach Sweden or Frankfurt. They have left for Arab countries as maids and built restaurant and beauty parlour chains in these wealthy desert cities.

He now finds a spot on the earthen midden of Bruce Lee and sits down on a charred eucalyptus beam. His back has started aching of late. He has also started to wear reading glasses and puts on thick t-shirts underneath his shirt because he constantly feels the cold gnawing at his bones. What a kick the past can deliver, Bruce! He chuckles to himself. The three-bedroom condo given to him as compensation for his house in Sangaterra was sold long ago. He bought a single room with the proceeds, one for which he now receives the rent at the end of each month. He lives in a tiny house near Arat Kilo in a village similar to this. It too has lost its children to the desert routes, and its communal fabric to urban renewal. The only difference is that the village is being brought down to be rebuilt as a modern residential zone. The neighbourhood is going to revive from its ashes with new people and a new lifestyle. Himself, he doesn't know if he can get back on his feet again – get his mojo back. He doubts *he* can rise from the ashes again. He is more old bull than bullish as he thoughtfully munches his *beleche* [a kind of *khat*].

Sammy Asfaw (1977–) is a translator, writer and teacher. He was born in Sangaterra Sefer.

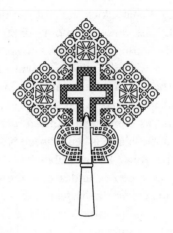

6

UTHIOPIA

Introduction

'Will your grace command me any service to the world's end? I will go on the slightest errand now to the Antipodes that you can devise to send me on: I will fetch a tooth-picker from the furthest inch of Asia: bring you the length of Prester John's foot . . . '

Much Ado About Nothing, William Shakespeare

Utopia *An imagined place or state of things in which everything is perfect. The word was first used in the book* Utopia *(1516) by Sir Thomas More. Synonyms: Garden of Eden, Paradise, Heaven on Earth, Shangri-La, Elysium.*

Ethiopia *A republic in north-eastern Africa close to the Red Sea; formerly called Abyssinia. In classical antiquity the term was loosely applied to all of the lands beyond southern Egypt.*

Uthiopia *A portmanteau word, a toponym for the land of Prester John, John de Mandeville, & the blood line of Solomon, where the lion of Juda roams and the troglodytes of Herodotus now make their abode in the condominiums of Menelik's booming capital.*

Ethiopia is etched on to the map first by the Greeks as a suitably remote location for the holiday resort of the gods, a place where the monster Cetus – that some see as the precursor of Saint George's dragon – devours Andromeda while her parents, King Cepheus and Queen Cassiopeia of Ethiopia, can do nothing but look on. Perseus delivers her, but the princess, instead of sailing happily ever after over the horizon with her Greek hero, is cast into the skies together with her mother for comparing their beauty to the goddesses'. Their fate? To be stared at for all eternity in the night sky as the Andromeda and Cassiopeia constellations – beautiful as well as remote and cold.

As we saw from the early Greek and Byzantine texts, Ethiopia is at first the country of the most remote of men, of deserts inhabited by troglodytes and the odd dog-headed human beast or monopodi. The Ethiopians take part in the siege of Troy, and some see in the Medusa head of serpents a fantastical depiction of the braided hair of an Ethiopian woman. In Egypt, a bas-relief portrays the Land of Punt as a bountiful source of elephants, precious gems and gold. Heliodorus, the first Greek novelist, witnesses a flight of fancy with pirate ships, Ethiopian princes and princesses. Texts such as the Periplus of the Red Sea, Byzantine ambassadorial accounts, Pliny and Rufinus and other church texts begin to sketch an only slightly less fantastical portrait of what has become the empire of Axum – recognised as the equal of Rome and Persia in a Manichaean fragment. Byzantium and Axum, allies in war, and in religion upon the conversion of the latter to Christianity, seem to be marching in military and spiritual lockstep, with their concerted effort to attack and disrupt Persian affairs in Southern Arabia. The invasion and settling of Yemen, during which the viceroy sent by the Axumite king quickly sets up his own court, is of short duration. The Axumites build a church in Sa'ana – Al-Eklis, of which you can still see the foundations today – and make an ill-advised attempt to invade Mecca, perhaps to redirect trade towards Sa'ana, using war elephants. This is recorded by the Holy Koran in Surat 105 Al-Fil, The Elephant, which also relates how the Axumites are routed by a huge flock of stone-throwing birds.

After the rise of Islam, Axum retreats from the Red Sea – although there are accounts of Axumite 'pirates' seizing Jedda in the eighth century – and moves inland and turns inward, even if there will be no major clash with the Muslims, or attempt to wage jihad until much later on, in the sixteenth century. Between the rise of Islam in the sixth century, and the founding of the Agew stronghold of Lalibela, except for a few hazy accounts, there are no travellers' tales, no ambassadorial accounts, no royal chronicles, to help explain the transformation of an antique Christian empire with a recent pagan past, into the staunchly Christian mountain kingdom that we find firmly clinging to a rockside in the twelfth century. There is no known account of what transpired in these lands from the fall of Axum to the rise of Lalibela – a blank slate from at least the eighth to the thirteenth centuries – an incredible six hundred years, during which kingdoms fell and rose, kings came and went, and Axum became something other, which would one day be called Abyssinia and later give birth to Ethiopia.

It is during this long period – let us call it Uthiopia – that myths are forged, which shed light on how the country understands and sees itself today, and what will become modern Ethiopia takes root. A 'Jewish' queen, named Judith, sacks Axum and forces the inhabitants to flee to the mountains of Lasta (a true account or a symbolic story?). The Agew, who speak a Cushitic tongue, carve out of the rock the churches of Roha, later renamed Lalibela. They are known as the Zagwe dynasty and as such, are an illegitimate interlude, before the rightful heirs of Solomon's line, who had been hiding out all the while in the kingdom of Amhara to the west, centred on Lake Haik and its famous monastery, take back what was rightly theirs. A warlord is crowned as Amda Tsion, Pillar of Zion, and an alliance forged with the church will last another seven hundred years. To the kings go the earthly spoils, but to the church more than enough is left over, and the kingdom becomes an example of a monastic society, in which vast resources are given over to the clergy. A powerful missionary movement is initiated, from the Monastery of Haik, by Tekle Haymanot, the well-named Plant of the Faith, and as the kingdom moves south and westward, the Church moves too, pros-elytising and building monasteries and churches in new lands. Saints abound: Tekle Haymanot himself stands on one leg for seven years, a feat which seems – after reading Francisco Alvarez' accounts of the mortifications monks inflict upon themselves, such as spending whole days immersed in water up to their chins – quite possible.

Most importantly, the clergy will write down/translate/reinterpret from Arabic texts the Fetah Negast, the Law of Kings, and the Kibre Negast, the Glory of Kings, in which Sheba and Solomon's story, and their link to the lineage of Amda Tsion, is revealed and proclaimed. We also find here the first mention of the Ark of the Covenant, and of its location in Ethiopia, another symbolic transfer, which places Ethiopia under the protection of God and makes them his newly anointed people. Ethiopia is the new Israel – a land of milk and honey – and its lands, including newly acquired territories and peoples, can partake in this promised land, if they assimilate and internalise this manifest destiny. And indeed, in Lalibela and in Gojam, not that long ago Agew-speaking territories, you would be hard pressed to find someone today who does not speak Amharic, or does not recognise – as an interiorised guide – the story, the founding myth, of Saba and Solomon.

At the same time as this myth making – this creation of modern Ethiopia from old sources – was underway, European writers took advantage of the blank slate that Ethiopia had become, and drew on it their own myths, starting with Prester John. Luis de Urreta thus has the king of Ethiopia live on a mountain of gold and lapis lazuli, which contains a library with all the books ever written, a story that could have been written by Borges, but Borges, alas, only makes a passing, oblique reference to 'Ethiopian troglodytes' in his short story *The Immortal*, in which the spring of eternal life and the spring of death are found, the former somewhere in the deserts of Nubia, the latter near a port on the Eritrean coast. Prester John himself seems to be the creation of a European scribe, eager to dispel the notion spread by El-Dani of there being a Jewish kingdom beyond Ghion, in Africa. Marco Polo talks of the 'numerous cavalry of the king of Ethiopia' before the Portuguese, seeking this fictional character, stumble upon the route to the Indies, and go on to save the Abyssinian Christian Kingdom – and the ruler they will go on calling the Prester until the mid sixteenth century – thus changing the course of history by means of their reading of a fictional text.

In Coleridge's 'Kubla Khan', on his Mount Abora, where an Abyssinian Maid on her Dulcimer sang, in Milton's *Paradise Lost*, and in Doctor Johnson's *Rasselas*, it seems that the old land of Ethiopia, burnt by the sun, and ploughed repeatedly for two thousand years till worn out, is a giant palimpsest upon which first the Greeks, then the inhabitants themselves and later everybody else, has been playing a vast geographical textual, Borgesian game. In Ethiopia – as in the Argentine writer's story in which a despot asks for a map to the scale of 1:1 to be made – a vast army of scribes, fictioneers and makers of true history have together conspired to build a fantastical, but real, country out of the disparate elements of a library and a few acres of land. In this interpretation, Luis de Urreta's limitless library is indeed a reality – as is Ethiopia herself. And today, the Zara Yacob of the video game *Civilisation IV*, the Prester John of Marvel Comics, and even Star Trek's own Grand Nagus – and the evil, mercantile Ferengi – show that the myth is alive and well. Prester John continues to boldly go where no myth has gone before.

John, Priest by the Almighty power of God and the Might of our Lord Jesus Christ, King of Kings and Lord of Lords, to his friend Emanuel, prince of Constantinople, greeting, wishing him health, prosperity, and the continuance of Divine favour.

Our Majesty has been informed that you hold our Excellency in love and that the report of our greatness has reached you. Moreover, we have heard through our treasurer that you have been pleased to send to us some objects of art and interest that our Exaltedness might be gratified thereby. Being human, I have received it in good part, and we have ordered our treasurer to send you some of our articles in return [. . .]

Should you desire to learn the greatness and excellency of our Exaltedness and of the land subject to our sceptre, then hear and believe: I, Presbyter Johannes, the Lord of Lords, surpass all under heaven in virtue, in riches, and in power; seventy-two kings pay us tribute [. . .] In the three Indies our Magnificence rules, and our land extends beyond India, where rests the body of the holy apostle Thomas; it reaches towards the sunrise over the wastes, and it trends toward deserted Babylon near the Tower of Babel. Seventy-two provinces, of which only a few are Christian, serve us. Each has its own king, but all are tributary to us.

Our land is the home of elephants, dromedaries, camels, crocodiles, meta-collinarum, cametennus, tensevetes, wild asses, white and red lions, white bears, white merules, crickets, griffins, tigers, lamias, hyenas, wild horses, wild oxen, and wild men – men with horns, one-eyed men, men with eyes before and behind, centaurs, fauns, satyrs, pygmies, forty-ell-high giants, cyclopses, and similar women. It is the home, too, of the phoenix and of nearly all living animals. We have some people subject to us who feed on the flesh of men and of prematurely born animals, and who never fear death. When any of these people die, their friends and relations eat him ravenously, for they regard it as a main duty to munch human flesh. Their names are Gog, Magog, Anie, Agit, Azenach, Fommeperi, Befari, Conei-Samante, Agrimandri, Vintefolei, Casbei, and Alanei. These and similar nations were shut in behind lofty mountains by Alexander the Great, towards the north. We lead them at our pleasure against our foes, and neither man nor beast is left undevoured, if our Majesty gives the requisite permission. And when all our foes are eaten, then we return with our hosts home again. These accursed fifteen nations will burst forth from the four quarters of the earth at the end of the world, in the times of the Antichrist, and overrun all the abodes of the Saints as well as the great city Rome, which, by the way, we are prepared to give to our son who will be born, along with all Italy, Germany, the two Gauls, Britain, and Scotland. We shall also give him Spain and all of the land as far as the icy sea. The nations to which I have alluded, according to the words of the prophet, shall not stand in the judgment on account of their offensive practices, but will be consumed to ashes by a fire which will fall on them from heaven.

Our land streams with honey and is overflowing with milk. In one region grows no poisonous herd, nor does a querulous frog ever quack in it; no scorpion exists, nor does the serpent glide amongst the grass, nor can any poisonous animals exist in it or injure anyone.

Among the heathen flows, through a certain province, the River Indus; encircling Paradise, it spreads its arms in manifold windings through the entire province. Here are found the emeralds, sapphires, carbuncles, topazes, chrysolites, onyxes, beryls, sardius, and other costly stones. Here grows the plant Assidos which, when worn by anyone, protects him from the evil spirit, forcing it to state its business and name; consequently the foul spirits keep out of the way there. In a certain land subject to us all kinds of pepper is gathered and is exchanged for corn and bread, leather and cloth [. . .] At the foot of Mount Olympus bubbles up a spring which changes its flavour hour by hour, night and day, and the spring is scarcely three days' journey from Paradise, out of which Adam was driven. If anyone has tasted thrice of the fountain, from that day he will feel no fatigue, but will, as long as he lives, be as a man of thirty years. Here are found the small stones called Nudiosi which, if borne about the body, prevent the sight from waxing feeble and restore it where it is lost. The more the stone is looked at, the keener becomes the sight. In our territory is a certain waterless sea consisting of tumbling billows of sand never at rest. None have crossed this sea; it lacks water altogether, yet fish of various kinds are cast up upon the beach, very tasty, and the like are nowhere else to be seen. Three days' journey from this sea are mountains from which rolls down a stony, waterless river which opens into the sandy sea. As soon as the stream reaches the sea, its stones vanish in it and are never seen again. As long as the river is in motion, it cannot be crossed; only four days a week is it possible to traverse it. Between the sandy sea and the said mountains, in a certain plain, is a fountain of singular virtue which purges Christians and would-be Christians from all transgressions. The water stands four inches high in a hollow stone shaped like a mussel shell. Two saintly old men watch by it and ask the comers whether they are Christians or are about to become Christians, then whether they desire healing with all their hearts. If they have answered well, they are bidden to lay aside their clothes and to step into the mussel. If what they said be true, then the water begins to rise and gush over their heads; thrice does the water thus lift itself, and everyone who has entered the mussel leaves it cured of every complaint.

Near the wilderness trickles between barren mountains a sub-terranean rill which can only by chance be reached, for only occasionally the earth gapes, and he who would descend must do it with precipitation, ere the earth closes again. All that is gathered under the ground there is gem and precious stone. The brook pours into another river and the inhabitants of the neighbourhood obtain thence abundance of precious stones. Yet they never venture to sell them without having first offered them to us for our private use. Should we decline them, they are at liberty to dispose of them to strangers. Boys there are trained to remain three or four days under the water, diving after the stones.

Beyond the stone river are the ten tribes of Israel which, though subject to their own kings, are, for all that, tributary to our Majesty. In

one of our lands, a highland, are worms called salamanders. These
worms can only live in fire, and they build cocoons like silk-worms
which are unwound by the ladies of our palace and spun into cloth
and dresses which are worn by our Exaltedness. These dresses, in
order to be cleaned and washed, are cast into flames [. . .] When we
go to war, we have fourteen golden and bejewelled crosses borne
before us instead of banners. Each of these crosses is followed by
ten thousand horsemen and one hundred thousand foot soldiers,
fully armed, without reckoning those in charge of the luggage and
provision.

When we ride abroad plainly we have a wooden, unadorned cross
without gold or gems about it, borne before us in order that we
meditate on the sufferings of our Lord Jesus Christ; also a golden
bowl filled with earth to remind us of that whence we sprung and that
to which we must return; but besides these there is borne a silver bowl
full of gold as a token to all that we are the Lord of Lords.

All riches, such as are upon the world, our Magnificence possesses
in superabundance. With us, no one lies, for he who speaks a lie is
thenceforth regarded as dead; he is no more thought of or honoured
by us. No vice is tolerated by us. Every year we undertake a pilgrimage,
with retinue of war, to the body of the holy prophet Daniel which is
near the desolated site of Babylon. In our realm fishes are caught, the
blood of which dyes purple. The Amazons and the Brahmins are
subject to us. The palace in which our Super-eminency resides is built
after the pattern of the castle built by the Apostle Thomas for the
Indian king Gundoforus. Ceilings, joists, and architrave are of Sethym
wood, the roof ebony, which can never catch fire. Over the gable
of the palace are, at the extremities, two golden apples, in each of
which are two carbuncles, so that the gold may shine by day and the
carbuncles by night. The greater gates of the palace are of sardius with
the horn of the horned snake inwrought so that no one can bring
poison within.

The other portals are of ebony; the windows are of crystal; the
tables are partly of gold, partly of amethyst; the columns supporting
the tables are partly of ivory, partly of amethyst. The court in which
we watch the jousting is floored with onyx in order to increase the

courage of the combatants. In the palace at night, nothing is burned for light, but wicks supplied with balsam [. . .] Before our palace stands a mirror, the ascent to which consists of five and twenty steps of porphyry and serpintine [. . .] This mirror is guarded day and night by three thousand men. We look therein and behold all that is taking place in every province and region subject to our sceptre.

Seven kings wait upon us monthly, in turn, with sixty-two dukes, two hundred and fifty-six counts and marquises. Twelve archbishops sit at table with us on our right and twenty bishops on the left, besides the patriarch of St Thomas, the Sarmatian Protopope, and the Archpope of Susa [. . .] Our lord high steward is a primate and king, our cup-bearer is an archbishop and king, our chamberlain a bishop and king, and our marshal a king and abbot.

ANONYMOUS

FROM *Kebre Negast*, or *Glory of Kings*, twelfth–fourteenth century

Concerning the king of Ethiopia and how he returned to his country

And the king of Ethiopia returned to his country with great joy and gladness; and marching along with their songs, and their pipes, and their wagons, like an army of heavenly beings, the Ethiopians arrived from Jerusalem at the city of Wakerom in a single day. And they sent messengers by ship to announce [their arrival] to Makeda, the queen of Ethiopia, and to report to her how they found every good thing, and how her son had become king, and how they had brought the heavenly Zion. And she caused all this glorious news to be spread abroad, and she made a herald to go round about in all the country that was subject unto her, ordering the people to meet her son and more particularly the heavenly Zion, the Tabernacle of the God of Israel. And they blew horns before her, and all the people of Ethiopia rejoiced, from the least to the greatest, men as well as women; and the soldiers rose up with her to meet their king. And she came to the city of the Government, which is the chief city of the kingdom of Ethiopia; now in later times this [city] became the chief city of the Christians of Ethiopia. And in it she caused to be prepared innumerable perfumes from India, and from Balte to Galtet, and from 'Alsafu to 'Azazat, and had them brought together there. And her son came by the 'Azyaba road to Wakerom, and he came forth to Masas, and ascended to Bur, and arrived at the city of the Government, the capital [city] of Ethiopia, which the queen herself had built and called 'Dabra Makeda' after her own name.

Concerning the rejoicing of queen Makeda

And David the King came with great pomp unto his mother's city, and then he saw in the height the heavenly Zion sending forth light

like the sun. And when the queen saw this she gave thanks unto the
God of Israel, and praised Him. And she bowed low, and smote her
breast, and [then] threw up her head and gazed into the heavens, and
thanked her Creator; and she clapped her hands together, and sent
forth shouts of laughter from her mouth, and danced on the ground
with her feet; and she adorned her whole body with joy and gladness
with the fullest will of inward mind. And what shall I say of the
rejoicing which took place then in the country of Ethiopia, and of
the joy of the people, both of man and beast, from the least to the
greatest, and of both women and men? And pavilions and tents were
placed at the foot of Dabra Makeda on the flat plain by the side of
good water, and they slaughtered thirty-two thousand stalled oxen
and bulls. And they set Zion upon the fortress of Dabra Makeda, and
made ready for her three hundred guards who wielded swords to
watch over the pavilion of Zion, together with her own men and her
nobles, the mighty men of Israel. And her own guards were three
hundred men who bore swords, and in addition to these her son
David had seven hundred [guards]. And they rejoiced exceedingly
with great glory and pleasure [being arrayed] in fine apparel, for the
kingdom was directed by her from the Sea of 'Aleba to the Sea of
'Oseka, and everyone obeyed her command. And she had exceedingly
great honour and riches; none before her ever had the like, and none
after her shall ever have the like. In those days Solomon was King in
Jerusalem, and Makeda was queen in Jerusalem, and Makeda was
queen in Ethiopia. Unto both of them were given wisdom, glory,
riches, graciousness, understanding, eloquence, and intelligence. And
gold and silver were held as cheaply as brass, and rich stuffs wherein
gold was woven were as common as linen garments, and the cattle and
the horses were innumerable.

How queen Makeda made her son king

And on the third day Makeda delivered to her son seventeen
thousand and seven hundred chosen horses, which were to watch the
army of the enemy, and would again plunder the cities of the enemy,
and seven thousand and seven hundred mares that had borne foals,

and one thousand female mules, and seven hundred chosen mules, and apparel of honour, gold and silver measured by the *gomor*, and measured by the *kor*, some six and some seven, and she delivered over to her son everything that was his by law, and all the throne of her kingdom.

How the nobles and governors of Ethiopia took the oath

And the queen said unto her nobles: 'Speak you now, and swear you by the heavenly Zion that you will not make women queens or set them upon the throne of the kingdom of Ethiopia, and that no one except the male seed of David, the son of Solomon the king, shall ever reign over Ethiopia, and that you will never make women queens.' And all the nobles of the king's house swore, and the governors, and the councillors, and the administrators.

HELIODORUS OF EMESA

FROM *An Aethiopian History* or *Aethiopica, c.* AD 270

Let this suffice concerning what was done about Syene, which, after it was come into so great a danger, by the clemency and equity of one man received so good a turn. This done, Hydaspes sent a great part of his army before and went himself into Ethiopia, the people of Syene and all the Persians following him a great way and praising him much and making many supplications for his good and prosperous health. First he took his journey along the banks of the Nile and such other places as were near unto the same. But after he came to the Cataracts and had sacrificed to the Nile and the other gods of the land, he turned aside and went through the middle country rather. When he came to Phylae he gave his army leave to rest and refresh themselves for two days, and sending away a great number of his meanest soldiers tarried himself, to fortify the walls and set a garrison. This done, he chose two horsemen, who should ride in post before him and in certain towns and villages change their horses, with letters to Meroe to certify them of his victory. To the wise men who are called Gymnosophists and are of the king's council he wrote thus:

> To the divine council Hydaspes sends greeting. I certify you of the victory I have had over the Persians. Yet I make no great count of my success but pay homage rather to the instability of fortune. I salute and commend by this letter your holy priesthood, which as at all times so now has told me the truth. I pray you also and, as far as I may, command you to come to the appointed place, that with your presence you may make the sacrifice more acceptable to all the people of Ethiopia.

Heliodorus of Emesa (born *c.* AD 250) is thought to have been Bishop of Trikka. The only certain (?) information pertaining to Heliodorus are the lines with which he closes the story itself: 'Here ends the

history of the Ethiopian adventures of Theagenes and Chariclea
written by Heliodorus, a Phoenician of Emesus, son of Theodosius,
and descended from the Sun.'

LUIS DE URRETA

FROM *Historia Ecclesiastica, Politica, Natural, y Moral,*
de los Grandes y Remotos Reynos de la Etiopia, Monarchia del
Emperador, Llamado Preste Juan de las Indias, 1610

All these famous libraries, and all of the others that are renowned and
celebrated, would lose their fame and glory, if they were compared
with the library of Prester John in the Monastery of the Holy Cross
on Mount Amara; for the books shelved there are uncountable and
infinite. It is sufficient to know that the Queen of Sheba began the
task of collecting works from many parts, and placed there many
books that Solomon had given her, and more still that he continued to
send. And from those distant times the emperors have continued
adding books with great refinement and care. There are three
enormous halls, each one more than two hundred paces in length, in
which there are books of every science, all in very fine, delicate, glossy
parchments, with exquisitely executed gilt lettering and decorative
embellishments; some are richly bound in hard covers; while others,
loose like legal documents, are rolled up and kept in silk bags: but
books made of paper are very scarce, and this modern artefact is a
novelty in Ethiopia [...]

The table I have placed in this chapter forms part of an index
and repertory that was catalogued by Antonio Grico and Lorenço
Cremones, who were sent to Ethiopia by Pope Gregorio XIII upon
the instigation of Cardinal Zarleto, to examine the library in the
company of others charged with further briefs, and who returned full
of admiration for having seen so many books: in their lives they had
never seen such a collection in so many different languages, all of
them handmade from full-sized parchment and as big as choirbooks,
arrayed on skilfully fashioned cedarwood shelves. The reason there
are so many books is due to the meticulosity and diligence of the
emperors who have collected them since the time of the Queen of

Sheba. And during the persecutions suffered by the Jews at the hands of the Babylonians, Assyrians and Romans, the emperors of Ethiopia would always endeavour to obtain their books [. . .]

Such was their concerned attention, that when the Emperor of Ethiopia named Mena heard that Charles V, the Holy Roman Emperor, had seized the city of Tunis, whose king Mulay Hassan entertained a copious and rich library, Mena forthwith sent his servitors to the markets of Egypt, Rome, Venice, Sicily and other parts, so that with his purse they should buy the books carried off by the soldiers, who, as these books were in Arabic, gave them away for free. In this fashion Mena added more than three thousand volumes on Astrology, Medicine, Herbs, Mathematics, and other interesting sciences. And now, as a result of this sustained diligence during who knows how many thousands of years, since the time of the Queen of Sheba until the present, one should not be alarmed if I say there are more than a million books, even if I still think that falls short, and far short, of the actual number [. . .]

They take great care of this library, for it is the most precious possession in the whole empire: more than two hundred monks from the Abbey of the Holy Cross are assigned as librarians, and attend to the upkeep, guard and protection from damage of the books; and every Monday three or four hundred soldiers from the guard stationed at the base of Mount Amara, come up to sweep the halls, dust and clean the books, and do whatever they are told to do. The monks are all very erudite and are assigned as librarians depending on the languages they know: they take care of the books in the language in which they are conversant; watch over them to see that the pages are not torn, or destroyed by bookworms; that the letters do not fade, which easily occurs since the books are of parchment; and generally address any other shortcomings [. . .]

When an emperor is crowned, he is presented with the keys of the treasury and the library at the same time, and then he entrusts the library key to the spiritual father of the Monastery of the Holy Cross, where the library is located, and entrusts him with the care, safe-keeping, surveillance and cleanliness of the library, declaring that he values it more than all his treasure, for even if the latter were insufficient, the empire possesses mines to make up the deficit, whereas the books of this library are unique in the world [...]

I only want to state that the treasure guarded on Mount Amara, in the Monastery of the Holy Cross, together with the library, is of such immense wealth, I dare to say, and say with confidence, there is no king in the world, in antiquity or presently, no empire or monarchy, even taking into account the four renowned global powers of Babylon, Persia, Greece and Rome, with all of their victories, triumphs and rich spoils of war, that ever held such a stock of gold and precious stones, like the treasure amassed and hoarded on Mount Amara [...]

According to Ethiopian tradition, it was the Queen of Sheba who began to hoard treasure on Mount Amara, and since those antique times, every year the emperors of Ethiopia add to the pile, amassing all the tributes and riches due to them, and disbursing nothing, for of this Prester John has no need; because the cities of the empire, following the antique custom, pay all the people of war, the guard of his person, his pavilions and the upkeep of Mount Amara. For the expenses of his court and house, are reserved the tributes of three powerful kingdoms, Sabba, Zambra and Gafate, which contribute more than enough for these outlays; but the resources of the other fifty-nine kingdoms remain free and untaxed, and are very abundant. As all of these populous kingdoms are rich in gold and silver mines, and the treasury on Mount Amara having been alimented for more than three thousand years, may the reader consider what quantities of gold have been hoarded, that for sure exceed all measure [...]

Well yes, in the days of the Queen of Sheba there were such riches in gold and silver; and from then until now taxes and tributes have been collected and hoarded. So, how many millions of gold and silver bars are there now? Even the treasurers and accountants of the empire themselves do not have the faintest idea, but always speak of it with admiration and acclamation. The treasure is kept in four large and spacious chambers [...]

In the old days, gold was stored in these chambers in the form of unsmelted ore, straight from the mine. The purest ore was from the Black River and some of the nuggets were quite large; but most of the gold was in the form of fine grains or flakes like wheat bran. They struck gold in the fields and forests, and took it to the treasury without smelting or refining it. This custom was maintained until the time of the Emperor David, when a Portuguese named Miguel da Silva advised him to melt it all down into bars so it could be kept more commodiously. The emperor did so, and the chambers were filled with square bars, measuring a hand's-breadth on a side and three fingers thick, stacked from floor to ceiling. The metal is so fine there are bars that can be folded and rolled like pastry, and indeed, the gold of Arabia and Ethiopia is already famed for being so fine and precious. So, making a reckless estimate based on what the Venetians and Portuguese who have seen them say, each chamber contains more than three hundred million bars, and as there are four chambers, that would amount to more than twelve hundred million gold bars.

Translated by YVES-MARIE STRANGER

Luis de Urreta (1570–1636) was a Dominican friar and theology professor in Valencia, Spain, who made a name for himself in the book he wrote about Ethiopia and the Prester John, in which he claimed to be relating what had been told to him by Antonio Greco and Lorenzo Cremonese who had travelled to Ethiopia on behalf of the librarian of the Vatican library, Cardinal Guglielmo Sirleto. Urreta made many tall and extraordinary claims about the country and its 'huge library on Mount Amhara', and its palaces of precious stones and metals. For all of its untruths, such was the interest in Ethiopia that the book was widely read and quoted, especially by the book's detractors, chief among whom was Pero Paez, the Jesuit missionary in Ethiopia, whose own *History of Ethiopia* often reads as a point by point refutation of Urreta's work, but should also be understood against the backdrop of the rivalry with the Dominicans who had previously been present in Ethiopia. Funnily enough, one of Urreta's most unlikely claims, that a copy of the long-lost *The Book of Enoch* could be found in Ethiopia, proved to be true.

SAMUEL TAYLOR COLERIDGE

FROM 'Kubla Khan: or a vision in a dream', 1816

In Xanadu did Kubla Khan
A stately pleasure-dome decree:
Where Alph, the sacred river, ran
Through caverns measureless to man
Down to a sunless sea.
So twice five miles of fertile ground
With walls and towers were girdled round;
And there were gardens bright with sinuous rills,
Where blossomed many an incense-bearing tree;
And here were forests ancient as the hills,
Enfolding sunny spots of greenery.

But oh! that deep romantic chasm which slanted
Down the green hill athwart a cedarn cover!
A savage place! as holy and enchanted
As e'er beneath a waning moon was haunted
By woman wailing for her demon-lover!
And from this chasm, with ceaseless turmoil seething,
As if this earth in fast thick pants were breathing,
A mighty fountain momently was forced:
Amid whose swift half-intermitted burst
Huge fragments vaulted like rebounding hail,
Or chaffy grain beneath the thresher's flail:
And mid these dancing rocks at once and ever
It flung up momently the sacred river.
Five miles meandering with a mazy motion
Through wood and dale the sacred river ran,
Then reached the caverns measureless to man,
And sank in tumult to a lifeless ocean;

And 'mid this tumult Kubla heard from far
Ancestral voices prophesying war!
The shadow of the dome of pleasure
Floated midway on the waves;
Where was heard the mingled measure
From the fountain and the caves.
It was a miracle of rare device,
A sunny pleasure-dome with caves of ice!

A damsel with a dulcimer
In a vision once I saw:
It was an Abyssinian maid
And on her dulcimer she played,
Singing of Mount Abora.
Could I revive within me
Her symphony and song,
To such a deep delight 'twould win me,
That with music loud and long,
I would build that dome in air,
That sunny dome! those caves of ice!
And all who heard should see them there,
And all should cry, Beware! Beware!
His flashing eyes, his floating hair!
Weave a circle round him thrice,
And close your eyes with holy dread
For he on honey-dew hath fed,
And drunk the milk of Paradise.

Samuel Taylor Coleridge (1772–1834), founder of the Romantic movement in England, is famous for *The Rime of the Ancient Mariner* and countless other poems, among them, *Kubla Khan*. Coleridge suffered from ill health his whole life as well as having an opium, or laudanum, addiction, said to have been caused by its frequent prescription for his physical as well as mental ailments. He suffered from what some have seen as depression, or what would today be called bipolar disorder. Many have seen the dreamy tropes of

344   Ethiopia: *through writers' eyes*

laudanum in *Kubla Khan*, a poem described as a fragment in a dream, which Coleridge said had come to him as he had fallen asleep in front of the fire in his cottage – before, sadly, being interrupted by 'someone from Porlock', and thus losing the thread of the story. Whether due to opium or not, Coleridge's vision of Kubla Khan, with his Abyssinian maid, remains to this day one of the favourite poems of the English language.

SIR JOHN DE MANDEVILLE

FROM *The Travels of Sir John de Mandeville*, *c.* 1360

Of the Royal Estate of Prester John. And of a Rich Man that Made a Marvellous Castle and Called It Paradise and of His Deviousnesss.

This emperor, Prester John, rules over a great land, and has many noble cities, good towns and numerous large islands in his realm. For the country of India consists of many islands due to flooding caused by the rivers that come from Paradise, dividing the land in many parts. He also has more islands in the sea; and the best city in the Island of Pentexoire is the royal city of Nyse, which is noble and wealthy.

Prester John has under him many kings, islands and different peoples of various conditions. The land is good and rich, but not so rich as the land of the great Khan. For merchants do not come here to buy merchandises as often as they do in the land of the great Khan, because it is so far to travel to; and on the other hand, in China they can buy whatever they need: cloths of gold or silk, spices and all kinds of goods. So, although there are more important markets in the land of Prester John, nevertheless men fear the distance and the great perils of the sea in those parts.

For in the sea there are massive rocks of a type of magnetic stone that attracts iron. Therefore, no ships pass by there that have either iron bolts or nails within them; if they do, instantly the magnetic stone attracts them, so the ships are stuck on the rocks. I myself have seen afar off in that sea an island, seemingly covered in trees, and the sailors told us that these were the wrecks of ships drawn to the magnetic rocks and trapped by the iron that was in them. Out of these shipwrecks and their rotten rigging grew so much vegetation it resembled a forest; and thereabouts there are many such rocks, and merchant ships avoid these passages unless they have good pilots.

Merchants also fear the great distance; and therefore they go to China, which is nearer; although still so distant that travellers from Genoa or Venice, by sea and land, take eleven or twelve months to reach China. However, the land of Prester John is even further and can only be reached by a dreadfully long journey.

The merchants pass by the kingdom of Persia, and go to a city called Hermes, for Hermes the philosopher who founded it. After that they cross the sea, and go to another city called Golbache; there they find merchandise, and parrots as plentiful as geese. If they continue further, they may travel securely enough; although in that country there is not much wheat or barley, and therefore they eat rice and honey, or cheese and fruit.

Prester John always marries the daughter of the great Khan; and the great Khan also, in the same manner, always marries the daughter of Prester John; for these two are the greatest lords under the firmament.

In the land of Prester John there are many precious stones, so large they are made into vessels, as platters, dishes, and cups. There are also countless other marvels, too complicated and long to describe; but of the principal islands, and his possessions and laws, I will tell you a little.

This Emperor Prester John is Christian, and most of his country also; however, they do not have all the articles of our faith as we have. Nevertheless, they believe in the Father, the Son, and the Holy Ghost; they are faithful and true to one another, and use no tricks, falseness, or any deceits.

He has under him seventy-two provinces, and in every province is a king. And these kings have kings under them, and all are tributaries to Prester John. And he has in his lordships many great marvels.

For in his country is the sea that men call the Gravelly Sea, entirely made of gravel and sand, without a drop of water, and it ebbs and flows in great waves as other seas do and it is never still nor in peace, in any season. Nobody has crossed that sea by boat or ship, nobody knows what lies beyond. Although there is no water, many different kinds of fish can be found on the sandbanks, just like in any other sea, and after cooking, these fish are tasty and delicious.

Three days' journey from that sea there are high mountains, out of the which flows a great river that has its source in Paradise; and this is a river full of precious stones that runs through the desert to make the Gravelly Sea; and it flows into that sea, and there it ends. The river flows three days a week, carrying with it huge quantities of stones, which as soon as it enters the Gravelly Sea, disappear and are lost for evermore. During those three days when the river flows, nobody dares to enter it; but on the other days people do.

Beyond that river, in the desert there is a wide plain of gravel surrounded by mountains. In that plain, every day at sun-rise, small trees sprout from the ground and begin to grow, and they grow till mid-day, bearing fruit; but nobody dares to pick the fruit, for it is enchanted; and after mid-day, the trees start to decrease in size and shrink back into the earth, so that at sun-set they disappear. And so they do, every day, which is a great marvel.

In that desert there are numerous wild men, of a hideous aspect; for they are horned, unable to speak, and grunt like pigs. There are also packs of wild dogs, and flocks of parrots, called *psittakes*. The parrots greet any travellers they encounter in the desert, and speak to them as clearly as if they were human.

The best talkers are the parrots with a large tongue and a foot with five claws; the other kind with three claws, talks very little and mainly shrieks.

When Prester John goes into battle against another lord, no flags are carried before him; but he has three great golden crosses encrusted with precious stones, and each cross is set in a richly decorated chariot. To protect the crosses, there are 10,000 knights and more than 100,000 soldiers, as we would protect a military standard during wartime. This number of men defending the crosses is independent of the main army. When Prester John is not at war, he rides with his own retinue, with only a plain wooden cross carried before him, in remembrance that Jesus Christ suffered death upon a wooden cross. They also carry before him a gold platter and a silver dish; the gold platter is full of earth, as a token that his noblesse, his power, and his

flesh, shall all turn to earth; the silver dish is full of jewels and precious
stones, as a token of his lordship, his noblesse, and his power.

He usually dwells in the city of Susa where he has his principal
palace, which is so sumptuous no man can conceive of it without
having seen it. Above the main tower of the palace are two round
pommels of gold, containing two large carbuncles, that shine brightly
in the night. The principal gates of his palace are of sardonyx; and
the borders and bars are of ivory; and the windows of the halls
and chambers are of crystal; and the dining tables are of emeralds,
amethyst, and gold, studded with precious stones; and the pillars that
support the tables are of the same precious stones. Of the steps up to
his throne, where he sits at dinner, one is of onyx, another crystal,
another green jasper, another amethyst, another sardonyx, another
cornelian, and the seventh, on which he sets his feet, is of chrysolite.
All these steps are bordered with fine gold, with other precious stones,
and oriental pearls. The sides of the seat of his throne are of emerald,
with gold borders encrusted with sparkling gems and great pearls.
The pillars in his chamber are of fine gold with precious stones, and
many carbuncles, that give great light by night to all people; but
although the carbuncles give enough light, nevertheless, at all times a
crystal vessel full of balm is burning, to perfume the emperor, and
expel all wicked airs and corruptions. The frame of his bed is of fine
sapphire, blended with gold, to make him sleep well and to restrain
him from lechery; for he will not lie with his wives, but four times a
year, after the four seasons, and only to engender children.

He also has a very fair and noble palace in the city of Nyse, where
he dwells when he likes; but the air is not as temperate as it is in the
city of Susa.

In his country and in the surrounding countries, men eat once a
day, as they do in the court of the great Khan. More than 30,000
persons eat every day in his court, without counting visitors. This
Emperor Prester John has seven kings with him to serve him, and
they share their service on a monthly basis. With these kings serve
seventy-two dukes and three hundred and sixty earls. Every day of the
year, there eat at the royal table, twelve archbishops and twenty
bishops. And the patriarch of Saint Thomas is treated there as the

pope is here. The archbishops, bishops and abbots are all kings in that country; and each of these great lords knows his duties; one is master of Prester John's household, another is chamberlain, another serves him food, another drink, another is steward, another is marshal, another is prince of arms, and thus is he most nobly and royally served. And his land extends in extreme breadth four months' journeys, and in length beyond measure, including all the islands of the world, that we suppose to be under us.

Near the Island of Pentexoire, there is another large island in the lordship of Prester John, called Mistorak. Not long ago there was a wealthy man living there called Gatholonabes, who was full of tricks and of devious deceits. He had a castle on a mountain, so strong and noble, that no man could design a fairer or a stronger. He had the mountain surrounded with strong walls; and within those walls he had the fairest garden that might be imagined; therein were trees bearing all manner of fruits, and many varieties of sweet-smelling herbs and flowering plants. There were pure water wells in that garden; and beside those wells he had built beautiful halls and charming chambers, with pictures painted in blue and gold, representing many different things and all kinds of stories. There were also artificial birds which sang delectably and were moved by hidden mechanisms, so that it seemed they were alive. Furthermore, he stocked his garden with live birds and animals for pleasure and enjoyment.

He also had, in that place, the fairest damsels that might be found, under the age of fifteen years, and the fairest youths that men might get, of that same age; and they were all richly dressed in clothes of gold; and he said they were angels.

There were three lovely fountains, made of jasper and crystal, diapered with gold, and set with precious stones and great oriental pearls. An underground pipe was connected to these fountains so that on demand, one would run with milk, and the others with wine and honey. And that place he called Paradise.

And when any good knight, who was hardy and noble, came to see this royalty, he would lead him into Paradise, and show him these wonderful things for his enjoyment, the marvellous and delicious songs of different birds, the fair damsels, and the lovely fountains of milk, wine, and honey, running plentifully. Many musical instruments could be heard playing in a high tower, so merrily, that it was joy to hear; and nobody could see the musicians. He said the music was made by the angels of God, and this place was Paradise, that God had promised to his friends, saying, 'I will give you a land flowing with milk and honey.' And then he would make them drink a certain drink, which instantly made them drunk; after which they seemed to have greater delight than they had before. Then he would tell them that if they would die for him, after their death they should come to his paradise; where they would be the same age as those fair damsels, and they should play with them and yet they would remain maidens. After that he would put them in an even lovelier paradise, where they would see the God of Nature visibly, in his majesty and bliss. Then he revealed his intention, and told them, if they would go and slay such a lord or such a man who was his enemy, or disobedient to his will, they should not fear to do it, or to be slain themselves in doing it; for after their death he would put them into another paradise, that was a hundred-fold fairer than any of the others; and there they would dwell with the fairest damsels that might be, and play with them for evermore.

Thus went many lusty young men to slay great lords, the enemies of Gatholonabes, and were themselves slain, in the hope of gaining that paradise. In this manner he often took revenge on his enemies using these subtle deceits and false tricks.

But when the worthy men of the country perceived this devious falsehood of the cunning Gatholonabes, they assembled their forces, assailed his castle, and slew him, and destroyed all the beautiful places in that paradise. The emplacements of the fountains and the foundations of the walls can still be clearly seen, but the riches are clean gone. And it is not long ago since that place was destroyed.

Sir John de Mandeville is the author of a compilation of marvellous lands and sights seen, written in Anglo-Norman French and first referenced between 1357 and 1371. Who he really was is subject to some controversy and *The Travels* have been variously attributed to

Jehan à la Barbe (a physician from Liège) and to Jean le Long, a travelogue-collecting Benedictine monk from Saint Bertin, where he remained Abbot until his death in 1383. Fictional or not, Sir John travels far and wide – from China to Sinai, from the Malay Archipelago to Trebizond and, of course, to Ethiopia. It seems the text was lifted from various sources: from the writings of Odoric of Pordenone, from the *Historiae Orientis* of Hetoum and, for Ethiopia, the Letter of Prester John, itself an anonymous invention. Be it what it may, it is said that *The Travels of Sir John* figured prominently by the bunk of Christopher Columbus, and he was widely read and quoted for several centuries.

FROM *The History of Rasselas, Prince of Abyssinia*, 1759

Description of a Palace in a Valley

You who listen with credulity to the whispers of fancy, and pursue with eagerness the phantoms of hope; who expect that age will perform the promises of youth, and that the deficiencies of the present day will be supplied by the morrow, attend to the history of Rasselas, Prince of Abyssinia.

Rasselas was the fourth son of the mighty Emperor in whose dominions the father of waters begins his course – whose bounty pours down the streams of plenty, and scatters over the world the harvests of Egypt.

According to the custom which has descended from age to age among the monarchs of the torrid zone, Rasselas was confined in a private palace, with the other sons and daughters of Abyssinian royalty, till the order of succession should call him to the throne.

The place which the wisdom or policy of antiquity had destined for the residence of the Abyssinian princes was a spacious valley in the kingdom of Amhara, surrounded on every side by mountains, of which the summits overhang the middle part. The only passage by which it could be entered was a cavern that passed under a rock, of which it had long been disputed whether it was the work of nature or of human industry. The outlet of the cavern was concealed by a thick wood, and the mouth which opened into the valley was closed with gates of iron, forged by the artificers of ancient days, so massive that no man, without the help of engines, could open or shut them.

From the mountains on every side rivulets descended that filled all the valley with verdure and fertility, and formed a lake in the middle, inhabited by fish of every species, and frequented by every fowl whom nature has taught to dip the wing in water. This lake discharged its superfluities by a stream, which entered a dark cleft of the mountain on the northern side, and fell with dreadful noise from precipice to precipice till it was heard no more.

The sides of the mountains were covered with trees, the banks of the brooks were diversified with flowers; every blast shook spices from the rocks, and every month dropped fruits upon the ground. All animals that bite the grass or browse the shrubs, whether wild or tame, wandered in this extensive circuit, secured from beasts of prey by the mountains which confined them. On one part were flocks and herds feeding in the pastures, on another all the beasts of chase frisking in the lawns, the sprightly kid was bounding on the rocks, the subtle monkey frolicking in the trees, and the solemn elephant reposing in the shade. All the diversities of the world were brought together, the blessings of nature were collected, and its evils extracted and excluded.

The valley, wide and fruitful, supplied its inhabitants with all the necessaries of life, and all delights and superfluities were added at the annual visit which the Emperor paid his children, when the iron gate was opened to the sound of music, and during eight days every one that resided in the valley was required to propose whatever might contribute to make seclusion pleasant, to fill up the vacancies of attention, and lessen the tediousness of time. Every desire was immediately granted. All the artificers of pleasure were called to gladden the festivity; the musicians exerted the power of harmony, and the dancers showed their activity before the princes, in hopes that they should pass their lives in blissful captivity, to which those only were admitted whose performance was thought able to add novelty to luxury. Such was the appearance of security and delight which this retirement afforded, that they to whom it was new always desired that it might be perpetual; and as those on whom the iron gate had once closed were never suffered to return, the effect of longer experience could not be known. Thus every year produced new scenes of delight, and new competitors for imprisonment.

The palace stood on an eminence, raised about thirty paces above the surface of the lake. It was divided into many squares or courts, built with greater or less magnificence according to the rank of those for whom they were designed. The roofs were turned into arches of massive stone, joined by a cement that grew harder by time, and the building stood from century to century, deriding the solstitial rains and equinoctial hurricanes, without need of reparation.

This house, which was so large as to be fully known to none but some ancient officers, who successively inherited the secrets of the place, was built as if Suspicion herself had dictated the plan. To every room there was an open and secret passage; every square had a communication with the rest, either from the upper storeys by private galleries, or by subterraneous passages from the lower apartments. Many of the columns had unsuspected cavities, in which a long race of monarchs had deposited their treasures. They then closed up the opening with marble, which was never to be removed but in the utmost exigences of the kingdom, and recorded their accumulations in a book, which was itself concealed in a tower, not entered but by the Emperor, attended by the prince who stood next in succession.

Samuel Johnson (1709–1784), better known simply as Dr Johnson, was a lexicographer, essayist, biographer, poet – 'arguably the most distinguished man of letters in English history', and the object of Boswell's famous *Life of Samuel Johnson*. He was also a cantankerous author of sallies, epigrams and the fiercest definitions ever written in a dictionary, the unsociable centre of literary life in London for decades and a monument of English letters – yes, but one important attribute is often left out when quoting the good irascible genius's list of accomplishments: Ethiopianist! Long before he was famous, Samuel Johnson's 'first' book was a translation of a small volume of travel: Jeronimo Lobo's *Itinerario or, Travels in Ethiopia*. In this work, which Johnson probably translated from the French and not from the original Portuguese, Lobo recounts in a simple manner his travels throughout Ethiopia, and, as if in passing, his visit to the springs of the Blue Nile. Lobo's book seems to have been the main or sole influence behind Samuel Johnson's later invention of Rasselas, a classic that has withstood the passing of years.

SAMUEL PURCHAS

FROM *Purchas, His Pilgrimages: or Relations of the World
and the Religions observed in all Ages and Places discovered,
from the Creation unto the Present*, 1613

Of the Hill Amara and the Rarities Therein

The Hill Amara has already been often mentioned, and nothing
indeed in all Ethiopia more deserves mention, whether we respect the
natural site, or the employment thereof. [. . .]

It is situated in a great Plain largely extending itself every way
without other hill in the same for the space of thirty leagues, the form
thereof round and circular, the height such, that it is a day's work to
ascend from the foot to the top; round about, the rock is cut so
smooth and even, without any unequal swellings, that it seems to him
that stands beneath, like a high wall, whereon the Heaven is as it were
propped; and at the top it is over-hanged with rocks, jutting forth of
the sides the space of a mile, bearing out like mushrooms, so that it is
impossible to ascend it, or by ramming with earth, battering with
Cannon, scaling or otherwise to win it. It is above twenty leagues in
circuit, compassed with a wall on the top, well wrought, that neither
man nor beast in chase may fall down. The top is a plain field, only
towards the South is a rising hill, beautifying this plain, as it were with
a watchtower, not serving alone to the eye, but yielding also a pleasant
spring which passes through all that Plain, paying his tributes to every
garden that will exact it, and making a Lake, whence issues a River,
which having from these tops espied Nilus, never leaves seeking to
find him, whom he cannot leave both to seek and find, that by his
direction and conveyance he may together with him present himself
before the Father and great King of waters, the Sea. The way up to it
is cut out within the rock, not with stairs, but ascending by little and
little that one may ride up with ease; it has also holes cut to let in light

and at the foot of this ascending place, a fair gate, with a *Corps du Garde*. Half way up is a fair and spacious hall cut out of the same rock, with three windows very large upwards: the ascent is about the length of a lance and a half: and at the top is a gate with another guard. The air above is wholesome and delectable; and they live there very long, and without sickness. There are no Cities on the top, but palaces, standing by themselves, in number four and thirty, spacious, sumptuous, and beautiful, where the Princes of the Royal blood have their abode with their families. The Soldiers that guard the place dwell in Tents.

There are two Temples, built before the Reign of the Queen of Sheba, one in honour of the Sun, the other of the Moon, the most magnificent in all Ethiopia, which by *Candace*, when she was converted to the Christian Faith, were consecrated in the name of the Holy Ghost, and of the Cross. At that time (they tell) *Candace* ascending with the Eunuch (whose proper name was *Indica*) to baptise all of the royal blood, which were there kept, *Zacharie* the eldest of them, was in his baptism named *Philip*, in remembrance of *Philip's* converting the Eunuch, which caused all the Emperors to be called by that name, till *John* the Saint, who would be called *John*, because he was crowned on Saint John's day: and while they were busy in that Holy work of baptising the Princes, a Dove in fiery form came flying with beams of light, and lighted on the highest Temple dedicated to the Sun, whereupon it was afterwards consecrated to the Holy Ghost by Saint *Matthew* the Apostle, when he preached in *Ethiopia*. These two Temples were after that given to the Monastical Knights of the Military Order of Saint *Anthony*, by *Philip* the seventh, with two great and spacious Convents built for them. I should lose both you and myself, if I should lead you into their sweet, flourishing, and fruitful Gardens, whereof there are store in this plain, curiously made, and plentifully furnished with fruits both of Europe plants there, as Pears, Pippins, and such like; and of their own, as Oranges, Citrons, Lemons, and the rest; Cedars, Palm-trees, with other trees, and variety of herbs and flowers, to satisfy the sight, taste, and scent. But I would entertain you, only with rarities, nowhere else to be found: and such is the Cubayo tree, pleasant beyond all comparison in taste, and whereunto for the virtue is imputed the health, and long life of the Inhabitants; and the Balm tree, whereof there is great store here: and hence it is thought the Queen of Sheba carried and gave to *Solomon*, who planted them in Judæa, from whence they were transplanted at Cairo long after. The plenty of Grains and Corn there growing, the charms of birds alluring the ear with their warbling Notes, and fixing the eyes on their colours, jointly agreeing in beauty, by their disagreeing variety, and other Creatures that adorn this Paradise, might make me glut you (as sweetmeats usually do) with too much store.

Samuel Purchas (*c.* 1577–1626) was an English cleric, who published several volumes of travellers' tales. Purchas himself never travelled more than 200 miles from Thaxted in Essex where he was born, but he collected seamen's yarns in Leigh-on-Sea, a nearby bustling port. *Purchas, His Pilgrimages* attained immediate notoriety, went through four editions before Purchas's death and sought to show the diversity of God's creation from the standpoint of the Anglican faith. Coleridge was reading Purchas when he fell asleep, and received his vision in a dream – *Kubla Khan*.

OTTO OF FREISING

FROM *Chronicle of the Two Cities*, 1145

We also saw there at that time the aforesaid Bishop of Jabala in Syria [. . .] He said, indeed, that not many years since, one John, a king and priest living in the Far East, beyond Persia and Armenia, and who, with his people, is a Christian, but a Nestorian, had warred upon the so-called Samiards, the brother kings of the Medes and Persians. John also attacked Ebactanus, the capital of their kingdom. When the aforesaid kings advanced against him with a force of Persians, Medes, and Assyrians, a three-day struggle ensued, since both sides were willing to die rather than to flee. At length, Prester John, so he is usually called, put the Persians to flight and emerged from the dreadful slaughter as victor. The Bishop said that the aforesaid John moved his army to aid the church of Jerusalem, but that when he came to the Tigris and was unable to take his army across it by any means, he turned aside to the north, where he had been informed that the stream was frozen solid during the winter. There he awaited the ice for several years, but saw none because of the temperate weather. His army lost many men on account of the weather to which they were unaccustomed and he was compelled to return home. He is said to be a descendant of the Magi of old, who are mentioned in the Gospel. He governs the same people as they did and is said to enjoy such glory and such plenty that be uses no sceptre save one of emerald. Fired by the example of his forefathers, who came to adore Christ in the manger, he proposed to go to Jerusalem, but he was, they say, turned back for the aforementioned reason.

Otto of Freising (*c.* 1114–1158), a German bishop and writer, was the fifth son of the Margrave of Austria and hence related to the Emperor Henry IV. His mother Agnes was also the mother, by her first marriage, of the German king Conrad III. Otto was thus connected to the most powerful German families of the time, and this would later play an important role when he entered the Cistercian order, soon becoming an Abbot and founding the Heiligenkreuz Abbey in 1133, with the financial support of his father. We know that as a young man he studied philosophy in Paris – but little else. He took part and was perhaps instrumental in Conrad III's ill-fated crusade of the same number, during which he met Hugh, bishop of Jabala, who told him of Prester John. The legend of Prester John is often thought to find its origin here.

BYRON KHUN DE PROROCK

FROM *Dead Men Do Tell Tales*, 1933

We passed the plantation of a French nobleman whose career was both thrilling and romantic. Bored with his secluded, half ruined, ancestral castle, and with almost no funds, he had come to Ethiopia twenty years before in search of adventure and a fortune. In an earlier age Henri de Monfreid might have turned pirate, but like Lord Byron's friend, Trelawney, his gift seemed to turn in his middle years toward writing. He began to put down episodes of his strange life, episodes which included gun-running from the Red Sea, slave raids, dope-running, and political intrigue. His stories were both fascinating and convincing adventure-romances. With the publication of his first book, he had become well-known; with the next, he became a vogue; and successful novels followed one after the other. Unexpectedly, he was ordered to leave his beloved, adopted Ethiopia – because of his secret negotiations with a foreign power, so it was rumoured.

Some distance beyond De Monfreid's plantation we passed the ancient Coptic monastery which is the home of the celebrated Bishop of Harrar, Abu Hanan. He was one of the most important men in all Abyssinia. With the brilliant mind of a politician and with the wealth and the power of the Church behind him, he was one of Haile Selassie's staunchest supporters.

A few miles beyond the monastery we came to the first of the sentries, the one farthest from Lidj Yassou's prison cage. At the sight of the two bottles of cognac I held out, the sentry smiled, came forward and took them, and disappeared without asking a single question.

At the second outpost, the soldiers needed several drinks of cognac before they were willing to accept the bottles and close their eyes to my presence.

'Our difficulties are increasing,' the young Armenian driver explained, 'because they have orders to search all cars for messages that get through from outside; that even includes myself, though I come up here every week.' He said it so guilelessly that, in view of the fact that he had been bribed to bring me with him, I smiled.

'Mohammedan and Italian agents are working to free Lidj Yassou and to start a civil war. They want to make him a puppet king,' he added. 'Tinker with the motor, clean the spark plugs, and keep busy when we reach the Military Governor's Palace. You'll find an oil can and wrenches under the seat. It'll take me some time to unload.'

Soon after he had given me those orders, we drove into the court-yard of a good-sized house built of stone and mud. When we stopped I got out, lifted the hood, and did as I was told, still managing to l ook around and see what was going on. Under the sharp eyes of a boss, a dozen Galla slaves began removing the cases of cognac and champagne. Through the trees, on the summit of a hill I could just see the Iron Cage. There was an air of excitement around, which seemed greater than could be explained by the mere arrival of the regular, weekly truck.

The driver came over and pointed to the carburettor as if he were explaining something.

'You're having luck. Lidj Yassou is celebrating another of his birth-days. He's giving a grand *gibr*, a banquet in honour of his women and his guards. He conveniently forgets the day on which he was born, so he can celebrate a number of times each year. It helps him to kill time, too.'

I began wiping down the motor with cotton waste, excited at the prospect of seeing Lidj Yassou when he was celebrating. The strange parties I had witnessed in this land had been genuine, but they had lacked the social prestige of royalty! 'The Mad Dog of Abyssinia' was an Ethiopian Nero and Rasputin combined in one person.

The feast was to take place inside the enclosure which surrounded the prisoner's cage. Under the strict and constant watch of spies, soldiers, and priests – several millions of the Mohammedan population still venerated him – Lidj Yassou was compelled to enjoy the spectacle from his second-storey prison.

As the men unloaded and checked the supplies, I counted twenty-two cases marked 'Pommery and Greno' and 'Hennessy'. Tables and benches were being carried from the barracks to the enclosure, and huge slabs of raw meat were placed in piles on the tables. Containers of odorous *intschera* – Ethiopian red pepper – and big barrels of *tedj* were brought out. The strong body odours of the workers combined with everything else to create a stench worse than that of a slaughterhouse.

The cases of luxury drinks were taken up the hill to the Iron Cage when the imprisoned ex-Emperor began to sip his first drink, the tedj was served to the natives below in the compound, and the feast began. Only Dante's description of Inferno offers any parallel to the spectacle. Heavy-lipped, gory mouths slavered from the reeking chunks of purple flesh and the copious draughts of tedj. One old man tried to emulate the death of the Duke of Clarence (who had drowned in a vat of Malmsey); he fell into a hogshead of tedj, and had to be pulled out by the feet by his shouting, laughing grandchildren.

In all the excitement, I slipped away from the truck, moved up nearer to the Iron Cage, and found a place from which I could see its occupants well. Lidj Yassou was lolling against a pile of silk cushions, surrounded by ten or twelve naked women who were offering him champagne and drugs. This fantastic prisoner was a mountainous, Bacchus-like figure with a bloated face – the result of twenty years of inaction, imprisonment, licentiousness, and drugs. In the hope of even a momentary restoration of his declining powers, he indulged in hashish and other drugs, and in obscene spectacles. From the Iron Cage there came a scream, followed by lewd laughter, which was far from pleasant to hear. Panic-stricken by my disappearance, the Armenian driver had searched until he had found me.

'Quick. We must get away from here before it gets any worse.' He took my arm.

'What's going on up there? Why did someone scream?'

'I'll tell you on the way.' He looked around anxiously.

We moved down the hill and got into the truck. Still the driver kept looking around. But whatever it was that he feared, nothing happened. We drove off just as the sunset turned the mountains purple, and no sentry delayed or searched us. As the driver manoeuvred the truck down the steep grades and hairpin turns, he talked as calmly as if he were sitting comfortably on some verandah.

'That scream you heard – Lidj Yassou is no longer capable of his favourite pastime, so he takes his pleasure by proxy. He has a male court favourite whose duty it is to take his pleasures while the former Emperor and his court look on. His present favourite is a huge Shan-kalla slave, and the scream you heard probably came from a young girl. Allah is supposed to bestow on the Emperor's diseased nerves and imagination the delights of the houris of the Mohammedan paradise while he watches.'

In the silence that followed this explanation, while we were getting farther and farther away from the horror house of Garamoulta, some lines of Keats stood out in my memory:

> The Shark at savage prey – the Hawk at pounce,
> The gentle Robin, like a Pard or Ounce
> Ravening a worm

Those simple, Harrar and Galla people, who lived in the valley oasis, were soon to be victims of the caterpillar treads of tanks, and vomit up their lungs from the poisonous chemical gas the Italians used. Intrigues between the Fascists and Lidj Yassou had been started; worn-out with disease, drugs, and excesses, he would have made a weak, easily managed puppet. But the Coptic priests were too intelligent to let this go on for long, and the Iron Cage was abolished. A sixteen-room palace was built for the ex-Emperor within the enclosure of a Coptic monastery. So far as she could, the ex-Emperor's sister, the Empress who is Haile Selassie's wife, protected her brother, but she could not prevent his being moved to the monastery grounds.

Count Byron Khun de Prorock's biography is related on page 63. His travels to Ethiopia took place when the former Emperor Iyasu V had been deposed for apparently converting to Islam and was imprisoned during the reign of his aunt, Zawditu.

JOHN MILTON

FROM *Paradise Lost*, 1667

Nor where *Abassin* Kings their issue Guard,
Mount *Amara*, though this by some suppos'd
True Paradise under the *Ethiop* Line
By *Nilus* head, enclos'd with shining Rock,
A whole day's journey high, but wide remote
From this *Assyrian* Garden, where the Fiend
Saw undelighted all delight, all kind
Of living Creatures new to sight and strange:

Paradise Lost, BOOK IV, LINES 280–287

John Milton (1608–1674). Samuel Johnson, never quick to heap praise on a fellow author, said of *Paradise Lost* that it was 'a poem which with respect to design may claim the first place, and with respect to performance, the second, among the productions of the human mind'. Milton was born in London, attended Christ's College, and read, studied and travelled widely. He spoke or had knowledge of Greek, Latin, Aramaic, Syriac and Hebrew, as well as Spanish, German, French and of course, his mother tongue, English. Milton first become a pamphleteer and publicist, with his poetry circulating clandestinely under the rule of Charles I, before gaining favour and employment as a civil servant during the Commonwealth. Come the Restoration, Milton lost public favour and gainful employment, but, by now completely blind, he seemed not to care much and remained very popular not just in England but on the continent as well. It was in these years, blind and impoverished, that John Milton wrote – or rather, dictated to his amanuenses – *Paradise Lost*, followed by *Paradise Regained*, and also one of his most loved poems to this day, *On His Blindness*.

YVES-MARIE STRANGER

FROM A review of *Tintin in Ethiopia*,
the *Abyssinian Review of Books*, 1966

As most people know from the widely beloved *Tintin in Ethiopia* (French serialised edition 1963–1966, English-language edition 1966), the Ark of the Covenant has been held in safety in Ethiopia since the destruction of Solomon's Temple in Jerusalem. The story goes that Menelik the first, the son of Solomon and the Queen of Sheba, brought it back to his mother's country with the scions of Israel's tribes, thus planting the seed of Israel in Africa and symbolically transferring God's covenant from Israel to Ethiopia.

All of this information is imparted to Haddock at the beginning of the story by a vehement Ethiopian barber, to whom the debonair captain has just imparted 'Oh . . . the tabernacle thing, that disappeared from Solomon's Temple, never to be seen again . . . ' While Haddock is comically fed *gursha* – hand-fed that is – by two sprightly Orthodox nuns who keep telling him to just say *ishi while the apoplectic barber wields a cut throat razor in an alarming fashion.* This is not to be Haddock's last force-fed ingestion of Ethiopian culture! But in case you are one of those adults who no longer thumb the classics of childhood, let me flip back through the album quickly.

The cartoon begins in Marlinspike, where Haddock and Tintin are reading about the Negus (Emperor Haile Selassie), and his recent triumphal trip to Europe. Calculus is bumbling about with his pendulum, darkly talking of a weapon to end all wars, and mistakes Haddock's *The Negus of Ethiopia* for *The Egg of Utopia*, and launches into a philosophical ramble on what came first, Utopia or the Egg?

Of course, this is only a prelude to their adventures in Ethiopia – Hergé's clear drawings make for wonderful depictions of Lalibela, the highlands, the Semien Mountains and Lake Tana – I particularly like the moment when Tintin and Haddcock are travelling on the lake in a papyrus *tankwa* to the Monastery of Narga, and mistake Calculus's submarine for a new species of hippopotamus. Another favourite is the Zar-spirit invocation in the Fasilides Castle of Gondar, when the spirit possesses Snowy.

But the most iconic scenes are certainly those in the Semien Mountains, where Tintin and Mamoush, disguised as Bleeding Heart Baboons, in the middle of a one-thousand-strong pack, are pretending to graze on grass and roots, when suddenly one of the Baboons shuffles up carrying a bottle, and turns out to be Captain Haddock, likewise disguised:

'Billions of Blistering Baboons! Plus two more!'

'Captain Haddock we presume!' chorus Tintin and Mamoush.

'I'm under some kind of aerial surveillance by a Pestilential Stool-pigeon!' whispers Haddock.

As a Bearded Vulture hovers above with a baboon skeleton dangling from its talons, Mamoush expounds:

'Captain, that's not a Pigeon with a stool, that's a Vulture with a load of bones, looking for somewhere to drop them, to crack them open. It can even do the same with live tortoises . . . '

'Ten Thousand Tormented Tortoises! Boneheads! Numskulls! We need a bomb shelter! Remember how Aeschylus was killed back in 455 BC by a falling tortoise, dropped on his bald pate by an irruptive Hirundo æthiopica . . . or was it a gyrating Gypaetus barbatus?'

'A bird is a bird is a bird, my friends,' shrugs Tintin nonchalantly.

High above, the hovering Bearded Vulture now gives the reader a bird's-eye view of what it may mean, in an æthereal and platonic vision, to be in Æthiopia, as it drops, with an unerring aim, its ballistic load of retributive bones on their heads:

'Wooaaagh!'

'It's a Boeing B-52!'

'Body-Snatcher! Duck-Billed Diplodocus! Guano-Gatherer! Misguided Missal! Syllabaric Barbarian! Buggy Abugida!'

(Their cover is blown. Exit pursued by Nine Hundred and Ninety-Nine Baboons.)

When Tintin's nemesis, restyled Ras Popoulous – complete with a head of dreadlocks – arrives on the scene, it becomes clear that the

theft of the Ark, in order to harness its devastating power and trans-
form the world into a dictatorship ruled by a crazed and reclusive
Russian Communist, is the real objective of the story, and not Tintin's
purported work to cover Haile Selassie's Jubilee celebrations.

The '60s were of course the height of the Cold War – and of Haile
Selassie's reputation in the non-aligned movement. The last image,
of the avuncular and wise emperor waving goodbye from the steps of
the Jubilee Palace, as Haddock, Calculus, Tintin and Snowy take
their leave, is particularly poignant when one remembers that the
emperor would be bundled from those same steps in this happy scene
just a decade later, and driven to prison in the back of a Volkswagen
Beetle. And how not to see in the conniving Ras Popoulous a prescient
precursor of Colonel Mengistu?!

There are some who see this late work, produced by the Studio
Hergé, as a tired version of *Tintin in Tibet*, and it has to be admitted
there are close parallels between the Semien shepherd boy Mamoush
and Chang, and some scenes do seem at times directly transposed
from earlier stories. For all that, it remains a startlingly accurate
portrayal of Ethiopia. The ethereal quality of Hergé's style seems
particularly suited to his subject here. Just think back to those iconic
scenes in the Semien in which Tintin and Mamoush, disguised as
Bleeding Heart Baboons, have to feast on grass and roots, in the
middle of a one-thousand-strong pack of baboons! As the Bearded
Vulture hovers above, it is the reader himself who is given a bird's-
eye view of what it means, in a perfect platonic vision, to be *in*
Ethiopia. Never has the particular light of the Ethiopian Highlands
been captured so well.

But I suppose one should not read too much into a comic book,
even when imagined by the great Hergé, and likewise, I don't think
much of interpretations that see in this work the cartoonist's act
of contrition for the colonial and ethnocentric *Tintin in the Congo*. In
my opinion, *Tintin in Abyssinia* is one of the most clear-sighted
depictions of Ethiopia there is, and I encourage anybody who wants
to get a good feel for the country to go out and get it immediately –
lest you be force-fed cultural *gursha* à la Haddock!

E. M. BERENS

FROM *Myths and Legends of Ancient Greece and Rome*, 1984

Perseus

Perseus then resumed his travels. His winged sandals bore him over deserts and mountains, until he arrived at Æthiopia, the kingdom of King Cepheus. Here he found the country inundated with disastrous floods, towns and villages destroyed, and everywhere signs of desolation and ruin. On a projecting cliff close to the shore he beheld a lovely maiden chained to a rock. This was Andromeda, the king's daughter. Her mother Cassiopea, having boasted that her beauty surpassed that of the Nereides, the angry sea-nymphs appealed to Poseidon to avenge their wrongs, whereupon the sea-god devastated the country with a terrible inundation, which brought with it a huge monster which devoured all that came in his way.

In their distress the unfortunate Æthiopians applied to the oracle of Jupiter-Ammon, in the Libyan desert, and obtained the response that only by the sacrifice of the king's daughter to the monster could the country and people be saved.

Cepheus, who was tenderly attached to his child, at first refused to listen to this dreadful proposal; but overcome at length by the prayers and solicitations of his unhappy subjects, the heart-broken father gave up his child for the welfare of his country. Andromeda was accordingly chained to a rock on the sea-shore to serve as prey to the monster, whilst her unhappy parents bewailed her sad fate on the beach below.

On being informed of the meaning of this tragic scene, Perseus proposed to Cepheus to slay the dragon, on condition that the lovely victim should become his bride. Overjoyed at the prospect of Andromeda's release, the king gladly acceded to the stipulation, and Perseus hastened to the rock to breathe words of hope and comfort to the trembling maiden. Then assuming once more the helmet of Aïdes, he mounted into the air, and awaited the approach of the monster.

Presently the sea opened, and the shark's head of the gigantic beast of the deep raised itself above the waves. Lashing his tail furiously from side to side, he leaped forward to seize his victim; but the gallant hero, watching his opportunity, suddenly darted down, and producing the head of the Medusa from his wallet, held it before the eyes of the dragon, whose hideous body became gradually transformed into a huge black rock, which remained for ever a silent witness of the miraculous deliverance of Andromeda. Perseus then led the maiden to her now-happy parents, who, anxious to evince their gratitude to her deliverer ordered immediate preparations to be made for the nuptial feast. But the young hero was not to bear away his lovely bride uncontested; for in the midst of the banquet, Phineus, the king's brother, to whom Andromeda had previously been betrothed, returned to claim his bride. Followed by a band of armed warriors he forced his way into the hall, and a desperate encounter took place between the rivals, which might have terminated fatally for Perseus, had he not suddenly bethought himself of the Medusa's head. Calling to his friends to avert their faces, he drew it from his wallet, and held it before Phineus and his formidable bodyguard, whereupon they all stiffened into stone.

Perseus now took leave of the Æthiopian king, and, accompanied by his beautiful bride, returned to Seriphus, where a joyful meeting took place between Danaë and her son.

EDGAR ALLAN POE

FROM *The Narrative of Arthur Gordon Pym from Nantucket*, 1838

The Writing is on the Wall

Mr Pym has given the figures of the chasms without comment, and speaks decidedly of the *indentures* found at the extremity of the most easterly of these chasms as having but a fanciful resemblance to alphabetical characters, and, in short, as being positively *not such*. This assertion is made in a manner so simple, and sustained by a species of demonstration so conclusive (viz., the fitting of the projections of the fragments found among the dust into the indentures upon the wall), that we are forced to believe the writer in earnest; and no reasonable reader should suppose otherwise. But as the facts in relation to all the figures are most singular (especially when taken in connection with statements made in the body of the narrative), it may be as well to say a word or two concerning them all – this, too, the more especially as the facts in question have, beyond doubt, escaped the attention of Mr Poe.

Figure 1, then, figure 2, figure 3, and figure 5, when conjoined with one another in the precise order which the chasms themselves presented, and when deprived of the small lateral branches or arches (which, it will be remembered, served only as a means of com- munication between the main chambers, and were of totally distinct character), constitute an Ethiopian verbal root – the root 'to be shady' – whence all the inflections of shadow or darkness.

In regard to the 'left or most northwardly' of the indentures in figure 4, it is more than probable that the opinion of Peters was correct, and that the hieroglyphical appearance was really the work of art, and intended as the representation of a human form. The delineation is before the reader, and he may, or may not, perceive the resemblance suggested; but the rest of the indentures afford strong confirmation of Peters' idea. The upper range is evidently the Arabic verbal root 'to be white,' whence all the inflections of brilliancy and whiteness. The lower range is not so immediately perspicuous. The characters are somewhat broken and disjointed; nevertheless, it cannot be doubted that, in their perfect state, they formed the full Egyptian word 'the region of the south.' It should be observed that these interpretations confirm the opinion of Peters in regard to the 'most northwardly' of the figures. The arm is outstretched toward the south.

Conclusions such as these open a wide field for speculation and exciting conjecture. They should be regarded, perhaps, in connection with some of the most faintly detailed incidents of the narrative; although in no visible manner is this chain of connection complete. Tekeli-li! was the cry of the affrighted natives of Tsalal upon discovering the carcase of the *white* animal picked up at sea. This also was the shuddering exclamative of Tsalal upon discovering the carcass of the *white* materials in possession of Mr Pym. This also was the shriek of the swift-flying, *white*, and gigantic birds which issued from the vapory *white* curtain of the South. Nothing *white* was to be found at Tsalal, and nothing otherwise in the subsequent voyage to the region beyond. It is not impossible that 'Tsalal,' the appellation of the island of the chasms, may be found, upon minute philological scrutiny, to betray either some alliance with the chasms themselves, or some reference to the Ethiopian characters so mysteriously written in their windings.

'I have graven it within the hills, and my vengeance upon the dust within the rock.'

Edgar Allan Poe (1809–1849). Poe's *Narrative of Arthur Gordon Pym of Nantucket* has baffled critics and readers alike, with its straight mix of maritime knowledge and seafaring yarns culminating in a Hollow Earth adventure in which the survivors of a shipwreck find an underworld entrance in the Antarctic. Edgar Allan Poe has long been celebrated in Europe – and especially so in France, where his works were translated by Baudelaire, and a sequel to *Arthur Gordon Pym* was written by Jules Verne, *An Antarctic Mystery* (*V.* by Thomas Pynchon, also seems to hint at *Arthur Gordon Pym* at times). The 'Ethiopian' script that wraps up his Narrative in such an elusive manner, seems to have been the adequate mysterious ending for Poe – always the lover of cryptography.

Chronology

c. 3.4 million years ago
: Lucy (*Australopithecus Afarensis*): early hominids in the Horn of Africa.

3000 BC Egyptians travel to the 'Land of Punt' to source wild animals and incense.

2500 BC Greek sources call the inhabitants of regions south of Egypt 'Ethiopian'.

1000 BC 'Semitic' settlements in the highlands close to the Red Sea.

500 BC Pre-Axum Temple of Yeha.

100 AD Emergence of Axum as a powerful Red Sea state.

*c.*330 AD King Ezana converts his state to Christianity.

451 AD Monophysitism is rejected at the Council of Chalcedon. Ethiopia falls in line with the Copts and becomes 'orthodox'.

520s AD Axumite expedition to subdue Yemen.

616 AD First Hejira of the Prophet Mohammed's early followers to Axum.

Tenth century
: A mythical (?) Queen Judith lays waste to Axum.

Eleventh–twelfth century
: Lalibela is built in the rock of Lasta as a capital of the Zagwe dynasty.

Thirteenth century
: 'Restoration' of the Solomonide dynasty.

1499 The Portuguese envoy Pero de Covilha arrives in Abyssinia.

1520 Dom Rodrigo de Lima's embassy arrives in Abyssinia. The Expedition's chaplain, Francisco Alvarez, will write an account of their seven years in Abyssinia.

1530s Ahmad ibn Ibrahim al Ghazi launches a wave of successful campaigns all over Abyssinia.

Sixteenth century–1840s
> Ottoman Imperial power in the Red Sea and surrounding lands waxes and wanes.

Sixteenth century
> Beginning of the great population migrations of the Oromo.

1541   The Portuguese troops of Cristóvão da Gama defeat the Muslim jihad.

1633   Foundation of Gondar. Expulsion of the Jesuits.

1855–68 Theodore II, Emperor of Ethiopia.

1868   Storming of Magdala by Napier's Indian expeditionary force. Theodore II commits suicide.

1878   The Berlin Conference ushers in the Scramble for Africa.

1889   Coronation of Menelik II as Emperor of Ethiopia.

1896   Ethiopia defeats Italy's army at Adua.

1896–1906
> Menelik gives Ethiopia the shape we know today in his own 'scramble for Africa'.

1911   Iyasu, grandson of Menelik II, becomes ruler of Ethiopia.

1916   Iyasu is deposed, and Menelik's daughter Zawditu rules with Ras Tafari as regent.

1917   The French-built railway arrives in the capital.

1928   Coronation of Ras Tafari as King Haile Selassie (Emperor in 1930).

1932   The last of the independent Oromo 'Gibe States', in southwest Ethiopia, Jimma, reverts to Ethiopia upon the death of the last ruler Abba Jiffar.

1935   Italy invades Ethiopia.

1941   Liberation of Ethiopia/Eritrea under British rule. Haile Selassie restored to the throne.

1950   Eritrea federated with Ethiopia.

1961   Eritrea's war of independence begins. Attempted coup in Addis Ababa.

1962   Haile Selassie annexes Eritrea as a province of Ethiopia.

1963   Haile Selassie inaugurates the first conference of the Organisation of African Unity.